THE NEW M

THE NEW

MEN OF POWER

AMERICA'S LABOR LEADERS

C. WRIGHT MILLS

with the assistance of
Helen Schneider

Introduction by
Nelson Lichtenstein

UNIVERSITY OF ILLINOIS PRESS
URBANA AND CHICAGO

Manufactured in the United States of America
1 2 3 4 5 C P 5 4 3 2 1

♾ This book is printed on acid-free paper.

Library of Congress Cataloging-in-Publication Data
Mills, C. Wright (Charles Wright), 1916–1962.
The new men of power : America's labor leaders / C. Wright Mills, with the assistance of Helen Schneider ; introduction by Nelson Lichtenstein.
p. cm.
Originally published: New York : Harcourt, Brace, 1948.
Includes bibliographical references and index.
ISBN 0-252-02692-6 (cloth : alk. paper)/ISBN 978-0-252-02692-8
ISBN 0-252-06948-X (pbk. : alk. paper)/ISBN 978-0-252-06948-2
1. Labor unions—United States—History. 2. Labor leaders—United States—History. I. Schneider, Helen. II. Title.
HD6508.M583 2001
331.88'0973—dc21 2001023086

for

J. B. S. Hardman,

Labor Intellectual

"When that boatload of wobblies come
Up to Everett, the sheriff says
Don't you come no further
Who the hell's yer leader anyhow?
Who's yer leader?
And them wobblies yelled right back—
We ain't got no leader
We're all leaders
And they kept right on comin'.'

—From an interview with
an unknown worker
Sutcliffe, Nevada
June, 1947.

CONTENTS

Introduction to the Illinois Edition by Nelson Lichtenstein ix

Introduction: What Are Labor Leaders Like? 3

PART ONE

1. The Political Publics 13
2. The Mass Public's View 31

PART TWO

3. The Houses of Labor 49
4. The Split Runs Deep 68
5. The Self-Made Men 84

PART THREE

6. The Liberal Rhetoric 111
7. The Racketeer Business 122
8. Labor's Image of Business 133

PART FOUR

9. Programs and Expediences 153
10. Party Ties 171
11. Communists and Labor Leaders 186
12. Old Parties, New Parties 201

PART FIVE

13. The Main Drift 223
14. Alternatives 239
15. The Power and the Intellect 266

Notes and Sources 293

Index 313

INTRODUCTION TO THE ILLINOIS EDITION

NELSON LICHTENSTEIN

The New Men of Power is a study of trade unions and their leadership, the American political scene, and the prospects for a radicalized democracy in the years just after World War II. It offered mid-twentieth-century readers a well-textured, fully realized portrait of a newly empowered set of strategic actors who, C. Wright Mills argues, led the nation's most important progressive institutions, "the only organizations capable of stopping the main drift towards war and slump" (3).[1] It was the first book of which Mills was the principal author, and it constitutes the first of his three great works on U.S. social structure. Published in 1948, it was followed in 1951 by Mills's masterwork, *White Collar: The American Middle Classes,* and then five years later by *The Power Elite,* his explosively controversial dissection of the nation's ruling strata.

Unlike his politically acute, agenda-setting volumes published during the 1950s, Mills's equally expansive probe into the meaning and future of U.S. trade unionism quickly fell into the shadows, both popular and academic.[2] Mills himself soon abandoned any interest or hope in the radical potential of the labor movement, especially after American trade union leaders seemed to make their postwar peace with corporate America. By the mid-1950s few observers would have called these unionists "a strategic elite," as Mills argues in a book whose very title by that time mocked the waning influence of a labor leadership firmly wedded to the Democratic Party, cold war orthodoxy, and the collective bargaining routine. As the generation of labor leaders who had built the new unions in the 1930s retired, labor seemed a stagnant force, largely defenseless against the political and economic hammer blows that befell the rank and file during the 1970s and 1980s.

That said, *The New Men of Power* bears rereading at the dawn of the twenty-first century. This is not because the contemporary labor movement has regained the power held by union leaders in the 1940s when Mills and his associates made the surveys and drafted the chapters that went into the book. By almost any standard the unions are far less powerful—in terms of relative membership, raw economic power, and political influence—than they were when *The New Men of Power* first appeared. Nor does the American working class face an immediate, consciousness-changing crisis, such as a new war or a new depression, which Mills himself expected to put the unions at the center of the nation's political thought and action.

Enough has changed, however, to make the ideas and speculations put forward in *The New Men of Power* useful and exciting once again. Today, as in 1948, the unions stand on the left side of American politics and culture. They are organizing again and recruiting a new generation of young activists who seek to infuse the labor movement with a radical élan. A new leadership has ascended to important posts in the trade union movement, and the old iron curtain that once divided official labor and the broad American left—academic, feminist, socialist, African-American, Latino, and gay—is rusting away. Faced with a new world of global production, a nearly useless labor law, and a corporate opposition that remains intransigently antiunion, many otherwise conventional union leaders have been forced to look for new allies and new ideas; likewise, social activists and intellectuals have come to see the revival of a powerful trade union movement as essential to their dreams for a better world.

The American Federation of Labor–Congress of Industrial Organizations (AFL-CIO) has therefore begun a self-conscious effort to reconnect with students, clergy, intellectuals, and many of those once-spurned veterans of the enthusiasms spawned during the 1960s and the years immediately thereafter. Between 1996 and 1998 a series of university "teach-ins" put AFL-CIO president John Sweeney and other top union officials on the same podium with people such as Betty Friedan, Julian Bond, Barbara Ehrenreich, Richard Rorty, Eric Foner, and Cornell West. The symbolism was impressive: when Sweeney told a 1996 Columbia University teach-in "We need your help," the audience of intellectuals, left-wing academics, and old-time radicals gave him the sort of lusty ovation no labor chieftain had heard from this kind of crowd in half a century. Three years later, when radical Teamsters and ecological Turtles joined forces on the streets of Seattle in a spectacular set of demonstrations against corporate power and the World Trade Organization, a new alliance seemed well on its way to fruition.[3]

A similar sort of creative excitement infused the labor movement in the mid-1940s when C. Wright Mills began his study of the trade unions and their leadership. By the end of World War II the blue-collar working class, as a proportion of all gainfully employed people, stood at its twentieth-century apogee. The unions themselves had grown nearly fivefold in little more than a decade, and at fourteen million strong they enrolled about one in three nonfarm workers. Politically, the trade unions defined the left wing of what seemed possible in American politics. Although the American Federation of Labor was now larger than the decade-old Congress of Industrial Organizations, the latter was a more dynamic social formation whose fractious leadership represented almost every left-of-center political tendency in the nation: FDR liberals, Catholic corporatists, old-line Socialists, a handful of Trotskyists, and a far larger Communist bloc. Most important, the great CIO industrial unions of that era—in the steel, auto, rubber, and electrical product industries—contained a remarkable layer of alert, politically conscious militants. They were the shop stewards, the committeemen, the local union officers, and the regional directors who gave leadership to an industrial underclass—immigrants or the sons and daughters of immigrants, African Americans, Appalachian whites, the unskilled and the uneducated—whose voice had long been mute.[4]

The unions that comprised the CIO and the AFL were therefore collective bargaining institutions, but in an era of New Deal economic regulation and wartime social control, they had become political to the core. The smashing electoral triumph won by Franklin Delano Roosevelt and the Democrats in 1936 prepared the way for the even more dramatic strike victories that came in Flint, Detroit, Akron, Youngstown, New York, and Chicago just a few months later. By the onset of World War II both the AFL and the CIO sought a hand in running the war economy. Labor's men (and a few women) served on the War Labor Board, took posts at the War Production Board, and filled many key positions in the Office of Price Administration. They were far less influential than their corporate counterparts, but in a political economy in which the idea of tripartite governance—involving organized labor, corporate management, and representatives of the New Deal state—proved ideologically potent, unionists were reaching for a kind of societywide power well beyond the traditional world of firm-centered contract bargaining. Indeed, the great set of postwar strikes that began late in 1945 were intrinsically political, designed not simply to raise wages but to make corporate prices, production, and planning subject to both union demands and government regulation.[5]

C. Wright Mills encountered this laborite universe by a path far more circuitous than those of many of his adult contemporaries. He had been born in Waco in 1916 and spent his youth in Forth Worth and Dallas, where he attended Catholic elementary schools and public high schools. Mills's Texas was devoid of the political passions others found so consuming during the 1930s. His education and his parents were conventionally middle-class, so Mills knew little of the ideological warfare that consumed so many college-age leftists during that depression decade. "I did not personally experience 'the thirties,'" he once remarked. "At the time I just didn't get its mood."[6] Mills was, according to the nomenclature of the 1940s, a radical "anti-Stalinist," but this set of politics, on topics both foreign and domestic, remained unburdened by the trauma and disillusionment that had transfigured so many other left-wing intellectuals at the end of the 1930s.

After demonstrating brilliance and hard work at the University of Texas, Mills took a sociology Ph.D. at the University of Wisconsin and quickly moved on to his first academic job at the University of Maryland. In Madison, Mills had encountered Hans Gerth, a left-wing German émigré who introduced him to the great European social theorists, especially Karl Marx, Max Weber, and Karl Mannheim. Mills thought Gerth "the only man worth listening to in this department." Later they would collaborate to translate and publish the writings of Weber, whose fruitful impress upon the Millsian worldview is evident in almost all his work. A self-conscious continental liberal who valued property, order, and individual liberty, Weber nevertheless sought to trace out the multifaceted process of bureaucratization and rationalization, identifying with both the emergence of high capitalism and state socialism. Despite Weber's central preoccupation with the forms of domination in modern society, the pioneering German sociologist still sought a way forward for human freedom. As Mills and Gerth put it in 1946, Weber "felt that freedom consists not in realizing alleged historical necessities but rather in making deliberate choices between open alternatives. The future is a field for strategy. . . . Yet the possibilities of the future are not infinite, nor are they clay in the hands of the willful man."[7]

At Wisconsin, Mills also took Selig Perlman's well-attended classes on socialism and capitalism. Although Perlman disdained the Left, or any sort of self-conscious intellectualism within the unions—his famous "job conscious" interpretation of the labor movement left little room for a visionary transformation of society—his brand of economistic institutionalism coexisted easily with a Weberian emphasis on functional role, legal constraint, and social status within any structure, including that of the unions. As *The New Men of Power* amply demonstrates, Mills did not share Perlman's anti-Bolshevik hostility to intellectuals as an alien, corrupting presence within labor's body politic, but he did take from Perlman's lectures an appreciation of the history and institutional flavor of the American unions, especially as they served to mobilize and sell the labor power of their members, thus making unionism functional to the capitalist marketplace. So even as a self-conscious radical, Mills would remain acutely aware of the organizational logic and economic forces that made for conservatism and defensiveness within these institutions of the working class.[8]

His real exposure to a radical understanding of labor's potential came at the otherwise provincial campus of the University of Maryland, just outside Washington, D.C. Here Mills encountered a vigorous set of young historians: Kenneth Stampp, Frank Friedel, and Richard Hofstadter, whose brother-in-law, Harvey Swados, later a well-known novelist and journalist, would remain a lifelong friend.[9] This circle soon put Mills in touch with a radical, anti-Stalinist world of writers, intellectuals, and activists centered in New York. He wrote for *Partisan Review*, *The New Leader*, and *The New Republic*, and he collaborated with Dwight Macdonald in founding *politics*, the amazingly influential "little magazine" whose critique of the warfare state, advocacy of radical pacifism, and search for new forms of democratic participation prefigured much of the political sensibility exhibited by the New Left a generation later. By 1945 Mills was reading *Labor Action*, the revolutionary broadside published by the "third camp" Trotskyists in Max Schactman's Workers Party.[10]

Many of the key ideas that would later appear in *The New Men of Power* are found in the wartime essays and reviews Mills sent north from College Park. In a 1942 issue of *Partisan Review*, he hailed Franz Neumann's dissection of the Nazi regime, in which an imbricated set of political, industrial, and military elites statified capitalism and eviscerated an independent working class. "If you read his book thoroughly," wrote Mills, "you see the harsh outlines of possible futures close around you."[11] Therefore, like Schactman, Macdonald, and Swados, Mills did not see World War II as a necessary defense against the fascist menace but rather as a step toward an American version of the militarized, Leviathan state. This is what Mills would call "the main drift." He would have served if the military's doctors had passed him through—because of his high blood pressure they did not—but Mills still thought the war "a god dammed blood bath to no end save misery and *mutual* death to *all* civilized values."[12]

At the core of Mills's analysis was a crisis theory of capitalist development. In its twentieth-century form, the system was inherently unstable, prone to a recurrent cycle of depression, war, and hothouse boom. Mills expected another slump in just a few short years, and, according to this analysis, so did the most sophisticated representatives of big business, who therefore backed an administratively guided political economy, a sort of postwar New Deal but with a much more authoritarian, business-oriented elite firmly in command. At various points in *The New Men of Power*, Mills calls this "a corporate form of garrison state" (233) or "a state capitalism with many corporate features" (237), but whatever the nomenclature, it is "the main drift" that leads eventually to what Neumann had called "totalitarian-monopolistic-capitalism."[13]

Mills's outlook, however, was not one of despair. Increasingly he looked to the labor movement, "the chief social power upon which a genuine democracy can rest today." Influenced by the Schactmanite Trotskyists, Mills saw within organized labor the potential for the emergence of a third camp that could resist both Stalinist and capitalist oppressions. He therefore applauded union militancy and rank-and-file insurgency. Mills defended the otherwise unpopular coal strikes led by John L. Lewis, and in a 1943 issue of *The New Republic* he pushed forward a theme that would strike repeated chords in *The New Men of Power:* unless the unions, "fructified by pro-labor intellectuals," demonstrated their independence and power, they would soon find themselves "incorporated within a government over which they have little control."[14]

Not unexpectedly Mills turned his sociological energies to a survey of labor leadership. Early in 1944, while still at the University of Maryland, he sent out questionnaires to more than two hundred top AFL and CIO officials. In effect, this was a pilot study for the much larger research effort that would go into *The New Men of Power,* and some of the findings appear in the book. Mills probably found what he expected: AFL leaders were a full generation older than those in the CIO, and leaders of the industrial union organization stood to the left of those in the older federation. However, among all union officials the Roosevelt New Deal had served to greatly reduce third-party radicalism. Still, Mills remained hopeful. In a 1945 speech based on the study, he discounted the "actual mentality and proclaimed ideology" of labor leaders, arguing instead that by their very nature mass industrial unions "fight for general economic policies which favor the mass of the semi- and unskilled working people."[15]

Mills was anxious to get out of College Park, so early in 1945 he leapt at the chance to take a research post at the Columbia University–affiliated Bureau of Applied Social Research (BASR) in Manhattan. There Mills really hit his stride, juggling two or three projects at a time, supervising a dozen or more researchers, and writing or speaking both for academic audiences and the unique New York world of labor intellectuals and radical activists. The BASR had been founded by Paul Lazarsfeld, another German émigré sociologist but one increasingly steeped in the Anglo-American empirical tradition that emphasized methodologically sophisticated survey research tackling concrete issues of contemporary public concern. Like Mills, Lazarsfeld studied how elites disseminated ideas and information to a mass public, though he was often more interested in showing how that process could be made more efficacious and efficient. In the mid-1940s, money for plenty of such work poured into the universities and research institutes from the federal government, although funding for the surveys in *The New Men of Power* came from a Guggenheim grant won by Mills himself, as well as from BASR and local New York sources. Mills put students, staff, and even friends to work on his many projects, including the surveys and research work that constitute the empirical heart of *The New Men of Power.* He recognized their contribution—he gives researcher Helen Schneider acknowledgment on the title page—but there's no doubt that Mills himself reaped, and pretty much deserved, the lion's share of the credit.[16]

J. B. S. Hardman was one of the first people Mills looked up in New York, and he proved both a collaborator and a model for the kind of labor intellectual Mills thought so central to the future of the labor movement. Hardman (né Jacob Benjamin Salutsky) came out of the great tradition of Jewish radicalism under the czars. He was born in 1882, studied law at the University of St. Petersburg, and rose to leadership in the 1905 Revolution in Vilna and Kiev. Exiled in 1908, Hardman sailed for New York, where he moved easily from radical, Yiddish-language journalism to editorship of *The Advance,* the organ of Sidney Hillman's Amalgamated Clothing Workers of America (ACWA). By 1944 Hardman, like Mills, had also come to see the need for the projection of a more programmatically radical agenda within the house of labor.[17] To vitalize the unions and prepare them for the postwar battles, he founded the Inter-Union Institute for Labor and Democracy (IUI) and began editing a new monthly, *Labor and the Nation,* which began publication in 1945. Here Hardman sought to give voice and coherence to the work and ideas of the anti-Communist, but socialist or social democratic, staff intellectuals, journalists, and academics who still represented an important current within the unions and among labor's close allies.[18]

Mills described Hardman as "a wonderful old man who runs a magazine down in the village." He joined the IUI and began to write frequently for *Labor and the Nation.* Indeed, his column for the magazine, "What the People Think," published a good deal of the survey research that would shortly thereafter appear in *The New Men of Power.* Mills and Hardman became good friends: Hardman opened doors for Mills throughout the labor movement, and the IUI provided at least a third of the funds the BASR used to conduct its labor surveys. Through Hardman, Mills won a more concrete feel for the texture of the existing labor movement. In *The New Men of Power* much of the introduction, "What Are Labor Leaders Like?" in which Mills plays brilliantly with the contradictory character of such officials, reflects the inner history of the ACWA's leadership, from pre–World War I insurgency to late New Deal statesmanship.[19]

But Mills did not just use Hardman for insights into the structure of the unions. He thought that through the IUI he might have found the vehicle through which radicals like himself could actually have an impact on the labor movement. "Many of the new research people," he wrote in 1946, probably indicating his own feelings, "are disaffected and morally unhappy: they will their minds to people they don't like for purposes they don't feel at one with. . . . What some of them really want is to connect their skill and intelligence to a movement in which they can believe; they are ready to give a lot of energy to an organization that would harness these skills in the service of the left. And the left to most of them means labor."[20] Thus the dedication in *The New Men of Power* is "for J. B. S. Hardman, *Labor Intellectual.*"

Taken as a whole, *The New Men of Power* reflects the dual nature of Mills's labor research project: an empirical set of core chapters that illuminates the character of modern unions and the state of mind of their leaders enclosed within the more speculative, programmatic chapters that offer a Millsian analysis of the trajectory taken by U.S. capitalism and its political leadership, along with Mills's own, barely covert "radical program for America today."[21] The survey research itself, both questions asked and the interpretation of the results, reflects a highly politicized probe into the mentality of the labor leadership. Mills, Hardman, and other like-minded observers wanted to know if an empirical basis existed for prodding the unions leftward, if and when a new economic or political crisis hit. This was not value-free sociology.

Mills and his team sent out more than a thousand questionnaires during the spring of 1946 to city, state, and national union leaders, and then they dogged the nonrespondents with at least two follow-up letters. More than 40 percent responded, an extraordinarily good return. The polling is now more than fifty years old, but we do get a very useful snapshot of American labor leadership at a moment when its future seemed in tension between new fears and old hopes. The men and women who had built many of the unions were still very much in charge, and they were willing to wage successful strike battles of unprecedented effectiveness. But conservatives in the corporations, in Congress, and in the press had opened up a growing assault against labor's new power, culminating in the passage of the restrictive Taft-Hartley Act in 1947.

Thus the survey results, taken at this crucial moment in labor history, bear reexamination today. Mills found that CIO union leaders were much younger than their AFL counterparts, that the industrial unionists were better educated, and that for most workers union activism was a more certain path to upward mobility than recruitment into the ranks of management. He also found that nearly nine of ten unionists, both from the AFL and the CIO, were born in the United States. This was politically important because, as other surveys also revealed, almost half of all Americans thought far more labor leaders were of foreign birth, and therefore infected with alien ideas and loyalties. This supposition was the subtext for the right-wing assault on the CIO and the Democrats during the 1944 presidential campaign, when FDR's opponents made the political and policy influence of the Lithuanian-born Sidney Hillman, then the high-profile chairman of the CIO Political Action Committee, a prominent part of their election year polemics.

As Mills and his staff undoubtedly expected, they found that more

CIO than AFL unionists were willing to contemplate formation of a labor party, but not before the 1948 campaign.[22] Indeed, his survey revealed that the political and organizational divisions between the AFL and the CIO unionists still ran deep and that merger of the two organizations was unlikely in the immediate future. But leaders of both organizations feared the power and intentions of big business, and Mills found that an extraordinary 69 percent of all industrial union leaders thought fascism a definite threat in the United States. The survey results reported in Mills's study lend little support to the idea that unionists and managers embraced a postwar "labor-management accord," at least before 1948.

In June and July 1947 Mills finished what he described as "a fairly good draft" of a book then titled "The Labor Leader: Who He Is and What He Thinks." It was written at a ranch outside Reno, Nevada, where Mills was staying while awaiting a divorce from his first wife, Freya, whom he had married when he was still an undergraduate at the University of Texas. In the offing was marriage to twenty-four-year-old Ruth Harper, a Mount Holyoke College graduate Mills met late in 1946 when he hired her to work on *White Collar,* for which he had already begun to assemble research data and interviews. Mills thrived in the high desert. Between jeep excursions, horseback rides, and sessions on a newly purchased guitar, he churned out a manuscript, 432 pages in five weeks. "It just rolls out," reported Mills to his parents. "Wrote it like free association," he told Dwight Macdonald. It was in Nevada that Mills encountered an old Wobbly who provided the epigraph for the book. It is a "honey," he wrote to Ruth, "'WE AIN'T GOT NO LEADER. WE'RE ALL LEADERS.' That has just the right irony for a book on labor leaders."[23]

The finished draft was not due at the publisher until early 1948, so Mills had time to send about half a dozen copies to friends and colleagues, including Macdonald, Gerth, Swados, Columbia's Robert Lynd, and William Miller, a historian of business who was one of Mills's best friends. We don't know precisely what revisions were made by Mills, but his attendance at the November 1947 convention of the United Automobile Workers (UAW) had a large impact on the final manuscript, especially the last two chapters in which he is both more hopeful and more radical concerning the unions than either his introduction or his survey research might otherwise warrant. Mills was a partisan of Walter Reuther, an ex-socialist who had already fought his way to the union presidency, but when Nathan Glazer, then an assistant editor at *Commentary*, asked him to write an essay on the UAW, Mills became even more attentive to the outlook and ambience of the young intellectuals and labor militants who comprised the general staff of the Reuther caucus within the million-member auto union.[24]

To Mills "the most impressive thing about the United Automobile Workers union is the spectacle it affords of ideas in live contact with power."[25] His excitement was justified. In 1947 the UAW was the nation's largest trade union, confronting the very largest corporations in the world. The membership was militant and the leadership young, fractious, and highly political. Mills called it "a union amazed by itself."[26] Indeed, the forty-year-old Walter Reuther, whose faction swept to power at the union's 1947 convention, almost perfectly exemplified what Mills saw as the new union man of power. Mills was not uncritical of Reuther—he thought the UAW chief might well "become a 'human engineer' for some sort of state capitalism guaranteeing industry disciplined workers," but he put these doubts aside to applaud the programmatically coherent victory of the Reuther caucus over the coalition of Communists and placeholders with whom they had been at war for a decade. Mills called it "a democratic rank-and-file revolt against a disintegrating machine." It seems likely that when he retitled his book *The New Men of Power* sometime during the winter or spring of 1948 he was thinking of Reuther and his circle of militant young comrades. Here he found the "union-made intellectuals," not the New York variety, "intellectuals without fakery and without neuroticism."[27] Among them were Nat Weinberg, the UAW's new research director; Victor Reuther, Walter's younger, more ideologically left-wing brother; Jack Conway, who had studied for a Ph.D. in sociology at the University of Chicago; and the autodidactic rank-and-filer Clayton Fountain, who had explored a half-dozen political sects before joining up with the Reutherite socialists.[28]

Mills saw such people as his natural audience, so in *The New Men of Power* he works hard to avoid the language either of academic sociology or of the conventional Left. Earlier, in applying for a Guggenheim grant, Mills asserted his wish "to rid myself of a crippling academic prose and to develop an intelligible way of communicating modern social science to nonspecialized publics."[29] Mills also sensed the exhaustion of Marxian language in his time, and he tried to come up with alternate words and phrases, even if his ideas were still thoroughly meshed with those of the socialist tradition. We therefore find no reference in *The New Men of Power* to the bourgeoisie, imperialism, the ruling class, the masses, and certainly nothing on the "labor lieutenants of capital." Instead we find phrases such as "the main drift" and "the grand trend" to describe the trajectory of a militarized capitalism. In a letter to his friend William Miller, who questioned the definition of the word "intellectual," much used in *The New Men of Power*, Mills responded, "by intellectual here we mean humanitarian socialist. What the hell else? So I'll say so in some innocent, hard-boiled way."[30] He feared that because his book was "so very political" it would be pigeonholed as merely sectarian, so his search for a new language of class and politics was designed to win him the broader audience he craved. When Arthur Schlesinger Jr. endorsed it as "genuinely democratic and boldly radical . . . stimulating and fruitful," Mills sighed with relief: "Well! Anyway, it shows we can get away with it among the liberals."[31]

Mills certainly put his politics front and center. This begins in the first chapter, "The Political Publics," and he renews his programmatic analysis in the whole last part of the book that contains his discussion of "The Main Drift" (chapter 13) and its "Alternatives" (chapter 14). In his account of the political publics Mills offers a panoramic view of what he sees as the decisive points on the postwar political compass. The phrase "political publics" is important to this typology and in Mills's mind is quite distinct from the more passive, uninformed "public opinion." The political publics are much more self-conscious, more politically alert—communities either of ideology or interest that bring to bear a particular sensibility to the issues of the day. They formulate the ideas and programs that operate on the consciousness of the passive, atomized mass. For Mills, ideas matter and so too does the raw organizational power of the public that seeks to put those ideas into practice.

Mills describes five such publics, but they are of radically unequal weight. The first two, the "far left" and the "independent left," consist of but a few thousand individuals, and as Mills describes them, it is clear that he is really talking about his friends, comrades, and erstwhile collaborators (15–16). Mills is a product of this left; he wrote for its journals, spoke at its forums, and took his friends from its circles. But he is hardly uncritical of this milieu. Although he was ideologically close to the Workers Party of Max Schactman (of which Harvey Swados was a member), he found the Trotskyists "bureaucrats without a bureaucracy" (16) and adherents to a "popish set of ideas" (15). Thus Mills never joined up, even as he took a good bit of his ideological gunpower from these neo-Leninists: the idea that labor had to see itself as a "third camp" hostile to both capitalism and Stalinism, the concept of a "permanent arms economy," the disdain for the liberal center, and the expectation that when the postwar slump finally came the ranks of the Left might well multiply many fold in the contest for power.[32]

Mills is much harsher on the independent left. One suspects his animus is largely directed at Dwight Macdonald and the circle of *politics* writers and readers of which he was once a founding member. By the late 1940s Macdonald had moved to a political dead end: like Mills he feared the encroaching power of a Leviathan, corporate-military state, but Macdonald had lost faith, not only in the labor movement, but in any political solution to the moral crisis enveloping the modern world. In stark contrast to the Reutherite intellectuals so hopefully come to power, Mills charged the *politics* circle with drift and hopelessness, "oscillating between lament and indignation" (17). Thus Mills sharply attacks their indifference to the trade unions and Macdonald's characterization of the unions as but another apparatus of control, a "bureaucratic net ensnaring the people" (18). Of course, Mills also foresaw this potential devolution, which may account for the vitriol with which he attacked its premature proponents.[33]

Mills identifies the Sturm und Drang of everyday headline politics with the next two publics: the liberals, whom he finds "continuously excited and upset" (19) but programmatically incoherent, and the practical right, who have no well-worked-out ideology but see politics as an immediate source of economic gain, legislative advantage, and antiunion muscle. The liberals read *The Nation* and *The New Republic,* pine away for FDR, and look to Henry Wallace with some favor (Mills wrote just before the Truman revival of 1948 had begun and before the apogee of the liberal, anti-Communist assault on Wallace, who was then running for president on a Communist-backed Progressive ticket). The practical conservatives, identified with main-street business and small-town virtue, find their champions in Robert Taft and the Congressional Republicans, who in 1946 had just swept the Democrats out of power for the first time in sixteen years. Considering the extent to which these publics monopolized the overt world of mid-1940s politics, Mills gives them rather short shrift. He caricatures both the ardent liberals and the fervent conservatives, missing the nuances that divide each camp and underestimating their staying power, most notably that of the practical conservatives, whose influence would grow dramatically in the years after Barry Goldwater rose to prominence. Mills's relative disinterest derives from his expectation that when the postwar slump really came, these noisy combatants would fade from the scene or join up with those on both the labor left and the sophisticated corporate right who had a more systematic set of political ideas and the organizational apparatus to advance them. Power, writes Mills, will "shift toward those who are ideologically and strategically prepared for it" (28).

Mills throws the Communists into the cat fight between liberals and conservatives. Today, most historians recognize that whatever the Communist Party's relationship to Soviet power, the party's social, cultural, and laborite ambitions represented something organic to the traditions of the American left. They were a motive force in the world of New Deal labor and 1940s liberalism, in the civil rights movement, and even in the nascent rebirth of feminism.[34] Mills had to acknowledge some of this—he devotes an entire chapter to the Communist Party's influence within the unions—but like so many of his friends on the anti-Stalinist left, he was essentially contemptuous and dismissive. From his Columbia perch, Mills saw the party as composed of Union Square hacks and a shifting residue of lower-middle-class members whose influence was less on the labor movement, where they were being eliminated, than on the excitable liberals, to whose political sentimentality they appealed. So Mills was an anti-Communist, but one who saw the enemy as pathetic rather than dangerous.

To Mills the most formidable public was undoubtedly that of the sophisticated conservatives, to whose analysis he returns again and again throughout the book. These were the men who presided over the great New York law firms, the executives who led the largest corporations, and the editors of the nation's most respected papers. Mills does not use the term "power elite" in *The New Men of Power*, but these conservatives practically defined it: "they work in and among other elite groups, primarily the high military, the chieftains of large corporations, and certain politicians. Knowing what they want, wanting it all the time, and believing the main drift is in their favor, these sophisticated conservatives try to realize their master aim quietly" (25).[35] Two decades later, New Left historians would label this kind of manipulation, which effectively consensualized so much of American politics, "corporate liberalism." Unlike the noisy right, this corporate/political elite sought not to destroy the unions but to tame them by recruiting and rewarding a labor leadership willing to deradicalize its own rank and file. Mills saw as their prime ideological weapons the new language of labor-management cooperation and the soporific rhetoric of contemporary liberalism, both of which served to demobilize labor and its leadership (see 111–21, 223ff.).

These sophisticated spokesmen for American capitalism were hardly liberals themselves; indeed, Mills thought their victory led inexorably toward an American version of Neumann's Behemoth. The elite's effort to stabilize capitalism and buy off the labor movement contributed to the rise of an essentially authoritarian corporate state. These conservatives wanted "a New Deal on a world scale operated by big businessmen" (241) that would keep open European and Latin American markets in order to forestall the coming depression. With the Marshall Plan in the offing, Mills now labeled this strategy "the spinal nerve of the sophisticated conservative's plan: its principle is a world profitable for U.S. business; its next steps are the massive politically guided loans" (243). The domestic counterpart of this corporate imperium is the generation of a garrison state that would regiment the unions and sustain full employment, but only through a "permanent war economy" (249).[36]

To counter the main drift, Mills envisioned a thoroughgoing labor-based radicalism in chapter 14's "The Program of the Left" (250–63). Here he borrows freely from the World War I–era guild socialists, from the circle of American Trotskyists associated with C. L. R. James, and from the left-wing Reutherites.[37] Because he fears that the nationalization of industry, as in postwar Britain, will lead to but another form of bureaucratism, Mills posits the "socialization" of industry through a combination of both workers' control and centralized economic planning. He wants an independent labor party, of course, but he also seeks to infuse the labor left with a syndicalist spirit. Consumer cooperatives, neighborhood price-control committees, and a thoroughgoing shop democracy are all part of his near-revolutionary vision. Mills knows that many readers will see sectarian utopianism here in the place of a more achievable, if prosaic, labor program. He justifies himself, however, by making an existential leap to those "who have decided to throw in with the 'little groups that cannot win.' In fact, the big groups never win; every group loses its insurgency; maybe that is all that is meant by winning. It is a question where one decides to keep placing one's weight" (265).

The power and brilliance of C. Wright Mills lies in his effort to understand the social forces at play in mid-twentieth-century America and the progressive calculus that might yet generate a democratic combination, even as he remains utterly aware of their reactionary potential. In the penultimate chapter, "The Power and the Intellect," he takes the measure of the salaried middle class. By 1948 Mills had already completed much of the research and some of the writing for *White Collar,* so his cautious optimism here should be noted.[38] The middle classes may well side with architects of the main drift, especially if and when the great slump arrived, but a bold labor program, designed to keep prices low and the corporations on the defensive, might well forestall a white-collar drift to the right and in its place generate a far more inclusive and dynamic labor movement, one that truly set the national agenda. Instead of being fodder for the fascists, Mills was hopeful that the burgeoning ranks of the salaried workforce might yet swell labor's power.

The labor intellectuals are crucial to this great turn, however, for without the ideas and program of a set of engaged, practical union thinkers the labor leadership would drift with the conservative, bureaucratic tide. Mills writes that within the unions these professional intellectuals "act as leaven, lifting it beyond mere pork-chop contentment," so as to turn the unions into "vanguard organizations" (286). Utopianism? Not if "the power and the intellect" are united. And that is why Mills found trade union leaders to be "the strategic elite in American society," even as he also warned, on the very last page of the book, that "never has so much depended upon men who are so ill-prepared and so little inclined to assume the responsibility" (291).

When it appeared late in the fall of 1948, *The New Men of Power* won a set of largely favorable reviews. The business press did not think much of the work, of course, but the reviews that did appear, in *Barron's, Nation's Business,* and elsewhere served to legitimize the importance of the project. More unexpectedly, even the magazines and newspapers of the liberal center, like *The Progressive* and *The Nation,* repeatedly skewered by Mills, offered the book a good send-off. The reviewer for *The Nation* gave the Millsian critique of liberal language and sentiment a thorough, favorable evaluation. Similar respectful reviews appeared in the major academic journals.[39] Ely Chinoy, then conducting the field research that would generate *Autoworkers and the American Dream,* the classic sociological study of blue-collar mentalité, thought the book "demands and accepts a place for trained intelligence not only in providing piece-meal and limited solutions, but also in suggesting major alternatives for dealing with basic questions."[40] But Mills may well have been most gratified by Irving Howe's piece in *Partisan Review.* Though not uncritical—Howe thought the book suffered from a "certain lack of maneuverability in argumentation"—he nevertheless anointed Mills for resisting the pessimistic tide then sweeping the ranks of once-radical intellectuals. According to Howe, *The New Men of Power* stood "in total opposition to such current inclinations as quiet-ism, ideal-community building, advocacy of 'preventive' atomic war, [and] a truce with the right because of fear of Stalinism."[41]

The programmatic radicalism of an Irving Howe or a C. Wright Mills had little future in mid-twentieth-century America. Even as Mills read the reviews of his book, he was turning his back on what he would later call the labor metaphysic. Given his cresting expectations, which certainly reached their laborite apogee sometime before the 1948 elections, the deflation of his labor-left perspective was swift and thoroughgoing. Mills was sorely disappointed by President Truman's unexpected reelection. He had voted for the Socialist Party candidate, Norman Thomas, but his real hopes had lain with the possibility that Reuther and other CIO union leaders would take immediate steps to build a labor-based third party. Had the GOP's Thomas Dewey won the White House, Mills and a goodly number of others on the non-Communist labor left, including the Reutherite intellectuals, expected the Democrats to dissolve and a new labor party to come roaring forward. But in the wake of the election Mills saw such a prospect as "quite dead." And as it became clear that no slump would materialize, the victory of the sophisticated conservatives was assured.[42]

As these developments snuffed out the prospects for a more expansive set of laborite politics, Mills elevated to canonical status the conservative, but contested, trajectory he had hypothesized for the unions in *The New Men of Power.* Writing in mid-1949, in his last essay for *Labor and the Nation,* he argued that the unions were losing their potential to remain a broad social movement and were becoming instead "another vested interest, an agency of political regulation at an economic price." Thus the organization of white-collar workers, which Mills had once seen as a key to a progressive transformation of the middle classes, would now become merely "unionization into the main drift: it [would] serve to incorporate them as part of the newest interest to be vested in the liberal state."[43] When Mills published *White Collar* in 1951 he wrote as if his political enthusiasms of the mid-1940s were some species of ancient incantation: "Trade unions are the most reliable instruments to date for taming and channeling lower-class aspirations. . . . The old radical faith that the mere enlargement of unions is good because it brings more workers into 'organizing centers' is now naïve, as is the belief that winning the white-collar people to unionism is necessarily 'a link to the middle class.'"[44] By the time his last book, *The Marxists*, appeared in 1962, Mills had written off not just the unions but the Western working class itself. Looking with expectation to the Cuban Revolution and other third-world insurgencies, Mills dismissed "wage workers in advanced capitalism [who] have rarely become a 'proletariat vanguard'[;] they have not become the agency of any revolutionary change of epoch."[45]

There was, of course, much basis for such a doleful perspective. The defeat or expulsion of the Communists from the CIO did not just eliminate an unpopular political current. It also chilled all ideological debate and put shackles on internal union democracy. Meanwhile, in 1950 the UAW, upon which Mills had staked such hopes, signed a five-year contract with General Motors—in *Fortune,* Daniel Bell dubbed it "The Treaty of Detroit"—whereby the Reutherites won a higher standard of living for blue-collar workers, but only in return for their assurance of industrial discipline and stability in GM factories. Then, as Mills's friend Harvey Swados would attest after his sojourn in a mid-1950s Ford plant, the working class itself seemed to have rejected, or forgotten, or psychically buried any spark of radical opposition to the status quo. So even if the postwar economy did encounter the great slump Mills prophesied, it was unlikely to generate the lurch leftward that he and so many other radicals had once expected.[46]

It is therefore a tribute to Mills's courage that, even as he turned away from the labor movement, he made no peace with what he conceived of as the main drift. He remained at odds with the power wielded by America's elite, at home and in the rest of the world. But without a powerful set of allies himself, or the prospect of such, his only stance was one of moral rectitude and intelligent dissection. He would "debunk, debunk, debunk," Mills wrote to his editor at Harcourt Brace, "go back to the Muckraker era, which may be one measure of our defeat." He transmuted this radical disappointment into what he held to be a "politics of truth." Writing in a 1955 issue of *Dissent,* Mills argued that the independent intellectual must serve as "the moral conscience of his society . . . asking serious questions, and if he is a political intellectual, he asks his questions of those with power."[47] This was a noble and worthy calling, and it would inspire a generation of New Left radicals a decade hence, but the Millsian perspective no longer sought the fruitful interpenetration of social power and critical intellect that had so animated *The New Men of Power.*

What remains of this book for our own day? As history and contemporary observation, Mills ignored or got wrong some important things. He was not interested in the social history of the working class—North or South, black or white, immigrant or native-born, women or men. He was unconcerned with the geographic mobility of capital and with the technological shifts in the production and distribution of goods and information that have so dramatically transformed the nature of work, both blue collar and white. Nor did he foresee the capacity of Keynesian fiscal policies to stabilize U.S. capitalism, at least in the first quarter century after World War II. Most important, Mills made too much of the distinction between the sophisticated conservatives and the practical right. While the United States never became the kind of authoritarian society he believed the main drift would inexorably generate, he was actually much too sanguine about the labor policies of the managerial elite that ran America's largest corporations, staffed its most prestigious law firms, and sat upon its highest courts. Mills feared that the fate of organized labor was one of a claustrophobic incorporation into a hierarchically structured political economy. But after only a single generation of labor-capital accord, even the most internationalist and technologically advanced capitalists adopted the exclusionary union-free program, if not the polemics, of the entrepreneurial conservatives.[48]

The New Men of Power nonetheless bears a careful look by a new generation of unionists, not to mention historians and social scientists. If the unions are to once again become key elements of a new progressive movement, it is important to recognize that they are not in and of themselves radical institutions. Mills himself might well have avoided some of his own disillusionment if he had taken to heart the epigrammatic analysis put forth in the book's introduction. Trade unions are hybrid institutions, half monopoly seller of labor, half nascent social movement; and their leadership is just as mixed, though not always in the same personage: "an army general and a parliamentary debater, a political boss and an entrepreneur, a rebel and a disciplinarian" (9). The unions alternately tilt their character toward stolid interest group or expansive social movement, but if and when they do move toward the latter, it is unlikely they will ever fully arrive there.

If the unions cannot substitute themselves for the Left—an independent party is certainly needed, or at least an independent political voice—they are nevertheless essential to the health of the democratic polity. Mills saw the relationship between an organized working class and political democracy in stark Germanic terms, as in fact it had all been played out in 1933 and the years afterward. But the interwoven fate of the labor movement and a viable democracy need not be so Manichean. The erosion of democratic institutions in the contemporary United States is organically linked, at work and in the political arena, to the evisceration of the labor movement. When less than one-tenth of the private-sector working class can speak directly on its own behalf, American politics begins to share some of the characteristics of those societies ruled by more overtly authoritarian regimes. Conversely, where democracy has been reborn in recent years—in Poland, South Africa, South Korea, Spain, and Brazil—its revitalization has been synonymous with the reemergence of a powerful, independent labor movement. In *The New Men of Power* we rediscover what Mills knew so well: the democratic stakes are always high when the labor movement charts its future.

Notes

I thank Dan Geary for much conversation, excellent comments, and useful archival guidance in the preparation of this introduction. Dana Frank, Kathryn Mills, John Summers, and Carl Bon Tempo also made helpful comments.

1. All citations for quotations from and discussions in *The New Men of Power* appear parenthetically in the text.

2. *White Collar, The Power Elite,* and *The Sociological Imagination* (1959) have been almost continuously in print and are still capable of provoking controversy. In 1971 Augustus M. Kelley reprinted *The New Men of Power* in hardcover, but sales were limited and the book soon went out of print again.

3. John J. Sweeney, "America Needs a Raise," in *Audacious Democracy: Labor, Intellectuals, and the Social Reconstruction of America,* ed. Steven Fraser and Joshua Freeman (Boston: Houghton Mifflin, 1997), 13–21; Denise Magner, "Labor Leaders and Academics Seek a New Alliance," *Chronicle of Higher Education,* October 18, 1996; Steven Greenhouse, "Liberal Academics and Labor's New Leaders Pulling in Tandem Once More," *New York Times,* September 22, 1996; Steve Fraser and Nelson Lichtenstein, "Teamsters and Turtles," *New Labor Forum* 6 (Spring/Summer 2000), 23–29.

4. The literature is now far larger than when Mills wrote. Among those books that emphasize unionism's capacity to give voice to the heretofore inarticulate are: George Lipsitz, *Rainbow at Midnight: Labor and Culture in the 1940s* (Urbana: University of Illinois Press, 1994); Joshua Freeman, *In Transit: The Transport Workers Union in New York City, 1933–1966* (New York: Oxford University Press, 1989); Gary Gerstle, *Working-Class Americanism: Politics of Labor in a Textile City, 1914–1960* (New York: Cambridge University Press, 1991); and Nelson Lichtenstein, Susan Strasser, and Roy Rosenzweig, *Who Built America: Working People and the Nation's Economy, Politics, Culture, and Society* (New York: Worth Publishing, 2000), especially chapters 8, 9, and 10 on the Great Depression and World War II.

5. Numerous studies offer insight into the power, excitement, and program of the unions, both in Washington, D.C., and at the grass roots. See Robert Zieger, *The CIO, 1935–1955* (Chapel Hill: University of North Carolina Press, 1995); Nelson Lichtenstein, *Labor's War at Home: The CIO in World War II* (New York: Cambridge University Press, 1982); and, for a novelized treatment, K. B. Gilden, *Between the Hills and the Sea* (1971; rpt., Ithaca, N.Y.: ILR Press, 1989).

6. Irving Louis Horowitz, *C. Wright Mills: An American Utopian* (New York: Free Press, 1983), 5–6; Kathryn Mills with Pamela Mills, *C. Wright Mills: Letters and Autobiographical Writings* (Berkeley: University of California Press, 2000), 21–30. Mills is quoted in Richard Gillam, "Richard Hofstadter, C. Wright Mills, and the 'Critical Ideal,'" *American Scholar* 47 (Winter 1977–78), 72.

7. H. H. Gerth and C. Wright Mills, *From Max Weber: Essays in Sociology* (New York: Oxford University Press, 1946), 70. See also John Eldridge, *C. Wright Mills* (London: Tavistock, 1983), 22–25; and Joseph Bensman, Arthur Vidich, and Nobuko Gerth, *Politics, Character, and Culture: Perspectives from Hans Gerth* (Westport, Conn.: Greenwood Press, 1982), 9. The Gerth-Mills collaboration was not without its difficulties. See Guy Oakes and Arthur J. Vidich's *Collaboration, Reputation, and Ethics in American Academic Life: Hans H. Gerth and C. Wright Mills* (Urbana: University of Illinois Press, 1999)

8. Perlman famously denounced the "onrush of overpowering social mysticism" that enveloped intellectuals when discussing labor. See Selig Perlman, *A*

Theory of the Labor Movement (New York: Augustus M. Kelley, 1928), 281; Horowitz, *C. Wright Mills,* 43–45.

9. For an evocative portrait of Mills, from this period and later, see Harvey Swados, "C. Wright Mills: A Personal Memoir," Dissent 10 (Winter 1963), 35–42.

10. According to biographer Richard Gillam, Mills was greatly influenced by Schactman's theory of "bureaucratic collectivism," which described the system of class oppression that now existed in the Soviet Union and might yet emerge out of the crisis of capitalism in the United States. See Richard Gillam, "C. Wright Mills, 1916–1948: An Intellectual Biography" (Ph.D. diss., Stanford University, 1972), 330–31. As for his relationship with Dwight Macdonald, Mills may well have been instrumental in choosing the name—*politics*—for the magazine. See Mills to Macdonald, October 10 and October 25, 1943, in Mills and Mills, *Letters and Autobiographical Writings,* 51–54; see also Gregory Sumner, *Dwight Macdonald and the "politics" Circle* (Ithaca, N.Y.: Cornell University Press, 1996).

11. C. Wright Mills, "The Nazi Behemoth Dissected," *Partisan Review* (September–October 1942), reprinted in *Power, Politics, and People: The Collected Essays of C. Wright Mills,* ed. Irving Horowitz (New York: Oxford University Press, 1962), 177. On Franz Neumann, whose work greatly influenced Mills, see H. Stuart Hughes, "Franz Neumann between Marxism and Liberal Democracy," in *The Intellectual Migration: Europe and America, 1930–1960,* ed. Donald Fleming and Bernard Bailyn (Cambridge, Mass.: Harvard University Press, 1969), 446–62.

12. Quoted in Gillam, "Richard Hofstadter, C. Wright Mills, and the 'Critical Ideal,'" 72. On his willingness to serve as an officer, see Mills to Parents, June 29, 1943, box 4B353, C. Wright Mills Collection, Center for American History, University of Texas at Austin. See also Mills to Thomas McCormick, July 15, 1944, in Mills and Mills, *Letters and Autobiographical Writings,* 68.

13. Gillam, "C. Wright Mills," 373–74. In chapter 13, "The Main Drift," Mills forcasts the postwar statification of much of the union movement under a regime of neo–New Dealism. The postwar fear that the United States might turn into a "garrison state" was not confined to the extreme left, as Michael Hogan has demonstrated in *A Cross of Iron: Harry S. Truman and the Origins of the National Security State, 1945–1954* (New York: Cambridge University Press, 1998), 23–68 passim. See also Aaron Friedberg, *In the Shadow of the Garrison State: America's Anti-Statism and Its Cold War Grand Strategy* (Princeton, N.J.: Princeton University Press, 2000), for a "triumphalist" reading of how and why the United States avoided becoming a garrison state.

14. C. Wright Mills, "The Political Gargoyles: Business as a System of Power," *New Republic* (April 12, 1943), reprinted in *Power, Politics, and People,* ed.

Horowitz, 75–76. See also Mills, "The Case for the Coal Miners," *New Republic* (May 24, 1943), reprinted in ibid., 696–97. Mills soon ceased writing for *The New Republic* because the editors there thought of Lewis and most other strike-wielding wartime labor leaders as little more than self-serving labor bosses.

15. C. Wright Mills, "The Trade Union Leader: A Collective Portrait," *Public Opinion Quarterly,* 9 (Summer 1945), reprinted in *Power, Politics, and People,* ed. Horowitz, 77–96; Mills quoted in Dan Geary, "The 'Union of Power and the Intellect': C. Wright Mills and the Labor Movement," *Labor History* (forthcoming).

16. Paul Lazarsfeld, "An Episode in the History of Social Research: A Memoir," in *Intellectual Migration,* ed. Fleming and Bailyn, 270–337.

17. Hardman actually quit the ACWA because he so intensely objected to Hillman's de facto alliance with U.S. Communists, especially within the New York American Labor Party. In 1944 this put Hillman on the more conservative, pro-FDR, pro–Democratic Party wing of the CIO. See Steven Fraser, *Labor Will Rule: Sidney Hillman and the Rise of American Labor* (New York: Free Press, 1991), 522.

18. See Geary, "'Union of the Power and the Intellect.'"

19. C. Wright Mills to J. B. S. Hardman, December 9, 1945; Hardman to Mills, February 24, 1946; Mills to Hardman, February 26, 1946; Mills to Hardman, March 22, 1946; and the book outline by Mills and Hardman entitled "Politics and Labor: An Inquiry into American Social Dynamics" (1946), all in box 4B395, C. Wright Mills Collection. Hardman must have seen Mills as a younger comrade who could carry out his lifework. In a February 26, 1946, letter Mills wrote, "I have your letter from Wood's Hole in which you outline our life together for the next ten years." For the most thorough study of the ACWA, see Fraser, *Labor Will Rule,* 77–145 passim and 324–48 passim. Hillman was often called a "labor statesman."

20. C. Wright Mills, "The Politics of Skill," *Labor and the Nation* 2 (June–July 1946), 35, quoted in Gillam, "C. Wright Mills," 340. To this end Mills and Hardman prepared to collaborate on an ambitious survey of where labor stood and what could be done to make it more powerful. It was later published as J. B. S. Hardman and Maurice Neufeld, eds., *The House of Labor: Internal Operations of American Unions* (New York: Prentice-Hall, 1951).

21. C. Wright Mills to Frances and Charles Grover Mills, September 1948, in Mills and Mills, *Letters and Autobiographical Writings,* 120.

22. Mills was undoubtedly pleased to report that among CIO staff intellectuals (the research and education directors) three-fourths were in favor of a labor-based third party (311).

23. C. Wright Mills to Ruth Harper, June 7, 1947; Mills to Frances and

Charles Grover Mills, June 1947; Mills to Dwight Macdonald, July 1947, all in Mills and Mills, *Letters and Autobiographical Writings,* 105–8. Mills was not an ironist, so he strikes a false note here. More likely, his inclusion of the Wobbly epigraph reflects his equivocal relation to the labor leadership and their often-times self-interested politics.

24. C. Wright Mills to Parents, "Friday" 1948, box 4B353, C. Wright Mills Collection; Geary, "'Union of the Power and the Intellect.'"

25. C. Wright Mills, "'Grass-Roots' Union with Ideas—The Auto Workers: Something New in American Labor," *Commentary* 5 (February 1948), 240.

26. C. Wright Mills, "UAW Diary," box 4B349, C. Wright Mills Collection.

27. Mills, "'Grass-Roots' Union," 242, 244.

28. The UAW has been well studied. For detailed accounts of the union and its factional character right after the war, see Nelson Lichtenstein, *Walter Reuther: The Most Dangerous Man in Detroit* (1995; rpt., Urbana: University of Illinois Press, 1997); and Martin Halpern, *UAW Politics in the Cold War Era* (Albany: State University of New York Press, 1988).

29. "Research Experience and Training," November 7, 1944, in Mills and Mills, *Letters and Autobiographical Writings,* 80.

30. C. Wright Mills to William Miller, Spring 1946, in Mills and Mills, *Letters and Autobiographical Writings,* 98. See also Horowitz, *C. Wright Mills,* 216–17.

31. Mills to Miller, Summer 1948, in Mills and Mills, *Letters and Autobiographical Writings,* 117.

32. The second of the "two Trotskyist parties" (15) to which Mills refers is the Socialist Workers Party (SWP), whose leading personality was James Cannon. The SWP saw the Soviet Union as a "degenerated workers state"; the Workers Party argued that its character was "bureaucratic collectivist." From this distinction, much polemic would follow, with rather large consequences for many political intellectuals, both inside and outside these two sects.

33. For an account of Macdonald's political sensibilities at this time and the "New Roads" controversy, see Sumner, *Dwight Macdonald and the "politics" Circle,* 147–78 passim. Among Mills's newfound Trotskyist acquaintances and friends, Irving Howe and Louis Coser wrote blistering denunciations of Macdonald's "New Roads" series in *politics.* Along with Columbia colleague Robert Lynd, they defended democratic socialism, a progressive labor movement, and the power of a Marxist analysis. See Gillam, "C. Wright Mills," 330; Louis Clair (Coser), "Digging at the Roots or Striking at the Branches?" *politics,* 3 (October 1946), 323–28; Irving Howe, "The 13th Disciple," *politics,* 3 (October 1946), 329–35. For Howe's retrospective views, see Irving Howe, *A Margin of Hope: An Intellectual Autobiography* (New York: Harcourt Brace Jovanovich, 1982), 115–17.

34. Many books have been written on this connection. Among the best, or at least the most provocative, are Robin Kelley, *Hammer and Hoe: Alabama Communists during the Great Depression* (Chapel Hill: University of North Carolina Press, 1990); Daniel Horowitz, *Betty Friedan and the Making of the Feminine Mystique: The American Left, the Cold War, and Modern Feminism* (Amherst: University of Massachusetts Press, 1998); and Michael Denning, *The Cultural Front: The Laboring of American Culture in the Twentieth Century* (New York: Verso Books, 1998).

35. See also 247–48 where Mills argues for the interpenetration of military, corporate, and government economic planning elites.

36. Although this idea would soon come into common usage, even among liberals, at the time it was confined to left-wing circles. Here Mills's analysis parallels that later made influential by William Applemen Williams in *The Tragedy of American Diplomacy,* first published in 1957. See also Hogan, *Cross of Iron,* 1–23 passim.

37. Mills cites a factional document from the Johnson-Forest Minority within the Workers Party of Max Schactman (257). This factional group, led by C. L. R. James and Raya Dunayevskaya, argued that a more spontaneous organization of the working class, following some of the ideas first put forward by Rosa Luxemburg, would avoid the pitfalls inherent in Leninist centralization. Reorganized as Facing Reality in the 1950s, this sect became increasingly hostile to virtually all wings of the trade union movement. Ria Stone, quoted by Mills, was the pen name of Grace Lee Boggs, who wrote *Revolution and Evolution in the Twentieth Century* (New York: Monthly Review Press, 1974), with her husband, James Boggs.

38. Mills to Hans Gerth, August 1946, in Mills and Mills, *Letters and Autobiographical Writings,* 99.

39. Horowitz, *C. Wright Mills,* 219–22; Robert Nichols, "The Leaders of Labor," *The Nation,* 167 (October 2, 1948), 377–79.

40. Ely Chinoy, "The New Men of Power: America's Labor Leaders," *Canadian Journal of Economics and Political Science,* 15 (May 1949), 259–61. Like Mills, Chinoy was an anti-Stalinist of left-wing views, but by the time *Autoworkers and the American Dream* appeared in 1955, his generation was more likely to lay the "blame" for the failure of the socialist dream on the consciousness of ordinary workers than on the strategic errors of their leaders.

41. Irving Howe, "Possibilities for Politics," *Partisan Review,* 15 (December 1948), 1356–59. The slap at "ideal-community building" is another kick at Dwight Macdonald, whose *politics* magazine was then about to reach its literal dead end.

42. Gillam, "C. Wright Mills," 367–69. To Hans Gerth, who was supporting

Henry Wallace, Mills wrote, probably in the summer of 1948, "There is now no doubt that Reuther is coming out this fall for a new party! There is moreover no doubt that John Green of the ship builders [International Union of Marine and Shipbuilding Workers of America] and textile workers [Textile Workers Union of America, led by Emil Rieve] will string along. It may be, or at least it is not foolish to think that Reuther and co. will get hold of the CIO minus the CPs in the next few years. I cannot but believe that such an organization will or may well amount to something. And those people are madly looking for ideas" (Mills to Gerth, n.d., quoted in Gillam, "C. Wright Mills," 367).

43. "Notes on White Collar Unionism," *Labor and the Nation* (May–June 1949), 19, quoted in Gary, "'Union of the Power and the Intellect.'" As one might expect, Mills and Hardman grew apart, even as the political hopes that had given rise to *Labor and the Nation* eroded. The magazine ceased publication in 1952.

44. C. Wright Mills, *White Collar: The American Middle Classes* (New York: Oxford University Press, 1951), 318–19.

45. C. Wright Mills, *The Marxists* (New York: Delta Books, 1963), 128. Despite such well-publicized attacks on the labor metaphysic, Mills may well have been considering a new book on the world of work. John Summers has brought to my attention an unpublished book proposal written sometime after 1956 in which Mills sought to explore the internal structures of the working class and thereby challenge the received "job-conscious" wisdom of his University of Wisconsin teacher Selig Perlman. Of *The New Men of Power,* Mills wrote that it "has fallen by the way. . . . Yet it contains many things, perhaps buried in it, that I am loathe to let fall aside in the portrait of American civilization on which I have been at work" (Summers e-mail to Lichtenstein, January 30, 2001, quoting "Proposal for New Book," box 4B412, C. Wright Mills Collection).

46. Lichtenstein, *Walter Reuther,* 271–98; Harvey Swados, *On the Line* (1957; rpt., Urbana: University of Illinois Press, 1990).

47. C. Wright Mills to Lambert Davis, October 30, 1948, quoted in Gillam, "C. Wright Mills," 368; Mills, "On Knowledge and Power," in *Power, Politics, and People,* ed. Horowitz, 611, 612.

48. A Millsian division among employers is found in Howell Harris, *The Right to Manage: Industrial Relations Policies of American Business in the 1940s* (Madison: University of Wisconsin Press, 1982), but a more recent study by Sanford Jacoby finds a sophisticated form of antiunionism at work among main-drift capitalists even as Mills conducted his study. See Jacoby, *Modern Manors: Welfare Capitalism since the New Deal* (Princeton, N.J.: Princeton University Press, 1997).

THE NEW MEN OF POWER

WHAT ARE LABOR LEADERS LIKE?

WHILE OLDER spokesmen are still being heroized, new men are accumulating power in America. Inside this country today, the labor leaders are the strategic actors: they lead the only organizations capable of stopping the main drift towards war and slump.

Twenty-five years ago, the movement which they led was scattered and straggling, the country in which they led it was secure and hopeful, and the world was thought to have been made safe for democracy. Now, in the middle of the twentieth century, their movement involves one-third of the American people, the power of the world is one-half American, and democracy everywhere is unsafe and in retreat.

What the U.S. does, or fails to do, may be the key to what will happen in the world. What the labor leader does, or fails to do, may be the key to what will happen in the U.S.

To ask what sort of man the labor leader is, is also to ask what sort of organization he is running and what sort of country he is running it in. He is not a private citizen; he is a social actor, and the first condition of his action is the character of his union. The labor leader is a union-made product, and that is true whether he built his union single-handed and now treats it as his private property or whether he came into it late in life and still feels like a stranger in it.

The labor union is an army; the labor leader is a generalissimo. The union is a democratic town meeting; the leader is a parliamentary debator. The union is a political machine; the leader is a political boss. The union is a business enterprise, supplying a labor force; the labor leader is an entrepreneur, a contractor of labor. The labor union is a regulator of the workingman's industrial animosity; the labor leader is a salaried technician of animosity, gearing men at work into an institution and then easing that institution through the slumps and wars and booms of American society.

The labor leader is like an old-fashioned general: he recruits and commands an army. But there are all sorts of armies. The union is more like a loose-knit guerrilla outfit, run by a war lord, than like a modern armed force run by some bureaucrats especially trained in the skilled use of mechanized violence. Yet in any union, as in any army, there is a hierarchy and there is discipline. Generals cannot be generals without sergeants, and neither make up an army unless discipline connects each to the other and to a mass of soldiers. In this sense, unions are armies, with some of the best and some of the worst discipline that is to be found anywhere today. It is no small thing to be among the 180-odd generals—the presidents of the national unions—with 14,000,000 people organized as a reserve corps for industrial battle.

Probably half of those 14,000,000 are disciplined enough to quit work on a few hours' notice if so ordered. But neither armies nor unions are constantly at war nor always in a militant state. There are treaties, armistices, and diplomatic relations with the enemy. Yet at all times the union is organized and prepared for the possibility of industrial battle. It has its spies and its military secrets; and within certain limits, it can virtually conscript its soldiers for service in the line.

In one key respect the U.S. union is very unlike the U.S. Army: it elects its own generals and sergeants, sometimes every one or two years and sometimes during the very course of perilous battle. It is an army that votes by actual ballot and "with its feet"; by acting or refusing to act, it votes on the declarations of war and on the terms of the armistice. That is why the labor union is not only an army but also a town meeting, and why the labor leader is not only a general or a sergeant but also a parliamentary leader.

Almost always on paper, and often in real life, the American labor unions are democratic societies. Probably they are the most democratic societies of their size in the world; what other continuous, voluntary associations of equal size exist with which they might be compared?

Between the democracy of the town meeting and the discipline necessary for militant action, there is a tension which the labor leader has resolved in the way of formal democracies everywhere—by the political machine. There are not many features of a city political machine that cannot be matched by a union machine. Bill Crump, boss of Memphis, Tennessee, and Bill Hutcheson, boss of the Carpenters Union, have much in common. The union world is a world of political machines; the labor leader is a machine politician.

Machine bosses at the top require ward heelers at the bottom: the labor bosses have district and local "pork-choppers," their business agents and international representatives. These agents fix things with the locals and the districts; they carry orders and report back what they have picked up in the wards. Not all business agents and international representatives are party hacks on patronage: their formal job is to assist the locals in organizing and in arranging the points of contact with business. But many a business agent or international representative is part of the machine of the top man, and many another is eating pork chops, even though he lost out in his local, because he stood by the high boss.

Big machine bosses make deals with other big bosses and with little bosses. Jurisdictional allocations of the building trades unions are examples of such deals. One might say that the AFL, as well as the CIO, is an interlocking of large and small political machines. The deals by which these federations are tied together are often those of political machinists, entered into for the powers they bestow and the guarantees they offer the union leaders as political bosses.

✦

Yet the labor leader is not merely the war lord, the parliamentary leader, and the machine boss. The main and constant function of a union is to contract labor to an employer and to have a voice in the terms of that contract.

A union stands or falls by the success or failure of its contracting job. Everything in the world of the business-like unions revolves around that. At different times labor unions look like many different things, but as long as they operate as going concerns, as labor unions, they must in some way regulate the conditions of employment within an occupation or an industrial market for labor. And that means that the labor leader is a business entrepreneur in the important and specialized business of contracting a supply of trained labor.

Has Charles O'Neil, executive for the coal owners and a Republican, got any more business sagacity than John L. Lewis, executive for the coal miners and a Republican? And is it far-fetched to believe that, given the motive and the opportunity, young Walter Reuther, president of the Automobile Workers' Union, could do the job that young Henry Ford, president of the Ford Motor Company, is doing just as well or perhaps better?

The labor leader organizes and sells wage workers to the highest bidder on the best terms available. He is a jobber of labor power. He accepts the general conditions of labor under capitalism and then, as a contracting agent operating within that system, he higgles and bargains over wages, hours, and working conditions for the members of his union. The labor leader is the worker's entrepreneur in a way sometimes similar to the way the corporation manager is the stockholder's entrepreneur. In the world of business there are old-fashioned entrepreneurs and new-fashioned managers, and so it is in the world of labor.

A labor union is a combination in restraint of an unfree labor market. Labor markets are rarely free because in them the only kind of contract the individual laborer can usually make is the type lawyers call "distress contracts." The individual employee and the individual employer are too unequal in power to permit free bargaining. A labor union is a combination looking toward the creation of a free labor market by equalizing the power of employers and employees.

"Trade unionism," one of our leading labor leaders says, "needs capitalism like a fish needs water." If we understand by "trade unionism" unions as we now know them, he is quite correct. Trade unions and private property are now parts of the same system. Before there was private property there were no labor unions; and whenever the state takes on the functions of the entrepreneur, it is also likely to invade, conquer, and finally abolish the functions now performed by labor leaders.

The labor leader as we know him will not last any longer than the businessman as we know him. He is performing an entrepreneurial function, however specialized it may sometimes seem, and his fate is the general fate of the entrepreneur, plus certain special treatments.

During the late Thirties, the labor leader spoke the language and acted the part of a rebel, but this is a role he usually plays only during times of militant organization. In a less obvious way, however, and with many cloaking myths, the labor leader continually challenges the received business system. Whether he knows it or not, and often he seems not to know, he is fighting the power conferred on other types of entrepreneurs by the rights of property and the laws guaranteeing those rights. If he is for the closed shop, he must be against freedom of contract. If he is for an improvement of shop conditions and for a change in the ways of managing a shop, he is, in fact, encroaching upon the received prerogatives of the managers of property.

The union is a human institution established to accumulate power and to exert it. The leader of the union is not of the elite of money or of prestige, but he is a member of the elite of power. The labor leader is a powerful man: he accumulates power and he exerts it over the union member and over property.

Property owners pull the worker into their sphere and then manage his working life. Within the owner's shop, the workman is under the command of the owner or his agents. The owners make economic decisions within and between business enterprises, and these affect the worker. The employers dominate the labor market by dictating the workers' wages and hours; when they have monopoly advantage, they set prices behind the backs of the unorganized consumers. Their whole sphere of domination is enlarged and strengthened as they increasingly enlist the aid of the state.

Yet at each point where property owners strive to dominate, the labor union and its leader rebel against that domination. The union attempts to move in on it in the interest of the organized workers. It sets up rules and grievance procedures for the place of work. In some industries, such as the garment trades, it makes rules about the higher administrative functions of management, stating what they can and cannot do by way of production and merchandising. It defies the uncontrolled sway of property in setting the rates and regulations for wages and the conditions in the labor market. And as a pressure group it tries to counteract the power of property in the commodity market and over the apparatus of the state.

During mass organization drives, the labor leader whips up the opinion and activity of the rank and file and focuses them against the business corporation as a pedestal of the system and against the state as the crown of the system. At such times, he is a man voicing loudly the discontent and the aspirations of the people next to the bottom, and he is seen and recognized as a rebel and an agitator. Yet, in fact, all the time that he is the leader of a live and going union, the labor leader is in conflict with the powers of property: he is a rebel against individual business units and their unmolested exercise of the powers which property conveys. In his timidity and fear and eagerness to stay alive in a hostile environment, he does not admit this, and he often believes that he is not a rebel in the senses named, but the fact remains that he is. He is serving the function of a modern rebel by virtue of what his organization must do to live; modern rebels need not be romantic figures.

Yet even as the labor leader rebels, he holds back rebellion.

He organizes discontent and then he sits on it, exploiting it in order to maintain a continuous organization; the labor leader is a manager of discontent. He makes regular what might otherwise be disruptive, both within the industrial routine and within the union which he seeks to establish and maintain. During wars, he may hold down wildcat strikes; during upswings of the economic cycle, he may encourage sit-down possession of private property. In the slump-war-boom rhythm of modern American society, the labor union is a regulator of disgruntlement and ebullience, and the labor leader, an agent in the institutional channeling of animosity.

The labor leader is an army general and a parliamentary debater, a political boss and an entrepreneur, a rebel and a disciplinarian. We can move with our camera across the universe of unions, taking snapshots of a variety of specialized actors; we can move through time, taking pictures of men at different moments in the course of union history. But in order to get a representative portrait of the labor leader today, we have to gather systematic information about a large number of labor leaders.

The 500 whom we have studied represent a cross-section of America's national, state, and city leaders.* They come from all regions of the country, from different-sized cities, from large and small, old and young unions. They are the men who have made union policy during the late war years and the recent years of the peace. This book is a collective portrait of these labor leaders, set in their American time and society.

We have tried to see the labor leader as part of the American scene and to relate him to what is happening to the whole of modern society. In order to understand him as a man and as a social actor, we have to understand the worlds in which he operates. As a social actor, he is known superficially to the general public and intimately to special political publics. These several publics are an important feature of the labor leader's milieu, and we must study the images they hold of him. But he is, above all,

* Our sample is discussed in the Notes and Sources, pp. 300-303.

the leader of a certain kind of organization: the labor union must be understood if the labor leader is to be understood. Publics and unions affect the kind of man and actor the labor leader is; they form the backdrop for the general role he plays in American society and, in particular, for the curious role he plays in his relations with businessmen and politicians.

In our method we have combined the statistical and the qualitative. Marx once remarked that the calculation of averages is the most explicit form of contempt for the individual. And yet, without "averages" the modern understanding is greatly enfeebled. In this book we have tried to avoid both the arbitrary trivialization that results when understanding is on the level of the anecdotal biography and the sterile contempt for individual reality that results when understanding is reduced to the statistical summary. We have tried to proceed as systematically, accurately, and carefully as possible in an inchoate field of study. We hope this is not inconsistent with our further aim to be politically relevant.

PART ONE

CHAPTER ONE

THE POLITICAL PUBLICS

THE AMERICAN labor leader, like the politician and the big businessman, is now a public figure: different groups hold various images of him. He is reviled and acclaimed by small and politically alert publics; he is tolerated and abused by the mass public. And always, like other men of power, he is carefully watched by men inside his own organization.

As a public actor and as a private man, the labor leader responds in various ways to the images others hold of him. How he acts publicly and what sort of private man he becomes is affected by which of the images he takes most seriously.

The labor leader may willingly trade external prestige for internal power and live within the narrow political world of the machine he has built inside his craft or industry. But even within this machine, the images held of him by others affect his conduct and his outlook. He must see himself as others see him even if these others are only "his own boys" in his own union. Sometimes the images held by his own boys are so pleasant to behold that the labor leader, even as other men, tries hard never to look beyond them. But everyone in the union is not his boy; and the opposition may rudely shove its contrasting images before him. It is hard to push such rude images away and still be seen in the mirror. To retain power means to deal successfully with these obtrusive views, for they may reflect something of the shifting ideas of the rank and file, and they may influence what this rank and file will come to believe.

Other leaders, especially those above him in the union world, also have images of the labor leader; and he will seldom make major decisions without worrying about how they may affect his reputation and his chances for advancement. And these other union people, as well as his own rank and file, may be seriously influenced by the opinions of people altogether outside the union world.

In one way or another, the labor leader takes these outsiders' opinions into account, for to him they are public opinion which, although often a distant force, may at any time work its influential way into the minds of the very people upon whom his continued status and future power most obviously rest. Outside the unions, two types of publics carry opinions of him: one is the small circle of politically alert publics; the other is the great American public of politically passive people.

Politically alert people are keenly and continuously interested in political affairs. They take active stands, identifying themselves with various political actors and trying to figure out what they would do if they had the power. When the politically alert change their politics, they change their principles and ideas, for they must state their views about specific events and policies in terms of the principles and ideas from which they can be deduced or in terms of which they can be justified. To them, voting is a collective realization of substantial convictions rather than the formal duty of an individual.

Unlike the mass population, which does not reason out an image of the labor leader and his organization in terms of a set of political principles, the small, politically alert publics do formulate such views. They connect their general expectations with the demands they make on specified political means, which include political men and thus, for them, include labor leaders. The images they hold of the labor world and of its leaders vary according to their general political orientation; their images of labor thus help us to classify the political publics as right, center, or left.

Political publics may be located by the publications they read and the organizations they support. The constant readers of the right-wing newsletters and the inner circle of the NAM, as over against the constant readers of the Trotskyist press and the members of small left parties, may thus be compared with each other and with readers of the *New Republic, Nation,* and *New Leader,* and members of liberal third parties which operate in various states.

We do not know just how many people are in the politically alert publics. We can only guess: on the basis of the estimated circulations of selected publications, trying to eliminate overlaps; and on the estimated memberships of the several organizations involved, attempting to eliminate the inactive members. On these two bases, we know that the number of the politically alert is only a minute fraction of the U.S. population.

That the great bulk of people are politically passive does not mean that they do not at given times and on certain occasions play the leading role in political change. They may not be politically assertive, but it would be short-sighted to assume that they cannot move, on surprisingly short order, into the zones of political alertness.

The general political outlook of the alert publics rests upon the type of demand that each of them raises and upon the kinds of people that each of them contain. Each holds a rather distinct view of labor and of labor leaders, and these views are linked with their social makeups and their larger political expectations.

The Far Left

The far or Leninist left, as represented primarily by the two Trotskyist parties, raises political demands that are specifically focused and continuous. Its followers know what they want and they want it all the time. They want capitalism smashed and socialism, with "workers' control," triumphant. To gain these ends, they demand "independent working-class action," which requires an independent labor party.

The members of this public operate on what is probably the most systematized view of political reality now available. Indeed, it is so well worked out that, for most occasions, people who believe but who are not very intelligent can formulate an attitude on any given issue. In this sense, the far left supports its adherents with an almost popish set of ideas.

At present, the far left is composed of younger men and women; it is centered very largely in metropolitan New York, with tiny cells in a few other cities. There probably has been a very great turnover among these little groups in the past. Although some of the college-educated in the far left work in factories, the membership is certainly not predominantly wage workers. The main source of supply has been one or two of the New York city colleges. As people of faith, members are dedicated, rationalized, and inflexible; they always have great political will and vast energies, and sometimes a little vision. Given their inconsequential power, they often seem like bureaucrats without a bureaucracy.

The far leftists hold that unions are one step toward class-conscious organizations and should be politically guided and developed as instruments for the struggle. The trade union leader, in their view, must become a leading member or a close follower of a radical political party, or should be fought by party-inspired rank-and-file militants. Since it is plain that union leaders seldom fulfill the role assigned to them, the typical far left treatment runs like this:

The framework within which the far left locates labor is political and manipulative. The far leftist is generally critical of the labor leader, although he is gentle toward the union rank and file. He most approves those unions which seem to have direct power over the conditions of labor; he may even see the closed shop as a sort of prototype and training ground for "workers' control" rather than as a mere hedging in of a labor market.

The major line of argument used by most far left splinter groups is: (1) labor leaders are not political enough, that is, not radical in their political views and activities; (2) labor's rank and file *is* radical, or potentially so, which means that the rank and file, if led by radical leaders, would become involved in a revolutionary movement; therefore (3) most of the present leaders do not respond to what the rank and file really want—and thus (4) most of the leaders of labor are really mis-leaders of the laboring class.

The Independent Left

By definition, the independent leftists are not explicitly clustered around any periodical or organizational center. Until recently, many of them read such magazines as *Politics* and *Partisan Review.* Now *Partisan Review* has more or less retreated from left-wing political life, and *Politics* has become admittedly tired of politics and even of life. Like the little magazines which carry their opinions, independent leftists come and go. In a way they are grateful parasites of the left: they seldom attempt organization but can feel strong only when left organizations are going concerns. Because of their lack of organization, they are prone to political hopelessness. When events or organizations do not drift their way, they are a powerless third camp of opinion, oscillating between lament and indignation. But when left organizations are on the move, the independent leftists are not without considerable influence.

In the main, the independents are upper-class and upper-middle-class people, many of them professional, some of them writers with independent incomes. In common with the far left, and in contrast to the other publics, there are many intellectuals composing the group. Since the late war, the independent left has grown somewhat, having been augmented by ex-liberals with pacifist and other moral incentives oriented to political contemplation, and by discouraged socialists of every brand. It is as if all bankrupt left movements, from the IWW on, have left behind a small and stalwart residue of leftist independents, and now no one knows how widespread the mood of rebelliousness is.

Although numerically small, this public is important as a casual censor of other left organizations and publics, which include among their members some of the bright young men now in trade unions. The independent leftists now raise political demands that are unfocused or general, although they are continuous. They feel that now is a time for left intellectuals to rethink the whole perspective of the left rather than demand specific actions. They have difficulty answering the question that matters politically:

Whom do you want to do what? At the present time, they find it easier to label good or bad the specific activities and formulations of active political groups. Since the latter are only seldom affected by this moral criticism, members of the independent left are often frustrated, although sometimes, we do believe, happily so. With them, political alertness is becoming a contemplative state rather than a spring of action: they are frequently overwhelmed by visions, but they have no organized will. Their expectations are generalized to the point of being moral; yet they are not simply moralists: they treat political events and trends as symptomatic of the bitter tang and hopeless feeling of current politics. For them the days are evil, but they do not have the organization with which to redeem the time.

The independents would like to be able to agree with the far left on the union question: the latter's view is so definite and seems to explain so much. It enables one to place one's resentment, strengthen one's leftward nerve, and yet, at the same time, to explain away the practical policies that labor unions so often pursue. But the independent leftists do not have the far left's faith; they have lost the view of labor's rank and file as the spontaneous initiator of what is right and proper, and they cannot, in a politically workable way, make specific demands of the labor leaders.

They see coming a great coalition of business, labor, and government; they see bureaucracy everywhere and they are afraid. To them unions seem one more bureaucratic net ensnaring the people, part of the whole alien and undemocratic apparatus of control. All the bureaucratic elite, in labor as in business and government, are against the rank and file; they are trying to manage it, and it is immoral that man should be the object of management and manipulation. He is the root, and he is being choked.

There is here an almost charismatic wish that man should be enthusiastic and joyous, and the independent leftists do not see how to reconcile this value with such everyday organizations as labor unions, or for that matter, modern industry and government. Of late they talk vaguely, but not very seriously, about anarchist and syndicalist ideas of decentralization. They feel overwhelmed by apparatus, and the trade union is also apparatus. Their image is rather formal; concentrating upon the form of existing organizations, they sometimes tend to discount the clashing interests among them.

The Liberal Center

The liberal center, as represented by *The New Republic, The Nation,* and *The New Leader,* is specific in its political attention; but the looseness of its ideas encourages its members to dissipate their political attention and activity among a great variety of issues and causes. Continuously excited and upset, the center is full of indignation, which constantly shifts to new objects. The liberals set up a continuous sequence of demands for a changing variety of equally great causes. Unlike the far leftists, they do not exploit these specific issues in propaganda for a wholesale, long-run program; nor do they, like the independent leftists, ensnare this variety of causes in a network of strict morality. They take the daily and weekly events very seriously, in and of themselves.

The liberals want changes, but the means they would use and the practicality they espouse are short-run and small-scale. That is why their hopefulness and energy often seem so tragic, and that is why the left in general sees the liberals' activities as petty bourgeois screaming. The far leftist sees liberalism as a mask; the independent leftist is either too worn out for the liberals' sort of thing or considers himself too intelligent to believe that anything is really gained by it.

American liberalism, for at least one long generation, has lived off a collection of ideas put together before World War I. The wellspring for one set of its ideas is Louis Brandeis; for the other, Herbert Croly. Since these men wrote, little new has been added to American liberal ideology. The Croly liberal stresses the role of government in regulating big organizations and strengthening small men. The Brandeis liberal gears his hopes to the magical role of the small businessman. Both still fight monopoly as such;

and both draw upon western populist ideas. These, along with social democratic notions, make up the longer-run ideological base of the liberal public.

The center includes liberal businessmen of the late New Deal type, who co-operate with labor unions and boast about doing so, as well as mild social democrats of the *New Leader* school and some from the genteel brotherhood of the *Socialist Call.* Between the liberal businessman and these socialist groups, such organs as *The New Republic* and *The Nation,* trundle along with great noise and little clear-cut orientation. Today the center manages to attract from the right the practical middle-class populism of Henry Wallace, and from the left a few younger social democrats and Socialist Party members who continually show strong tendencies of going over to the independent radicals. The Socialist Party members, like those of the far left, believe in the extension of democracy to all economic relations, but through parliamentary measures of socialization; the bulk of the liberal center, however, fights shy of even such measures.

In social makeup, the liberal center is mainly middle class. It includes salaried professionals, especially teachers and journalists. Many trade union officials are found here. Unlike the two left wings, the liberal center is well scattered geographically, with a concentration of old social democrats in the needle trades of New York and other large cities. And it contains a good many old-middle-class people—farmers and small businessmen. Both come from the Middle West, the farmers, centered organizationally around the Farmers Union, and the few businessmen, centered around such organizations as Businessmen for Roosevelt. Yet despite its avowal of the interests of the old middle class, the center's vanguard is now mainly the urban lower middle class of white-collar employees and skilled workers in New York, while its grass roots are still the people who used to read such papers as the Wisconsin *Progressive.*

One of the big reasons why the liberal is pro-labor is that in his middle-class way he easily identifies labor with "the public" or "the people." What helps labor helps you; labor is, after all, everybody—or almost everybody. The liberal sees trade unions as occupational and industrial pressure groups rather than as class organizations. He revolves around the theoretical view of unionism that Lenin called "economism," except that whereas Lenin condemned it, he blesses it and makes theory from it. Like most labor leaders and union members, he sees unions as primarily economic organizations, he appreciates their homegrown patchwork of ideology, and he believes in general that the unions should use political action only as a means of furthering their economic and welfare ends. Thus his chief aim is to inspire the labor leader to have more political vision, which means to be excited about longer-range views—for example, to think of 1949 in 1948. And of course he wants the labor leader, or the government, to clean up labor's own house so labor leaders won't be so much like patronage politicians.

In the liberal view, the trade union leader is seen on the whole as following a safe and sane policy and knowing what he is about. The liberals accept the trade union status quo; although they would like to see them reformed in spots, they would not use the unions for purposes other than those for which they are now being used.

The liberal center is labor's home, although labor is sometimes not comfortable there. Comfortable or not, the liberals are the public that most reliably supports the policies pursued by the labor leader. Some liberals were once further to the left on all political matters than they are now, and their guilt about their own rightward leanings rebounds to the labor leader's advantage. In many liberal minds there seems to be an undercurrent that whispers: "I will not criticize the unions and their leaders. There I draw the line." This, they must feel, distinguishes them from the bulk of the Republican Party and the right-wing Democrats, this keeps them leftward and socially pure. Among such people, it is conventionally inappropriate to criticize the activities of labor leaders, except as exceptions which prove the general rule of the labor leader's wisdom. Anyone who ventures to criticize labor is considered to be playing into the hands of reactionaries whose blackness makes the liberals seem so white.

The liberal center, especially in metropolitan areas, is split between those who are anti-Communists and those who in various degrees follow the wondrous party line.

The Communists

It is very difficult to locate the CP as a specific unit on any U.S. political scale. Its outlook and activities are those of a foreign national bloc within the lineup of U.S. politics, and in any long-term view, it has not had much consistency of position. It is more an influence on one segment of the liberal center, displaying much of the smaller bourgeois psychology of this center, than it is a defined political public with definite U.S. roots and position. To be sure, historically its inner circle has taken a view close to the Leninist left; but now its core is merely pro-Russian, while its big fringe operates politically with a section of the liberal center. This deceptive split between the inner circle and the larger periphery, with its frequent vulgarity, tends to upset independent radicals who, if they had to choose, would prefer the position of the Leninist left—if only they could believe in it.

The Communists are the only political public we are considering which is centered around one party. Formed in 1919, after a split with the Socialist International, the American CP claimed in 1934 to have 25,000 members. By 1938, the claim was 75,000. The tactic of national unity and the subordination of class struggle to national unity during the recent war raised the claim to 80,000. At the present time, the CP probably does not have 60,000 members. Party membership, according to one informed student, "has always had a tremendous turnover. Thus you have a hard core of perhaps 10 per cent who have been members for 15 years, a fairly solid ring of 30 per cent or 40 per cent who have been in from 2 to 10 years, and a vaporous penumbra of people who join the party because of some local strike or lynching (or clambake), lose interest, and are dropped when they fail to pay dues."

We do not know enough about the social makeup of the American Communist Party to attempt to describe it, but we do know that during the Thirties, many top intellectuals and professional people were involved. By the middle Forties, many of these people had left, leaving a lower-middle-class metropolitan residue as the core of party strength.

The Communists are now the most important minor party in the union world. As we shall see in detail when we discuss "The Communist and the Labor Leader" in Chapter Eleven, they have formed definitely powerful cliques in several unions. Like the Leninist left, from which they have historically descended, they see the unions as instruments for their aims. And this has been the case whether, as before Russia's entrance into the late war, they worked hard building unions to fight in the class struggle against the bourgeoisie and its government, or whether, as after Russia's entrance, they stood with management and government, trying to discipline the labor force.

The anti-Communist liberals, along with conservatives in general, probably tend to exaggerate the strength of the CP; but there is no doubt of its influence upon a large section of the liberals or of its importance in the labor union world today.

The Practical Right

In conventional American politics, the noisiest fights go on between the practical right and the liberal center; these fights *are* politics to politically passive people when they occasionally, as during elections, enter the political arena. The practical conservatives can duel noisily with the liberals because they have the same short-run, shifting attention and the same agitated indignation. The practical conservatives always enter politics with an economic gleam in their eyes. During Democratic administrations and during depressions, they display the psychology of the cornered animal; during Republican years and during wars or booms, they are gruff but ebullient.

The occupational core of the practical conservatives is the middle-sized and small businessmen, especially those in retail trade; their organs of communication include most of our daily newspapers; their organizations are local Republican Party cells and businessmen's luncheon clubs. They are thus the largest, most effectively organized, and most respectable of our political publics.

The most intelligent spokesmen of the practical conservatives are publicists for the benevolence of capitalism, who lean heavily upon the standard American success story and the beneficent role of the small businessman. The ideas at the disposal of these unreconstructed conservatives are not so cogent as those of the liberal center, and they are constantly looking for competent and hirable ideologists. The days of Robert Taft are the yearned-for days of Herbert Hoover, but Taft is not quite up to becoming Hoover's intellectual heir. Yet this leader of the practical conservatives does as well as he can. Indeed, he managed to make the Taft-Hartley Act an excellent expression of the practical conservative mentality, including in it some three-fourths of the matters "pressed on us very strenuously by employers."

Ideologically, the practical conservatives are wild-eyed Utopian capitalists; strategically, they are practical men. They have much will and a continuity that comes from much backward vision. "Remembering" imaginary situations, they long for the golden age of Harding, Coolidge, and Hoover. Their ideas are a hodgepodge of anything they can use to throw at the enemy. They do not, at the present time, have any real ideas about preventing war or stopping the drift to another depression; the condition of the foreign world is improbable nonsense to them, and the economic cycle a great bafflement invented by theoreticians of the New Deal.

The practical conservatives know what they want: to make more money out of business and to put down the radicals and labor leaders who get in the way. Many of them are not so much politically alert as they are economically excitable in a political way. Unlike the liberals and the left, they attend to politics primarily as means to their own immediate economic ends. They represent pure and simple anti-unionism, fighting labor because they know how very practical most of labor's activities are. They deeply resent labor's encroachment on managerial prerogatives and labor's effort to get out of business what the traffic will bear. They use political slogans, but their meaning is usually economic.

The Sophisticated Conservatives

The sophisticated conservatives, represented by magazines like *Fortune* and *Business Week*, are similar to the far left in that their political demands are continuous and specifically focused. They leave the noise to the practical right; they do not attempt to arouse the people at large; they work in and among other elite groups, primarily the high military, the chieftains of large corporations, and certain politicians. Knowing what they want, wanting it all the time, and believing the main drift is in their favor, these sophisticated conservatives try to realize their master aim quietly.

Many of the spokesmen of the sophisticated right are occupationally of the trade association world. They tie in solidly with the industry-armed forces-State Department axis, and move personally as well as politically in those circles. The interchange between the military and big industry is more widespread and easier than most observers realize; intermarriages, as well as explicit career moves, would have to be taken into account in any thorough study of these connections. Since this tiny political group is not at present attempting directly to enlist public support, the terms of its real ideology are not well known. Probably as they see it, the high military and the big management should unite and form a new elite. During crises they would expect support from among all those practical conservatives of the type whose names appear in the Congressional investigations of rough stuff in industry, especially the La Follette hearings of the Thirties; and if they are smart about labor, they might hope to win over a bloc from the liberal center.

The difference between the practical and the sophisticated conservatives vis-à-vis labor is that the latter see the world of unions and leaders from a more political, a more manipulative, and a longer-term point of view.

The sophisticated conservatives hold that unions are a stabilizing force and should be encouraged as a counter-force against radical movements. They believe that the unions might well become the bulwark of the system they want to preserve and develop along twentieth-century lines. They would have the trade union leader end up in their personnel and public relations departments, as a junior lieutenant of the captain of industry, from where, at an appropriate time, they could kick him out and replace him by a more reliable man.

Some of the sophisticated conservatives speak their views in terms of the national scene. For example, at a recent hearing before the House Labor Committee, an employer who had fought a political union said to the Congressmen: "You would play right into the hands of the radicals if you passed legislation that would destroy unionism." Unions, he went on, "are essential to the national economy."

Others speak in more local terms; they see the labor leader as a sort of aide to their own personnel manager—as part of their managerial force, a specialist in peacefully disciplining the rank and file. This view spread rapidly during the late war, when it seemed to many members of this public that management and labor were co-operating nicely, on the basis of cost-plus and other government contracts.

The sophisticated conservatives see the labor leader so much in a political light that although they quibble about money, they are willing to pay for services rendered. They believe that pension plans, good lighting, and personnel counseling are better than socialism. Unlike the practical conservatives, who fear encroachment upon their managerial prerogatives, the sophisticated conservatives think that, by taking in the labor leader as a junior partner and a needed front, they can keep the situation under control.

The sophisticated conservatives hope that the labor leaders, in their fear of the practical right and in order to hold their organizations together, may be ready to accept the lure offered by co-operative big business with its emerging liberal front. They have read carefully what liberal labor spokesmen have so often and solemnly said: "You get the kind of labor union and leader that you demand; if you give us the Mohawk Formula, you'll get rough, tough labor outfits." The sophisticated conservatives, unlike the liberals, have examined the other side of this true coin: "If you give us co-operation, you'll get co-operative unions and co-operative leaders." They have studied carefully stories of how the steel union had to kick out the rough leaders who became troublemakers after the contracts were signed. That is the sort of practice the sophisticated conservatives are banking on, and many of them are willing to risk the first step.

The sophisticated right has two points in common with the far left: in their imagery, both split the labor leader from the rank and file of labor; and in their strategy, both would use the leader to manage the working men and women in the union. The left would use the labor leader to radicalize or to release radical forces among the workers (depending upon the relative weights given spontaneity and organization). The right would use the labor leader to de-radicalize or to keep radicals away from the workers (depending on how spontaneously radical the workmen are believed to be).

The Politics of Slump

The practical conservatives now have the political initiative, and their major political enemy is the liberal center. Today these are the only two alert publics of visible importance in American political struggles. The far left and the independent left are negligible in size and unimportant in political strength. Such effectiveness as the Communists have, they enjoy through the liberal center's unimaginative lack of political ideas. For the time being, the sophisticated conservatives are pleased to allow the practical conservatives to carry the burden of their fight. That is where matters now stand. But to be politically oriented, it is necessary to gauge the future as well as contemplate the present.

Under conditions of slump, the size and significance of the political publics may undergo great change with bewildering swiftness. The liberal view of historical continuity should not obscure the fact that history, at times, is discontinuous, and that in our time its pace has been enormously accelerated.

It is a safe guess that in the next American slump the areas of political alertness will expand. Joined by members of the now passive mass public, the politically alert will suggest programs and attempt to build organizations to make them effective. The politically alert will compete for the people, whom events, such as the timing and the severity of the slump, will move one way and then another. In terms of political publics, the question is: Who will catch the people when the system fails them?

Under the impact of slump, power may shift toward those who are ideologically and strategically prepared for it. Then the ideas of minor political groups, now unimportant in size and strength, may become politically relevant and their roles may become decisive in the shaping of events. Already the political publics are being ideologically polarized to left and right. For ideas and programs, you have now to go to the sophisticated conservatives or to the far and independent left. When the slump arrives, the ideological polarity may become a practical polarity.

This is true despite the strong, if often unwitting, efforts of the liberal center and the Communists to confuse the issue before the struggle gets fully under way. Liberals may think that they are walking upright down the middle of the road, but, in fact, many of them are crawling along the edge of the right-hand ditch. Their attention is wholly absorbed by the awesomeness of the power of Russia and the United States; in the name of realism, they would abdicate domestic political quarrels in favor of the national unity needed to save the world for whatever those in charge of the American political economy may have to offer it. The liberal ideas now available to Americans obscure rather than clarify what is happening in the world, and their rhetoric has already been taken over by the sophisticated conservatives.

During boom or wartime, the sophisticated conservatives' policy of "living with labor" tends to prevail; during early slump and during fear of slump, the practical conservative, with his policy of "busting up labor," edges into the foreground, making his economic clamor, and carrying the struggle for the right against labor. That is why the sophisticated conservatives can be quiet, and even talk the language of the liberals.

After the slump comes, the sophisticated conservatives will gain in importance and participate in the fight as a general staff. They have a program for slump. It involves the building of a war economy during peacetime while speaking all the liberal phrases. They will see their chance and will be shrewd enough politically to attempt to capture the labor leaders for this program. As the severity of the slump increases, they will tempt the labor leader with bigger bait, offering him security for his organization and tenure for himself, if he will only come over and help discipline the rank and file in a responsible way. In the meantime, the sophisticated conservatives will discipline the practical conservatives, whom the labor leaders fear. If they can handle the labor leader and use his organizations to keep the rank and file acquiescent, the sophisticated conservatives think they can hold things steady until the wars come again.

But the practical conservatives have no program with which to meet a slump. Their "program" only leads into slumps, not out of them, and they are easily frightened. In a slump, they will probably swing behind the sophisticated planners of the new conservative order, although groups of fascists, recruited from the lower middle classes of smaller cities, will compete with the sophisticated conservatives for the allegiance of the rank and file of the right.

During the slump, all left-wing groups, as well as the Communists, will compete for the loyalties of the larger liberal center, which will probably move leftward in a body. The far left, and especially the independent left, will grow again. Many programs will be set forth, but none of them will matter much unless they are connected with going organizations. Therefore the entire left and liberal forces will converge on one point: they will compete for the allegiance and the support of the labor leader, and for the rank and file of the labor unions.

That is why the labor leaders are now a strategic elite. They are the only men who lead mass organizations which in the slump could organize the people and come out with the beginnings of a society more in line with the image of freedom and security common to left traditions. In the American political drama, the labor leader has been thus far less a leading actor than a stage prop. He has been a man to whom things happened rather than a man who made new beginnings. Now he is strategic not only because he is powerful, potentially more than actually, but because his fortunes are bound up with the fate of the rank and file of unionized workers. He cannot weather any sizable slump without trying hard to be responsive to the demands of this rank and file.

In a slump, there is a question of power and there is a question of intellect. A program would assert how each of the two are to be developed and how ideas and people are to be united into a going concern. The labor leader is now the only possible link between power and the ideas of the politically alert of the left and liberal publics. How will the labor leader behave in the coming slump? That is the key political question for those who want to know what is in the works for American society in the middle of the twentieth century.

CHAPTER TWO

THE MASS PUBLIC'S VIEW

THE LABOR leader does not appear as a distinct and durable image to the mass public. The people at large are more likely to make blurred moral judgments than distinct political demands. Their impressions are not stable or part of any thought-out political view, but these very conditions make them all the more amenable to influence.

Nobody knows which way the mass public will turn in the slump or what it will expect of the labor leader, but in considerable part, the way the labor leader will turn depends upon the political temper of the people and upon what action he believes the people will allow or expect of him. The politically alert public which can shape the mass public's interpretation of the slump will thus be the public in the best position to influence the strategy of the labor leader.

Political opinions trickle from smaller alert publics to the passive mass of the people in three major ways:

First, the liberal and leftward publications, as well as the right-wing newsletters, are read by editors and writers for mass-circulation organs and by radio commentators. The contents of the politically sophisticated media are thus passed on, although in the process they may be sharply reslanted.

Second, writers for the magazines and papers that serve the politically alert publics graduate, in the typical course of their careers, to better-paying positions with media that serve the mass public. The labor editor of one of the nation's foremost business journals is a former Trotskyist, and one group of magazines having enormous circulation seems to have consciously followed the practice of recruiting and training bright young men from leftward circles.

Third, in their daily lives, the members of the two types of public meet one another, for the politically alert are not socially isolated people; on the contrary, they are the ones who lead what temporary mass organizations exist, and they are the ones who in neighborhood, shop, and office are most likely to initiate serious political discussion. The politically alert infiltrate the mass public and reveal to its members in face-to-face conversation something of their own political opinions and imagery.

But other influences besides the politically alert and their organs are shaping the impressions of the mass public. To understand its images of labor, now and in a slump, we have to pay attention to the contents of the mass media of communication and to the direct experience which the people have with labor leaders and labor organizations.

Labor in the Mass Media

The mass media are not kind to the labor unions or labor leaders. As a general rule, they ignore the peaceful and stable features of the union world while reporting in detail the deadlocks, the strikes, and the seizures. Violence is the meat and gravy of labor news; labor peace is seldom part of that news, unless the media have first created the expectation of violence that didn't come off. The media tend to report those labor actions which seemingly indicate great and irresponsible power on the part of the unions and the labor leaders rather than any constructive work they may do.

A study has been made of the handling of labor news on all four major radio networks during a sample period of 1944. The content of the 33 news programs having the largest national audiences were examined in detail. This study discloses that:

"Important items" of labor news are likely to hit most news programs, although there is little continuous labor reporting . . . except by a few markedly anti-labor commentators who constantly hammer away at labor questions. The division of opinion that is expressed about who is going to win in conflicts of business and labor is about 50-50, whereas in the division of opinion as to who is right and who is wrong, there are five times as many comments unfavorable to labor as there are favorable. In quoting anti-labor opinion, the commentators as a group draw heavily upon statements by government officials, prominent Republicans, big businessmen, and anonymous "rank-and-file union members"; whereas, in quoting opinions sympathetic to labor, the commentators draw almost exclusively upon statements made by labor leaders.

The general impression of labor presented for mass consumption by these typical and nationally heard radio news programs is that "labor is sometimes strong and sometimes weak, but what it does is nearly always morally wrong and no one approves of labor, except the labor leaders themselves."

While no comparable study of the handling of labor news by typical newspapers has been made, certain general conclusions can be drawn from a spot inspection of widely read dailies of various political hues. Their types of coverage range from hysterical name-calling and excited shouts of doom to objective reporting. But there are two generalities which almost all these papers have in common:

First, they do not cover labor news in the continuous and detailed way in which most of them cover business news. There are occasional labor columns, but there are no "labor pages" as there are business pages. Naïvely, from the standpoint of news service to the mass readers, this cannot be excused on the ground that more people are vitally concerned with business than with labor. Only 6 or 7 per cent of the working population of the nation are themselves engaged in business, whereas something like 33 per cent are involved with unions.

Second, although the policies of the big dailies range from conservative right to vaguely liberal, their stand on labor news typically runs like this: the union as an institution might not be such a bad thing, or it is a good thing in principle; but certain unions and a good many labor leaders have gained too much power which they are using recklessly and selfishly, without proper regard for the effects of their actions upon our general welfare. Various papers place different weight on the several clauses of this summary, but in general, it contains the common denominator of the newspaper's handling of labor. Anti-unionism in the press is something like anti-Semitism in everyday life. The qualifications, made ostensibly for exceptional cases, effectively swallow up the abstract statement of approval.

In the Republican papers, smearing labor is part of smearing the Democratic administration. The chaotic and fearful conditions often presented in connection with labor are not taken to be solely the fault of the newly powerful labor leader; they are also the fault of the administration's policy, or the administration's lack of policy, or of the New Deal's "abject surrender to ambitious, unscrupulous labor leaders" and its persistent encouragement of labor "to go after more and more dough."

Torrents of criticism are let loose in some of the more popular papers against "Murray's CIO" as a "pet of the New Deal." The Communist issue is ridden hard: the CIO is "overrun with Communists" and is suffering severely from "Red rot." More august papers solemnly warn, whenever they comment on any evidence of labor militancy, that unions are "cutting their own throats" and playing into the hands of their enemies when they do these things against the "public interest," and that a "handful of men in key positions must not be permitted to flout the entire nation."

The mass media are not only purveyors of news; they are also media of popular culture. In their entertainment as in their news, they are anti-labor. In radio soap opera, in the comic strips, movies, and pulp fiction, labor unions and labor leaders are almost never brought into the picture in any way. Even the factory worker is practically unknown in the dramas of popular culture. Mass culture heroes either have no stated occupation or they are professional, business, or white-collar people. By their omissions and in their whole manner of dramatizing the American scene, particularly their heavy accent upon individual effort and individual ends, the mass media are biased against the labor world, and make it appear strange and sinister.

Yet it does not necessarily follow that the mass media are as effective as their editors or certain spokesmen for labor would have us believe. The people have experiences which enter into and form their views of labor; when experience repeatedly proves the media wrong, people come to distrust the media. But just how many people have any experience with unions and union leaders? Suppose there were no mass media of communication: What would the mass public know about labor unions?

In and Out of the Unions

About one-third of the U.S. adult population either belongs to some labor union or lives in a family containing a union member. Presumably these people have more opportunity than others to experience the union world from the union side of the picket line or conference table.

We do not know how many people employ workers belonging to unions, but we do know that, along with their family members, about 9 per cent of the adult population are involved in managing or employing workers. Most of these people handle very small labor forces; and since only about a third of the workers are in unions, it is generous to estimate that 6 or 7 per cent of the adult population have more of a chance than others to experience unions from the business side of the tension.

Seven per cent from the business side, 33 per cent from the union side: this leaves some 60 per cent of the U.S. population who are not members of unions and have no direct business experience with unions. These 60 per cent are known in business-labor disputes as the public. Whether they know it or not, they have as large a stake in the outcome of such disputes as those who are directly involved; many of them have close or distant friends who are among the 33 and the 7 per cent. They are clearly subject to cross-pressures from the business-involved and the union-involved people whom they know.

Yet for their images of the labor organization and for their feelings about the labor leader, they must rely largely upon the contents of the mass media, upon hearsay from friends or passers-by, and upon occasional glimpses at, or inconveniences from, picket lines.

To say that 33 per cent of the people are union-involved is not a precise indication of the character of experience they have of the inner workings of labor unions or of the operations of the labor leaders. The kinds of experience that various types of union members have, as well as the proportions that fall into each type, vary according to the specific way a particular union is organized, the work processes within its industry or trade, and the extent to which the union encourages membership participation. We can, however, roughly distinguish three groups among the union-involved people: the inactive members; the active members, known in some unions as the activity; and the voluntary, unpaid rank-and-file leaders of the unions.

1. The inactive members neither regularly attend their locals' meetings nor participate in any continuous feature of the life of the union except the grievance procedure and the payment of dues. The only labor leaders they are likely to see at close range are the unpaid shop stewards or committeemen who serve them in the grievance machinery. A great many of them undoubtedly do not even know the head of their own local or the name of the president of the national union to which they belong.

Although these inactive members may not see the leaders at close range, and may think of them as "just some more big shots," nevertheless union members—and for that matter, factory workers at large—are pretty unanimously convinced that labor leaders are fighting for the workers' bread and butter. Ninety-two per cent of the unionized workers in factories and 82 per cent of the non-union workers believe that the union heads are doing something of benefit to labor.

The pay-off is what most affects the union member's attitude toward his union. The majority of workers seem to know that they get more money and better conditions and more of a chance to kick effectively with a union than without. Some 88 per cent of union members in factories think their best chance of making a living lies in joining a union; about half of all workers, union and non-union, agree that the unions do fight for higher wages and that they have improved wage standards.

Many American workers look upon the trade union in the way that many middle-class people look upon the insurance policy. They don't want to bother about it, but if it doesn't demand much personal sacrifice, they are willing to receive the benefits of membership. Like the insured, or for that matter, like stockholders, the union members may not exercise their right to vote and to participate in the management of the concern, but that does not mean they don't want to belong.

Similarly, this does not mean that these inactive members are not loyal to the union. The test of union loyalty is not regular attendance at meetings or regular exercise of the privilege of voting. Many loyal citizens of the United States do not vote, much less attend political meetings. The key test of loyalty comes during battle and during crises: Will the members support the union during strikes? Will they join the picket line or cross it? Experience demonstrates that this solidarity, although varying greatly from one period to another and from one union to another, includes from half to three-quarters of the people in the unions.

II. The active members of the union, a relatively small number, attend meetings more or less regularly and usually come out for local union affairs. They are good union members, well sold on at least the rudimentary ideas of pure and simple unionism. They are the old standbys and the young militants, and when there is trouble, they will all be there. They take the extra shift on the picket line, their wives and daughters man the soup kitchens during times of trouble. These members of "the activity" overlap with the rank-and-file leaders, and some of them graduate into the circle close to the officials. They carry the gossip of the union and they know the leaders of the local to talk to; they gather, carry, and repeat what they hear about the leaders, and during factional squabbles, they take sides.

III. The rank-and-file leaders of the union, in addition to doing all that active members do, donate much time to the union's routine work. They are the shop stewards, the men representing the union within the place of work; they are "the union on the job," dealing every day with foremen and union members, handling grievances. As observers for the leaders of the local union, reporting and even advising, they "localize and adjust developing trouble." Some sit on the executive boards of the locals and on various standing committees, or are delegates to various other labor bodies. All these rank-and-file leaders know labor from the bottom up. Many of them, as we shall see, are the future full-time leaders of their unions.

There are no good studies on American unions as a whole, or on any number of individual unions, to tell us how many union members fall into the inactive, active, or leader classifications of membership. A partial study has been made of the membership of British trade unions. It is interesting to know that in a country whose labor movement, in parliamentary election, has taken over the government itself, among the unions for which data is available only from 15 to 25 per cent of the membership usually votes on the various issues.

For American unions, the figure would undoubtedly be lower. Many of the newer unions are filled with members who in no way have needed to sacrifice or struggle in order to create their union. Indeed, some were among the minority who voted against the union in NLRB elections. As a whole, American unions have done little to educate their members, and the labor press is almost as dull as the typical local union meeting. It is a generous guess to estimate that 15 per cent of the union members, in addition to rank-and-file leaders, are continuously active.

The cadre of rank-and-file leaders—the members of local executive boards, standing committees, delegates to various bodies, and shop stewards—numbers slightly over 2,000,000 men. Calculations, based on this estimate of the number of people holding these positions in U.S. unions, show that about 15 per cent of the union members are unpaid rank-and-file leaders. Inside the unions, then, the 14,000,000 members fall roughly into three categories: 15 per cent are rank-and-file leaders; 15 per cent are active members; and 70 per cent are inactive members.

Adding all estimations, on the base of the total adult population in 1945, the following crude portrait emerges:

Union-involved		33%
Leaders	3	
Active	3	
Inactive	27	
The public		60
Business-involved		7
Total U.S. population		100%

Labor's General Score

No matter what the mass media say or what the public opinion polls indicate, the facts of union membership show clearly that a considerable proportion of the American people think enough of unions to want to join them. Over the last dozen years Americans have joined the unions by the millions. In 1935, only 9.4 per cent of the wage and salary workers of the country were in unions; ten years later 34.4 per cent were members. That kind of fact must be taken into account, along with the generally bad press and radio coverage given the unions. The lineup of the people according to their chances of experiencing the union world is a counterweight to media-implanted biases.

It is obvious that everyone who has joined a union has not done so simply because of a favorable attitude toward the unions. During the latest surge of union organizing, workers joined unions primarily: (1) by way of elections under NLRB supervision, and (2) by way of union membership maintenance clauses in contracts given war industries. Under the NLRB, a majority vote prevailed, which means that possibly as many as 49 per cent of those entering the unions in this way might not have voted for a union. Under the maintenance-of-membership clause, the people who did not want to join were given a fixed period of time during which, if they wished, they could cancel their membership. Even considering these facts, a definite majority of union members must be favorable to the general idea of unionism.

From the early days of the CIO to the middle years of the late war, the public was repeatedly asked the same question about labor unions by public opinion polls. It is not a very precise question, but it is the only one that has been repeated—eleven times—in exactly the same form over such a long period of time. The question runs bluntly: "Are you in favor of labor unions?"

Throughout this period, from 1936 to 1943, slightly more than two-thirds of the people have been in favor of labor unions. These were years of sharp moves in industry, of slump and war and boom in the nation. They were the years of strong union militancy and growth. The figures over this period range from a low of 67 to a high of 78 per cent, not showing any trend up or down. Unions are now recognized as part of the institutional machinery of American society.

We have to turn to other questions in order to get more current opinions on labor unions, for the blunt question has not been repeated recently. The nearest to it, asked in 1947, revealed that 73 per cent of those having any opinion approved of the general idea of labor unions. A very good question was asked during 1946: "Suppose you had been acting as a referee in labor-management disputes during the past three months: do you think your decisions would probably have been more often in favor of labor's side or more often in favor of management's side?" The people answered:

	JAN. 1946	JUNE 1946	NOV. 1946
Labor	26%	37%	37%
Management	45	37	34
Don't know	29	26	29
Total	100%	100%	100%

When a question about labor involves a decision about conflict rather than the acceptance of a general principle, fewer people favor labor and about one out of three people cannot make up their minds. But examine the trend: during the year 1946, business lost support: from 45 per cent in January to 34 per cent in November, and this in spite of the many postwar strikes during that period. Something else is involved in the attitude of the mass public toward labor unions. The price rise may well have affected the people's view. Coping with overtaxed budgets probably increased their sympathy with organized labor's attempt to raise its wages during this period when price control was virtually killed.

All the other general questions on labor unions which we have examined, from 1936 to 1948, seem to uphold the point that the mass public is definitely in favor of the idea of labor unions. Yet two qualifications must immediately be made: (I) their general approval does not preclude many specific criticisms of unions, and (II) all classes are not equally pro-labor.

I. The public attaches specific qualifications to its general support of unions. In 1939, 71 per cent of the mass public felt the unions needed reform, as against only 52 per cent who were for reforming government and 30 per cent, manufacturing industries. In 1943, when the public was asked if there were any organizations in the country which might cause harm if not curbed, 50 per cent said "Yes," and over half of those who answered "Yes" were aiming at labor or at labor leaders. Again, late in 1946, when asked about a list of things that might need "government attention," the regulation of labor unions ranked high on the public's list.

Apparently the public does not make up its mind about labor issues in terms of black or white, as many columnists and commentators do. That is true even of strikes, which according to the content of mass media should in most cases be rejected on principle. In November, 1946, 62 per cent of the people said that if they were a member of Congress they would vote against a bill to prohibit "all strikes for any reason whatsoever." But

43 per cent would prohibit strikes against the telephone company, while 32 per cent would prohibit strikes in the automobile industry. The two types of strikes they are most against are those in companies taken over by the government (59 per cent against) and "general strikes where all the unions in an area go out on strike together" (56 per cent against). Yet even in these cases, some 16 per cent of the mass public hasn't made up its mind.

Various industrial situations evoke different reactions from the public. For instance in 1946, in the case of a small electrical company, only 19 per cent would favor government arbitration and require both parties to accept the decision, but 30 per cent would favor such an arrangement for a large electrical company, and 46 per cent for the railroads. The public's general approval of the idea of unions does not mean that it does not discriminate according to specific cases or that it necessarily sees these cases in a simple way.

II. Class bias underlies the images people have of unions. This bias is not revealed as clearly in opinions on the general idea of unions as it is in opinions on specific issues, and particularly on strikes or other matters of conflict.

On the blunt question, "Are you in favor of labor unions?" there is only a slight difference of opinion between the rich and the poor. In the late Thirties, 71 per cent of the upper, 75 per cent of the middle, and 82 per cent of the lower class answered "Yes." In the early Forties, 73 per cent of the upper, 69 per cent of the middle, and 71 per cent of the lower class answered "Yes." The class difference is greater in the Thirties, a time of labor militancy, than during the middle years of wartime unity. Over these years, class differences in opinion narrowed, but with inflation and the anxiety of another slump, they are widening again. The least favorable occupational group is of course the farmers: in 1941 only 50 per cent answered "Yes" to the general question. The most favorable are the poorer unskilled workers: in 1937, 86 per cent of them answered favorably.

During the 1937 steel strikes, the mass public was asked whether its sympathies were with the strikers or with the companies: 18 per cent of the upper but 44 per cent of the lower classes were in sympathy with the strikers. Sentiment for the strikers was four times as strong among people on relief as among people in the upper brackets. On the 1946 question concerning which side a person would favor in labor-management disputes if he were a referee, 75 per cent of the upper classes but only 31 per cent of the lower classes favored management. In January, 1947, 26 per cent of the general public, 34 per cent of the manual workers, and 52 per cent of the union members favored the closed or union shop.

The extremes in the class continuum of labor opinion are represented by businessmen and farmers on the one hand, and unionized working people on the other. Seldom do poll-takers find special groups holding such divergent opinions as in this instance. Businessmen, for example, in November, 1946, were more than two to one of the opinion that labor puts the greatest pressure on Congress and receives the most Congressional consideration. But among union members, two to one believed that business has the advantage on both points. Almost regardless of what sort of question is asked, the public is divided in its opinions of unions along class lines, and again along lines of union membership.

The general public approves of the principle of unionism, but its opinion during crises and on specific features of labor action is split along class lines, while many have no definite opinions. Of all the features of unionism about which there is public doubt, first is the labor leader himself.

Images of the Labor Leader

The labor leader is no American hero. When the people are asked to compare him with the business leader or stereotyped images of other social actors, he generally comes out badly. The public tends: (1) to approve of unions or of labor in general; (2) to split the unions and labor as a whole from the labor union leaders; (3) to blame the things they do not like about unions on the labor leaders. In these respects, the public seems to follow the press and radio. The labor leader gets little credit for peaceful everyday work, but when he is on the spot, the mass public focuses upon him and often makes him the object of blame and censure.

Yet there is another aspect to the people's image: they readily admit they don't know anything about labor leaders. This fact must be considered along with the generally negative image that seems to prevail. For instance, in 1940 a full 51 per cent admitted not knowing whether or not labor leaders in their community were doing a good job in representing labor, 57 per cent didn't feel they had any basis for judging whether labor leaders were honest in handling union funds, and 51 per cent were quite uncertain about how many labor leaders deal fairly with employers.

The public's ignorance concerning the labor leader is pointed up when questions are asked concerning individual labor leaders. More people can tell you all about The Labor Leader than can tell you who the president of the AFL happens to be: only 43 per cent of the people in 1942 knew who he was, and only 24 per cent were able to identify the president of the CIO. In 1945, only 20 per cent could name the correct organization for Walter Reuther, and only 37 per cent knew that James Petrillo was head of the Musicians Union.

There was one labor leader, however, whom the public could identify: 63 per cent knew that John L. Lewis runs the Mine Workers Union. John L. Lewis is probably the best-known labor leader in the United States. He is also among the least liked. In 1941, five times as many people, and in 1943, nine times as many, disapproved of Lewis as approved of him.

Which other leaders are liked most, which least? In trying to answer such questions, we are able to winnow from the polls three groups of labor leaders: (1) Philip Murray and William Green are well known and popular; (2) John L. Lewis, head of the Miners, Harry Bridges, West Coast Longshoremen, and James Petrillo, Musicians, are well known and unpopular; (3) very little known but fairly well liked are A. Philip Randolph, David Dubinsky, Walter Reuther, A. F. Whitney, and Joseph Curran.

Green is more widely known than Murray, but Murray is slightly better liked. Among the well-known and unpopular leaders one man is associated by the public with the Communist Party and another with the legitimate racketeer aspect of union life. Apart from the heads of the two union blocs, who receive publicity all the time, these are the types most likely to appear in the newspapers. Out of some 360 men prominent in the union world, the public at large is acquainted with a dozen at most.

This unfamiliarity does not prevent the mass public from having opinions about The Labor Leaders. The poll-takers seem to aim their questions at two aspects of labor leadership: power and morality. In both cases, their best questions ask the public to compare labor leaders with businessmen and sometimes with government officials.

Just before U.S. entry into the late war (May, 1941), more people were worried about the power of the labor leaders (75 per cent) than about the power of large corporation heads (59 per cent) or of government officials (32 per cent). Of course, the public unanimously holds the opinion that businessmen and labor leaders should have a social conscience and a sense of social responsibility. However, in March, 1946, when it was asked what proportions of businessmen and of labor leaders had these qualities, 59 per cent said that more than half of the businessmen did, but only 7 per cent said the same of labor leaders.

No poll-taker has yet devised a set of questions which would enable the mass public to allocate specific responsibilities to labor leaders and businessmen. In the closest attempt, during March, 1946, from a given list, the public overwhelmingly picked such things as "the economic health of industry" and the "general welfare of the community" as the joint responsibility of "both business and labor." In every one of the seven areas of responsibility asked about, the majority believed that both labor and management were responsible. In only one area ("productivity per worker") did more people think labor should be more responsible than business.

In their image of the role of the labor leader, the people have not figured out what a good labor leader really ought to do—which is not surprising, since those labor leaders who think they know have not told many people about it. The people, union and non-union, have a vague idea that the labor leader has too much power and that in some way he fails to live up to his social responsibilities. Yet the public cannot define what the responsibilities of the labor leader actually are or what kind of job the labor leader actually does.

This is how organized labor and its leaders stand with the mass public: too many of the people have now been affected by the practical benefits of unionism to accept the negative treatment in the mass media of communication. Some two-thirds of the public can usually be counted on to support the idea of labor unionism. When the unions are in a conflict, or the people are called upon to take a stand, many of them are undecided, but they by no means stack all the cards against the unions. The unions have much more support among the lower and lower middle classes than they do among the upper classes and, despite the general absence of education inside the union, their own members are fairly loyal.

Much public doubt about the labor leader as a newly powerful man is due to the fact that he is a social actor without a publicly defined role. Yet vigorous action on his part, when publicly connected with the interests of the people (as, for instance, lower prices), does not alienate but rather draws the people to his side. There is no reason not to believe that under slump conditions, broad and energetic action properly communicated to the public would greatly enlarge the sphere of union influence and support.

PART TWO

CHAPTER THREE

THE HOUSES OF LABOR

NO MATTER what political publics may demand or the general public support, the labor leader can neither follow the first nor accept the second unless he is strong. No man is strong in the world of U.S. labor unless he has or is thought to have a strong union back of him. The power of the labor leader is bound up with the power of the union which he leads.

It is only because of his organization that the political publics make demands on the labor leader and the general public keeps him in focus. All his action, political and economic, is action with an eye on the state of his union.

The Internationals

Workers come together to form local unions, which are the district units of nationwide unions. These national unions may be affiliated with the American Federation of Labor or the Congress of Industrial Organizations, or they may remain independent of both. The locals within a national union are under the control of the national headquarters, and the AFL and CIO are creatures of their respective national unions Thus the key organization in the world of U.S. labor is the national union, which is often called the international because it may have members in Canada as well as in the United States. The 180-odd national unions, or internationals, are self-governing: they alone decide what they will do. The men operating these internationals are the men who run the union world of American labor.

Heading the international are the general officers, the president and the secretary of the union, who usually also serves as treasurer. In smaller unions the president, the secretary, and the treasurer may be the same man, but generally there are two top officers. In larger unions there are also one or more vice-presidents. Elected by a national constituency of union members, the national officers are often somewhat independent of pressure from particular local unions.

Attached to international headquarters are varying numbers of general organizers or "international representatives." Their job is to organize new locals and to serve as liaison agents between national headquarters and the lower segments of the organization. As links between the national officers and the scattered locals, they advise and service the locals, many continuously working assigned districts. These "international reps" are usually appointed as salaried employees, although in a few unions they are elected by the union's national convention. In many unions, they are attached primarily to given national officials and make up the cadre of the machine within the international.

The international's headquarters usually maintains an office staff. In the smaller unions, this staff may be altogether clerical and secretarial, but in the larger internationals, it is augmented by a sizable corps of professionals, appointed by the general officers. These professionals are lawyers, editors of the union's newspaper, and in an increasing number of unions, economists, statisticians, and research directors; they are the inside-the-union "intellectuals."

The international is composed of local labor unions, the bottom unit of labor organization. These locals contain the workers of a given plant or the craftsmen in a given labor market. The president and the secretary-treasurer of the locals are elected by the rank and file. In small locals, these officers continue to work at their trades, serving as part-time union leaders; in larger locals, the top officers are important members of the labor leader fraternity. Their job is to administer the affairs of their locals, and apart from collective bargaining, they are the labor leaders whom businessmen and personnel directors meet in the everyday round of work.

Most locals of any size usually have one or more business agents, who in older unions are generally elected by the members of the local or in newer unions (which have often grown fast and from the top down) are appointed by the national officers. In either case, the business agent is generally a full-time, paid organizer. He is a general manager and contact man. He provides the continuity and general supervision of the local's administration. His duties are as wide as the activities of the local. He sits with the executive board and the elected officers; he participates in every important meeting between the union and the companies; he is generally the depository of continuous union experience.

The locals have certain members working in the plants who hold the position of shop steward. They are usually chosen by the membership in the plant, although in some cases they are appointed by the local or international officers. These shop stewards are the backbone of the rank-and-file leaders, and as volunteers they help the union administer its domain. They do not receive union salaries, and although they have no formal voice in running the local, they do have a chance to acquire a following and gain influence.

There is a bewildering variety of organizational arrangements between the top national officers and the local labor leaders. Intricate mazes of delegate bodies crisscross one another in a pattern of elected and appointed authority. For example, there may be joint boards composed of all the locals in the international that have jurisdiction over a set of related crafts or occupations. These boards are composed of delegates from all the locals involved, and their purpose is to promote or secure united action among these locals. The boards may have firm control of their locals, may sometimes actually run them, or may be weak and dependent upon the constituent locals for their existence. In some unions, the boards are headed by men appointed by the international's president.

Some internationals may also have district councils, which have jurisdiction over the locals within a given territory. Coal, for instance, is divided into 30 district organizations, the heads of which nominally are elected by the locals but actually a majority are appointed by the president of the international. Steel has 40 district offices, and in each of them, a representative from the international holds forth.

One national union, for instance, has 251 locals, 19 joint boards, and 7 district councils, located in 238 cities, 32 states, and 4 Canadian provinces. This vast bureaucracy is a virtual job empire, securely integrated with a leading American industry and tying together an international' labor union. In such internationals, there is much room for the "fixing" operations of a machinery of patronage built up and maintained by national officers.

All internationals began in one of three ways: (1) A number of independently organized locals banded together to form a new national organization. (2) An organizing committee, attached to some existing labor body, created a new international by going out and organizing a number of locals and setting them up as more or less autonomous organizations. (3) Spontaneously organized locals appeared in an industry or occupation and were then gathered together by an organizing committee attached to some going labor body.

The international heads make decisions on broad questions—when to begin an organizing drive or when and how to handle a strike situation. The locals oversee initial as well as continuous grievance dealings, policies about participation in city politics, and dues collection. Such influence as the locals have over the national officers is mainly through the elected delegates they send to conventions; such power as the international officers have depends upon how much control they can exercise over a strategic combination of locals. The control of the international over its locals varies greatly from union to union. In general, however, power has shifted to the international officers and to their appointees in the union hierarchy. Thus the histories of the various internationals are case studies in the shaping of various types of bureaucracy.

Sizes and Shapes

Fifty years ago, U.S. unionism was a small-scale affair. In 1900, there were 99 national unions, having a total of 833,600 members, 5.3 per cent of the wage and salary workers of the nation. In the five years after 1900, organizing surged, and from then until the first World War, the unions steadily made small gains. During and immediately after the first World War, membership boomed. Nineteen-twenty is the historical peak: 133 internationals had enrolled 4,961,000 members, 17.6 per cent of the wage and salary workers of the country.

The business boom of the Twenties was a bleak trade union slump: membership dropped from the 4,961,000 in 1920 to 3,400,000 in 1925. The early years of the depression did not spur union growth. By 1935, the percentage organized was at its interwar low: 9.4 per cent of the wage and salary workers were in unions.

The big story for American labor unions begins just after 1935, the year of the great springboard, when the CIO drive got under way. All labor organizations were ramrodded to increased efforts: in the next decade total U.S. union membership rose from 3,400,000 to 13,600,000. The windfall years of the war did not altogether account for this jump—by 1938, the internationals had already climbed to 7,800,000. What happened during the war was merely a continuation of the trend that started during the later depression years. In 1944, some 34.4 per cent of all wage and salary workers in this country were members of labor unions.

Of the 182 internationals that were operating nationally in 1943, 55 per cent were founded before 1914, 14 per cent were founded between 1914 and 1934, and 30 per cent were organized after 1935. However, the growth in union membership has greatly exceeded the growth in the number of internationals. In 1900, 99 unions had an average membership of 8,400; in 1944, 182 unions had an average of 75,000 members. The average size of the 1944 international was almost nine times the average of 1900, but there were not even twice as many internationals in 1944 as in 1900.

✦

These figures mean that a new institution is now part of the lives of many workers in America. Such numbers are the sure way to speak of the accumulated power of the unions. Behind them lie all the mechanics of slump and war and boom. Behind them lie all the struggles of the organization drive. Laws have been changed because of them. And theoreticians of business power worry over them late at night.

The Rival Houses

The all-powerful internationals of the union world are banded into two big agglomerates of American unionism—the American Federation of Labor and the Congress of Industrial Organizations, which derive their power from the internationals that compose them. Yet these blocs have power in and of themselves, and they exert it through wide-flung agencies.

The way in which the internationals have been grouped into these blocs has made for certain crucial differences between the types of unions and the types of leaders that prevail in each. In understanding any given labor leader or any given union, it is important to know whether he, or it, is inside the AFL, inside the CIO, or outside of both.

The AFL was founded in the Eighties by Samuel Gompers, its president (except in 1894) until his death in 1924. For 36 years Gompers ran it, and in doing so, set many basic patterns of U.S. unionism. He is the spiritual grandfather of many of today's labor leaders. In 1924, William Green became the head of the AFL, and as of 1948, he has occupied the post for 24 years. From the turn of the century through 1935, about 80 per cent of the union members in this country belonged to AFL unions. Shortly after 1936 (the CIO was launched in 1935), the figure dropped to around 50 per cent and has since remained at approximately that level.

A leader's power in the labor union world rests primarily upon the number of workers organized under him. The powers within the AFL high councils obviously would have been disturbed if the millions of workers in the mass production industries had been taken into the AFL as big new industrial unions.

Yet governmental acts passed during the middle Thirties encouraged labor leaders to organize, and spontaneously formed locals were cropping up in whole brackets of industry. Quite clearly sections of the government as well as the workers were asking for unions.

The AFL was not able to meet a challenge of such magnitude. Its executive board, composed of international heads, the high powers in the trade union world, tried several times to loosen the jurisdictional tensions and to spread the unorganized workers among the existing job empires within the AFL, but it had no success.

Many AFL unions were of the craft type, but there was a secular requirement for industrial-type unions. A craft union is composed of workers who have identical types of skill and training, each worker carrying through to completion some whole process of work. An industrial union is composed of all the people who work in an industry, regardless of their skill, training, or function within the work-process. The diamond workers or the coopers are in craft unions; the automobile or the steel workers are in industrial unions. Between these polar types are many forms of union organization, composed of varying combinations of skill. For the sake of simplicity, we shall call the intermediary forms "amalgamated craft unions," for they are mainly composed of workers from related crafts. The men's clothing workers—the pressers, cutters, lapel makers, and so on—are in the Amalgamated Clothing Workers of America.

The type of union organization that prevails is more important for the jurisdictional problems it may lead to than for the pure sociological type it represents. John L. Lewis, head of the AFL organizing committee in the middle Thirties, though a conservative unionist, saw what was happening and what was demanded. He called for industrial unions, that is, for unions outside the existing domains, or unions which, if organized inside the existing domains, would certainly require new sets of machinery and would thus cause trouble within the upper circles.

Trouble or not, Lewis went on organizing, enrolling workers in steel, rubber, automobiles, regardless of their fields of employment within these industries. The executive board of the AFL told him to stop organizing in this wholesale and unjurisdictional manner. He refused. At the conventions of 1934 and 1935, he fought for industrial unionism. He lost the debates. In 1936, the ten unions involved were branded "dual unions," the worst phrase the other leaders could mouth, and expelled from the AFL. Three other unions left voluntarily. These 13 became the CIO, nucleus of the second house of labor and in time, almost as big as the first. At one stroke the AFL lost about 40 per cent of its total membership. John L. Lewis, the founder of the new CIO industrial aristocracy of labor, was its president until 1940. Since then, Philip Murray has been in command.

Not all labor leaders and unions are inside one of these blocs. Some are independent or unaffiliated with any labor body. In the first quarter of 1947, 12 per cent of all union members were in independent unions, 39 per cent were in CIO unions, and 49 per cent were in the AFL.

Each international belonging to the AFL or the CIO is a sovereign body, and the federations do not often attempt to interfere in its internal business. The federations are dependent upon the internationals for monetary support. Why, then, are these autonomous and supreme internationals willing to pay from their treasuries to get a charter from the AFL or the CIO?

The American Federation of Labor and the Congress of Industrial Organizations try to assure an exclusive jurisdiction to the unions holding charters for given job empires. The Federation and the Congress will usually combat any union that tries to move in on the territory of another, even if vast portions of that territory are not being worked. But the leaders of an unaffiliated union may at any time find themselves facing a rival union backed by the money, organization, and unionizing talent of the AFL or CIO. If insurgents should form a majority within an international, the AFL is strongly inclined to continue recognizing the original leaders upon whom the charter was bestowed. Thus membership in the AFL or the CIO insures against rivalry from without and insurrection from within.

The AFL and the CIO represent labor before the legislative bodies of the states and of the nation. In so far as the member unions participate in decisions on legislative programs, they are part of what united political front labor has. Both affiliations help member unions in strike situations. They have no right to call upon the member unions to strike in sympathy, but they can, and do, back up the striking union with money and organizational talent. By its Union Label Department, the AFL helps its unions maintain the union label on goods that the members produce and boycott non-union-produced goods.

Both organizations lend their talents and money to their internationals for organizing purposes. In 1944, the AFL employed some 175 organizers; the CIO, 180. Usually, the organization of new fields is carried on by organizing committees; the people organized are then held in federal locals, directly attached to the bloc involved; and eventually they are assigned to existing unions or set up in new unions of their own. In addition, the locals of the member internationals can obtain the aid of the state and city bodies maintained by each of the two blocs.

The States and the Cities

All the locals belonging to affiliated internationals also belong to one of the AFL's 50 state federations * or to one of the CIO's 36 state industrial councils. Within each city, the locals belong to one of the AFL's 749 city centrals or the CIO's 232 city industrial councils.

Thus a local is part of an international, and through it, part of the AFL or the CIO. The same local may also belong to an AFL city central or a CIO city industrial council, which in turn belongs to a state federation or a state industrial council. Membership in these city and state organizations is optional, but the

* One for each of the 48 states, Alaska, and Puerto Rico.

majority of the locals of internationals attached to the AFL or the CIO send delegates to the state and city bodies.

The primary task of the state bodies is political. They hold annual conventions at which legislative programs are formulated. The city organizations are more concerned with economic matters, but they, too, formulate policies concerning city politics; in both political and economic matters, the city units are the city-wide agencies of the locals composing them, and the clearing houses for political and negotiating purposes. Next to the local unions, the city units touch the members of the union more intimately than any other sections of the union hierarchy.

Both the city and the state organizations of the AFL and CIO are under cross-pressures. Their leaders borrow from and bestow power upon the internationals, the blocs with which they are affiliated, and the locals under their nominal jurisdiction. All these organizations, having members in the domain of a city body, may be represented in state federations or in one way or another influence them. The composition of power in the AFL is such that it always tries to prevent city or state bodies from usurping power from any international. The city organizations are under the surveillance of the executive councils and can be expelled by them.

The internationals or the locals overshadow the city and state organizations in the handling of strikes and the framing of contracts. At most, the city and state agencies may attempt to integrate and help locals by providing techniques and information. If the head of a city central did more than that, the various internationals whose locals were involved would exert pressure on the head of the affiliate body of the offending city central, and then Green or Murray would act against the offending city central.

What Is Organized?

Labor leaders care nothing for the academic purity of definitions used to mark off the types of organizations which they lead. What they claim are job areas. They describe their jurisdictions, which is to say, the particular empires of jobs to which they have staked a claim. They do not do this to let the workers know where to go: they are talking to other labor leaders.

In the modern industrial world, and to a lesser extent in the world of labor unions, the craft has ceased to be the key unit of work and organization. Labor leaders, whether they want to or not, have to follow the contours of the industries that are open for organization. If they don't, and there is pressure for unionization, their unions will be by-passed by the mass of industrial workers. That is what happened in the middle and late Thirties. By 1940, only 9 per cent of the total union membership in the U.S. were in craft unions.

	UNIONS	MEMBERS
Craft	26%	9%
Amalgamated craft	53	48
Industrial	21	43
Total	100%	100%

The average craft union in 1940 had about 16,200 members as compared with the average amalgamated's 43,000 and the average industrial's 98,500 members.

The craft unions are not only the smallest but also the oldest: 77 per cent of the craft unions, 60 per cent of the amalgamated craft, and 47 per cent of the industrial unions were organized before 1914. Only 7 per cent of the craft unions were organized after 1935, as compared with 20 per cent of the amalgamated craft and 28 per cent of the industrials.

Within each of the three types, the older union is generally the bigger, but there is a difference in the relation of the present size and age according to the type: the older craft unions are on the average ten times as large as the newer craft unions, whereas the older industrial unions average less than twice as large as the newer ones.

✦

Most unions of the craft type are in the AFL; there is not one in the CIO, although it has many unions that are amalgamations of related crafts. Yet in 1936 it was not the principle of craft versus industrial unionism that caused the split; it was power among labor leaders, based on jurisdictional domains. Hutcheson's Carpenters Union, for instance, is a semi-industrial organization. It covers everything from the growing tree to the finished product: "Once wood, it is always the right of the carpenter to install it. . . ." These are the words of the same carpenter who is reputed to have said, "I'll see Lewis in hell before I see industrial unions." Power based on jurisdiction—that is the main issue which keeps the two organizations apart. It has remained the point of disagreement throughout the several formal attempts which, since 1936, have been made to get them together again.

In the early Forties, the members of the three major types of unions were divided between AFL, CIO, and independent unions in this way:

	CRAFT	AMALG.	IND.
AFL	65%	79%	13%
CIO	..	11	84
Independent	35	10	1
Total membership	100%	100%	100%

Clearly, amalgamations of crafts have occurred within and between a great many unions in order to minimize jurisdictional troubles, increase union strength, and make possible co-ordinated demands and actions. The median year of origin for craft unions is 1898, for amalgamated crafts, 1901, and for industrial unions, 1915.

Historically, labor unions have centered in construction, mining, and transportation, with manufacturing lagging. That pattern has now been reversed: between 1930 and 1940, the percentage of all union members who were in manufacturing rose from 24 to 43 per cent. Now for the first time, the manufacturing industries contain the bulk of the people who in one way or another are behind the power of the labor leaders.

Because craft-type unions predominate in the AFL, it is stronger in the building trades, mining, certain professional fields, personal service, and in transportation. The CIO is stronger in mass-production industries such as steel, textiles, automobiles, electrical equipment, and rubber. Here is the industrial composition within each union bloc:

	AFL	CIO	IND.	TOTAL
Raw materials	13%	9%	..	13%
Manufacturing	29	75	7%	43
Building and construction	23	..	..	13
Transportation and communication	17	8	64	17
Trade	2	3	..	2
Service	17	5	29	14
Total membership	100%	100%	100%	100%

Only 29 per cent of the AFL workers in 1940, against 75 per cent of the CIO workers, were in manufacturing industries. Furthermore, only one-third of the AFL manufacturing workers, compared with virtually all of the CIO manufacturing workers, were in industrial unions.

The question "What is organized?" may also be answered in terms of the white-collar and wage-worker components of the union membership. In 1900, 3.2 per cent of the white-collar employees and 5.8 per cent of the wage workers were in unions; today, 43 per cent of the wage workers, as compared with 15 per cent of the white-collar people, are unionized. There are many more lower-middle-class people in the unions than is generally realized: approximately 13 per cent of all union members are in white-collar unions.

There is some evidence that among wage workers, those having higher income and status are more likely to join unions, but among white-collar workers the reverse is true. The unionized ranks of both strata tend to come together, as it were, in a lower-middle-class grouping: this is the trade union bloc of the nation.

Before the CIO organizing drives, unions were, in the main, a monopoly of the skilled workers in certain industries: they were a trade aristocracy of labor. With the rise of the CIO, for the first time a large-scale arena for communication among many wage and salary workers was created. The progressive features of the CIO are due, in some part, to the fact that it has organized more than merely the skilled craft elite, just as its retrograde features are due, in some part, to the fact that it has not organized the lowest ranks of the wage workers but has become a new aristocracy of some of the industrial workers.

The Leaders and the Led

Some members of some unions are mere objects of manipulation; some participate actively in running the union. Some of the leaders are appointed and some are elected; some are paid and some work voluntarily. But always the relations between the leaders and the led are governed mainly by three facts: (1) the dues or the per capita tax which the local members pay to the national union and the money expended in locals by officers; (2) the elections and referenda, held in the locals, which formally determine the officers in the union hierarchy and their activities; (3) the machines the national officials may or may not control, which extend into the various locals.

The control of the first two, money and elections, is set forth in the constitutions of the unions. The possibilities of building up and of maintaining the often crucial third factor—the machine—are also somewhat limited, if only formally, by the terms of the constitution.

At the convention, the business of running the union as a town meeting or as a leader's machine takes place. Therefore the frequency and the procedure of these conventions are crucial in relations between the leaders and the led. Some 32 per cent of the internationals hold a convention once each year, 36 per cent once every two years, 26 per cent every three to five years; the remaining 6 per cent set their next convention during a given convention or by referendum of the membership. There are cases where unions have not called conventions for long periods of time, but only a handful of internationals are guilty on that score.

The convention is the supreme authority and the only legislative body of the international. The delegates to the convention are usually local officers who, in the larger locals, are often accompanied by active rank-and-file leaders. Usually, "fixing" a union convention requires as much political maneuvering as does any Republican or Democratic Party convention.

Between the members in the local and the officers in the international headquarters, money is a continuing link: the locals are assessed by the internationals, and the latter pay for various local purposes out of the national treasury. One of the key powers of the national officers is this disbursement of national treasury funds. In unions as elsewhere, there is a finance of democracy and there is a democracy of finance.

All the money with which the internationals are run is collected by the locals. A per capita tax per member is paid by each local to its international each month. All this money comes from the fee that the worker pays when he joins or when he is reinstated, the regular dues (usually monthly), and special assessments that may be made for particular purposes.

Power has shifted from the locals to their internationals; centralization of money has put power in the hands of the international officers, who in turn may use it to strengthen their position in locals where their administration is weak.

Centralization of funds also tends to spread the risks of the union's life more evenly among the locals. By putting strike funds in the hands of national officials, the locals weaken their own power but also increase, by a sort of insurance system, their chances of weathering a period of strife. This is especially important when unions face big corporations whose executives enjoy virtually absolute authority over far-flung plants.

The democratic election of union officers is often accompanied by factional fights. Democracy within the unions, as within the nation as a whole, is usually a democracy of machine politics imposed upon a mass of apathetic members.

This process can be observed in the re-election of union officers. Regardless of the merits of an incumbent, regardless of how successful he has been in running his office, if he does not face the scrutiny of opposition in an open and free election, he is less likely to remain alert to what previous generations have called the "will of the majority."

The fact is that opposition in union elections is the great exception. The rule is lengthy tenure in office. The best study available shows that between 1910 and 1941, of 764 officers who won the elections in 7 AFL unions, 634, or 83 per cent of them, ran for office unopposed. These were all national officers. In the 63 presidencies, 86 per cent were unopposed elections.

The elected leaders of the internationals thus show vigorous ability to perpetuate themselves in office. Daniel Tobin, the successful candidate of the Teamsters in 1907, is still boss, and no one has opposed him since the election of 1910. Sidney Hillman, late president of the Amalgamated Clothing Workers, was unopposed in office for over 25 years. William Mahon, head of the Street Railway Workers, has been head for over 40 years and unopposed for over 30. William Hutcheson, chieftain of the Carpenters, has been their president since 1916; D. B. Robertson, president of the Locomotive Firemen, was first elected to that position in 1922 and has served continuously since; G. L. Berry of the Printing Pressmen's Union has held his office since 1906. For over a quarter of a century, John L. Lewis has habitually expelled disruptive elements that might upset his rule of the Miners Union.

This lack of democratic opposition occurs whether the election is by convention or by referendum ballot of the membership. The reasons for this have never been studied systematically, but the scattered facts about a miscellany of individual cases can be pieced into a coherent story of why unions tend to become autocratic and centrally controlled.

As a union grows larger, there often tends to be less interest among the membership at large; effective desire for democratic participation is lowered. The appeal to join a union is seldom ideological. Bread-and-butter reasons for joining as well as for remaining a member go along with lack of interest in union affairs as democratic mechanisms.

As membership increases, there is also a greater possibility for more patronage to be controlled by union leaders. They can reward their friends and punish their enemies. In fact, the machine power built up in this manner may even make possible punishment severe enough to break men as union leaders. Thus when John Brophy tried to unify the opposition to John L. Lewis in 1926, Lewis declared the endeavor "a disruptive effort" and expelled Brophy and his confreres from the union.

In passing, it must be mentioned that intra-union discipline is often essential for effective dealing with thoroughly autocratic business institutions. The managers of corporations are not democratically elected by the stockholders to represent their interests. And in this respect, the unions are often practically forced to borrow from their opponents an autocratic type of rule in order to insure unity of action.

Over the last hundred years, the American unions have spread out with the national markets; on many of those markets, no local organization can stand alone. The distribution of power between the electorate in the locals and the labor leaders at national headquarters is thus in large part dependent upon the type of industry and upon the size of the competitive labor market areas.

If power in most of the older internationals has gravitated from the local to the national headquarters in the course of time, in many of the newer unions power has been concentrated at the top from the beginning. In many cases the men at the top today are the men who formed the union. In unions of either sort, a sudden flood of new members tends to invite the leadership to tighten its grip.

Though many labor leaders retain office only because of their grip on the union machine or because of the indifference of members, or both, some leaders also gain additional security from the loyalty of a hero-worshiping rank and file. In almost all cases of long tenure, the men in power have been sanctified by some battle through which they successfully led the union. They struggle with the birth of the union, they lead a large strike, or they organize vast numbers of new workers. The prestige John Mitchell gained from leading the great anthracite strikes at the turn of the century was so great that he could not be successfully challenged as head of the Miners.

Democracy unambiguously means control of a responsible leader by the whole rank and file. That requires a machinery that forces the leader to remain alert to the wants of the members, that keeps him responsible. Another kind of mechanism sometimes obtains equally popular results. It is dangerous and may exist in the tightest dictatorships, but in American labor unions it seems to occur more frequently than the first-mentioned. This second type evolves when an unchallenged leader consistently acts in the general interests of the membership. It may result from a leader's doing either what the members are interested in or what is to their interests. It may come about by an identity of mental processes between the leaders and the led ("Hutcheson thinks just like an old carpenter") or by the members' absolute trust in the leaders ("Ole John L. may be rough, but he's always working for us") or by the successful accomplishment of what all the members agree is the most important matter ("He got us the dough, didn't he?").

When considering the undemocratic rule and long tenure of many union chiefs, one should remember that on occasion rank-and-file leaders have upset the rule of the big shots of the union world. Now, however, there is no general surge of rank-and-file revolt against labor leaders. The old left wing of the AFL, composed of socialists and anarchist-syndicalists, is no more. Anyone who has watched a successful CP revolt knows that the CPers are not for rank-and-file democracy any more than the vested interests they replace. And like the old ruling class of Great

Britain, the aristocrats of American labor "buy up" the militant, lower-rank upstarts who look potentially powerful.

But unions, like other American institutions, have to ride the cycle of slump and war and boom. When times are bad but there is demand that they be bettered, labor leaders must compete with each other and with new leaders for rank-and-file allegiance. Slump makes the rank and file show its muscle, and the leaders of American unions jump to more democratic action.

CHAPTER FOUR

THE SPLIT RUNS DEEP

WHAT HAPPENS when labor leaders fail to look outside their own bailiwick to the demands of the rank and file is demonstrated by what happened to AFL leaders in the last slump. Their failure to respond resulted in a new crop of labor leaders at the head of a new organization. The CIO was born of slump, in jurisdictional competition with the AFL over the industrial workers. Now there are two houses of labor; the solidarity of labor, of which the left speaks, is not a fact of American labor unionism.

The AFL and the CIO are not two differently shaped vessels filled with similar kinds of leaders. The split between them runs deep: it divides different types of men. They differ in their personal characteristics, in the union experience they have had, and in their social and political outlooks. Two simple differences between the AFL and the CIO leaders are most decisive, carrying heavy implications for other personal and opinion characteristics. One is age. The other is education.

Ambitious young men within an organization argue that old age and long tenure in office lead to entrenched tyranny if not to the personal quality of "fatty degeneration." Things now move fast in industrial battles, much faster than old leaders can learn. Old leaders learned a long time ago and under a set of conditions that no longer prevail. They are uneducated; their very experience is a trap: they are victims of a trained incapacity.

Older leaders, on the other hand, to glorify old age and long tenure, argue that good leadership is a rare quality that once found ought to be kept. Experience, they say, is always the best and often the only teacher. There are no books to teach a young man how to be a great labor leader. A union is complicated and its leader is responsible for keeping it in good shape; the only sure man is one who has kept it going through the years. A lot of younger men coming into the union will throw overboard that rich experience. They will wreck the ship.

Experience and Atrophy

One might answer the dilemma of age and experience by saying that the unions need both the young and the old; if the two would co-operate, the proper balance could be achieved. In the labor leader world of today, that liberal answer does not seem possible, short of an organic merger. The statistical fact is that young men run the CIO and old men run the AFL.

Seventy-three per cent of the men who lead the CIO, as compared with only 35 per cent of AFL leaders, are under 45 years of age.*

Years of age:	AFL	CIO
Under 35	4%	20%
35-44	31	53
45-54	33	17
55-64	23	8
65 and over	9	2
Total cases	219	169

Young organizations: young leaders. The average CIO union was 12 years old in 1946; the average AFL union, 50 years old. The fact that one of the commonest ways to become a labor leader is to help found a union explains in part the sharp age differences between the AFL and the CIO. Young leaders who have built and are running a young organization tend to select young men for their associates. Under those conditions, rapidly expanding unions give young men chances to climb rapidly.

On each level of leadership, the CIO men are younger than their counterparts in the AFL. Here are the proportions of leaders on each level of leadership who are 45 years of age or over:

	AFL	CIO
National	80%	39%
State	73%	24%
City	56%	25%

The American Federation of Labor today forms an almost perfect hierarchy of age. Eighty per cent of the national, 73 per cent of the state, and 56 per cent of the city leaders are over 45 years of age. Age

* For a discussion of our sample of labor leaders, *see* Notes and Sources, pp. 300-303.

parallels the levels of leadership with almost bureaucratic precision.

There is already a tendency for the CIO to become an age hierarchy; in due course, no doubt, it will develop into one. But today, a decade after its beginning, the gradation is not yet clear-cut.

The age differences between the leaders of the two organizations decrease as we go down the hierarchy: between national leaders of the AFL and CIO there is a 14-year age difference; on the state level, the difference is 10 years; and on the city, it is less than 8.

The successful American labor leader enters the union world early and stays late. The typical leader of an AFL international took his first job in a labor union during the year 1918; in the CIO, the men now on the top level typically entered the unions in 1935.

Median year of first trade union job:	AFL	CIO
National	1918	1935
State	1929	1939
City	1933	1939

There are fewer differences in the experience of the leaders at the bottom than at the top of the two hierarchies: 17 years of experience separates the top of the AFL from the top of the CIO, 10 years in the middle level, and 6 years at the bottom. In the career of the labor union leader, there are two kinds of turnover at the bottom: he either goes up or he goes out of the hierarchy.

As the AFL is an age hierarchy, so it is a hierarchy of experience: the further up the line a leader is, the longer he has been in the movement. Apparently the CIO is too young for this development to be pronounced.

The independent unions do not have state and city officers as do those affiliated with the AFL or CIO. Our information therefore concerns only leaders of the independent internationals. In age and union experience, these presidents and secretaries are between the national leaders of the AFL and the CIO: their average age is 50 years, compared to the 57 of the AFL and the 43 of the CIO; and they got into unions in the median year of

1930, which, again, is in between the years of 1918 and 1935 for the AFL and CIO national officers. On the basis of this intermediate age and experience of the independents, no theory that they might bridge the gap between the AFL and CIO can, however, be developed. There are specific reasons why each of their unions is not in either of the two houses of labor. Moreover, in their general outlook, the heads of the independent unions resemble the AFL leaders much more closely than they do those of the CIO.

How do the ages of top trade union leaders compare with those of corporation executives and governmental officials? The presidents of AFL internationals in 1945 averaged about 57 years of age, exactly the same age as the 1940 average for the presidents of 100 corporations for which we have information. These corporation heads were in charge of the first 10 railway lines, the first 10 utilities, the first 5 companies in oil, steel, chain stores, mining, and the first 60 industrials. The average age in 1939 of 62 federal administrators, the heads of the bureaus, was 54.

The age lineup, then, is like this: corporation executives and AFL presidents: 57; government officials: 54; CIO presidents: 43. If we may consider these figures roughly comparable and representative of the three hierarchies of officialdom and power, it is clear that the CIO men are almost a new generation operating within and between the three hierarchies of power.

Education and Wisdom

Measured in the lifetime of a man, high schools are a new thing for the masses of the people. Colleges are even more recent. In 1940, only 10 per cent of the U.S. adult population had gone to college and only an additional 29 per cent had had some high school training. Since mass participation in formal schooling is so recent, it follows that the younger an adult is, the more likely he is to have finished a higher grade in school. Older people may have more of the wisdom reputed to come with age and experience, but younger people have, on the average, spent more years in school.

The AFL labor leader is older than the CIO leader and, accordingly, not so well educated. Here is the labor leaders' formal education compared to that of the U.S. adult population:

	U.S. ADULT POPULATION	AFL	CIO
College	10%	25%	33%
High school graduate	14	14	23
Some high school	15	26	24
Grammar school	57	34	20
None	4	1	..
Total cases	73.7 million	227	172

Fifty-six per cent of the CIO leaders, and 39 per cent of those in the AFL, have graduated from high school or gone to college. Both the AFL and the CIO leaders are better educated than the general adult public, of whom only 24 per cent have gone through high school or beyond.

This tendency for the CIO to be run by better-educated men is true of both its old and its young leaders. Actually, the differences in educational accomplishments between the AFL and the CIO leaders are more pronounced among the younger men in both organizations than among the older. Not only were the "original" leaders of the CIO better educated, but the younger men who have risen in the CIO are better educated than the younger men who have come into the AFL hierarchy.

Proportion completing high school:	AFL	CIO
Under 45	49%	62%
45 and over	36%	38%

These educational differences hold true for each level of leadership within the two organizations. Here are the proportions with some high school or higher education:

	AFL	CIO
National	57%	91%
State	64%	84%
City	70%	74%

The educational hierarchy inside the AFL is quite different from the hierarchy within the CIO. In the CIO, the levels of leadership are paralleled by levels of education: the further up you go, the better educated the men are, despite the older age groups at the top. But in the AFL, the further up you go, the older and less educated are the leaders. This inverted educational hierarchy in the AFL is due in large part to the age gap of some 10 years between the top and bottom positions. In the CIO, there is not such a big age difference between the top and the bottom; education and age are both graded in terms of organizational structure.

The presidents and secretaries of the independent unions, although somewhat younger than the AFL leaders, have completed almost the same median grade of formal schooling: for the independents it is 9.4 years; for the AFL, 9.3. In the CIO the median grade is 12.5 years.

The labor leaders are better educated than the adult U.S. population, but none of them, except the national leaders of the CIO, are as well educated as the heads of the business corporations with whom they deal. In 1940, over two-thirds of a sample of 200 top business executives had gone to college. And neither the labor leaders nor the business executives are as well educated as the government officials, who practically without exception have had college educations.

The AFL is a gerontocracy: at its top are older men who are relatively poorly educated and who have authority over much younger men who are relatively better educated. Age and education cause some tension within the AFL.

The CIO is a professional bureaucracy: at its top are slightly older men who are quite well educated, and these better-educated leaders exercise authority over slightly younger and less well-educated men. Age and education are graded according to organizational structure.

In understanding the behavior of the leaders of the AFL and the CIO, it is necessary to bear in mind that they operate in two different kinds of hierarchies. The differences are not merely organizational: the two houses of labor are inhabited by different types of men, related within each organization in different ways. The facts of age, education, and types of hierarchy make for further differences between AFL and CIO leaders. In the sphere of ideas, the first split can be seen in the way these two types of leaders view the possibility and morality of unity between the two organizations.

Political Dialogue on Unity

The mass public does not know much about labor's big split; certainly it has not formulated any detailed opinions concerning it. Questioning would probably discover only the general feelings that cluster around the symbols of "unity" and "disunity." In 1947, 55 per cent of the public felt the AFL and the CIO should "join in one organization"; 25 per cent felt they should not; 20 per cent had no opinion.

The special political publics have more definite views. But the big difficulty with talk of getting together is that everyone wants unity to serve some special purpose; in all political publics, as well as in the union world, the issue is: Unity for what?

The members of the liberal public feel that a solid front would be more politically and economically effective, and they favor the principle of unity. The anti-Communists among them want the alliance to break the power of the Communists; and those who, knowingly or not, follow the Communist dispensation, want unity to install "the progressives" in the most important posts available.

The far left wants amalgamation because a rift in the union world means disunity among the wage workers as a class. Merger is necessary to strengthen the whole working class and to defeat the efforts of employers and government to regiment the labor movement. In speaking of unity, the leftists lean toward terms favorable to the CIO rather than the AFL because *industry* is, in their minds, half-way along the road from *craft* to *class*, and because they believe that the CIO has been more politically alert, even if its leaders have only toyed with ideas of independent political action.

Although the practical right hasn't formulated any view, it contains the people who most favor continued disunity. Like many of the sophisticated right, the practical conservatives want continued friction in so far as it serves to make a deeper split and, in the end, to fragmentalize the potential power of the labor unions as a movement. Indeed, there is much in the idea that the present disunity serves rightward interests. Disunity, in fact, was a major purpose behind the practical right's Taft-Hartley labor law of 1947.

The argument over unity, however, is not merely an argument between the right which wants disunited and therefore weak labor and the left which wants labor unity in which there is said to be strength. Even politically sophisticated leftward thinkers are by no means agreed. Some independent left intellectuals believe that under prevailing conditions, unification of the AFL and CIO would be an essentially conservative move. Others take an opposite view. Among left intellectuals today the most significant arguments, pro and con, are the following:

Against Unity: Power in the union world rests upon the number of workers under a leader. The AFL is somewhat larger than the CIO, and many independent unions would favor the AFL. Therefore, power in any merged organization would rest more nearly with the AFL than with the CIO type. The top AFL leaders would thus gain a lot of autonomous power that is now within the structure of the CIO and free for action in an alert leftward manner. The leftward element in unions might be buried by a merger.

For Unity: To have power the unions must be big enough to cope with their opponents. The possibilities of effective leftward action by unions depend upon their strength compared with that of business. Industry is now mass; business is now unified. So the unions must become a mass organization under a unified command. To support fragmentalized unions in the hope that some small unions would thus have a greater chance to be or to become radical is to give up real possibilities for sectarian gestures: such left elements as exist are of little use in the smaller unions.

It is also assumed that the AFL is more uniform than it actually is. In a showdown, at least four or five fairly large AFL unions would go with the CIO.

Against Unity: Enlargement of unions leads to more conservative policies because more of the leaders must become administrators. More leaders must pay most of their attention to holding the big unit together. Moreover, in a large organization, huge funds are at the disposal of the leaders: there are more chances to build patronage machines, more chances for cautious attitudes to flourish among leaders who feel responsible for safeguarding a richer organization.

For Unity: There are as many conservative leaders among small independent unions as there are among huge unions. What is said about the funds is correct, but it is simply another way of saying "absolute power corrupts." Does that mean less power corrupts less? There are as many petty tyrants as big tyrants. Little men with small riches often guard them as cautiously as larger men with big riches.

Against Unity: The competition for new members between the AFL and the CIO has greatly aided the organizing work of the last decade. During the rush and rivalry over organizing, the unions in both blocs have paid less attention to strict jurisdictional lines than they might have if there had been a common head to whom to appeal. After 1936, even the AFL enlarged the jurisdiction of many of its unions, amalgamated crafts, and spent money organizing. This argument is not merely historical: with only one-third of the workers in unions, organizing should be intensified. Competition enlivens the activities of the labor leaders.

For Unity: Organizational efforts have been intensified not by disunity and competition but by the new idea of mass organization and the new tactics which the CIO put into vigorous practice. The opposing argument would mean that the postwar organizing drive in the South was helped by the competition between the AFL and the CIO, which is obviously not the case.

Against Unity: If the unions were fused into one big union, the public would regard this bloc as a monopoly Behemoth; it would look much stronger than it would be. The one big union would be severely attacked, political demands for public control of unions would be increased. The labor leaders, in their sharp fear of government encroachment on the free private enterprise of running a union, might seek to lead a union life of quiescence and compromise. They also might even be more likely to make secret deals with amalgamated employers' associations.

For Unity: The argument is like two others: if Negroes become militant, the whites will crack down; if Jews speak for their rights, anti-Semitism will increase. Both statements may be true in the short run. But in the long run, they are a renunciation of all power and struggle, a declaration for the cautious existence. Not strength but weakness, not militant action but powerlessness increases Jim-Crowism, anti-Semitism, and anti-unionism. Not apparent strength but genuine power will enable unions to stand the shock of attack and to return it. Unity is the way to such power.

Thus, among the politically sophisticated, one finds a wide range of possible attitudes toward labor unity, including points of view far more subtle than those which determine the opinions of the labor leaders themselves.

Should We Get Together?

Neither the abstract ideas of a handful of left-wing leaders nor any pressure from the rank and file, but the threat of powers outside and the movements of big men inside the unions drive the labor leaders to talk of unity.

Every time Congress sounds anti-labor the union leaders show some will toward unification. But when there is peace on the Congressional front, and the unions in both blocs seem to be doing well, the will is lost. In 1947, an anti-labor Congress came into power; lured by fear of anti-union forces and plied with good will toward one another, the labor leaders again talked of unity, but again nothing came of it.

The movements of certain bigwigs in the 10-year drama stir up talk and sometimes renew efforts. When John L. Lewis, founder of the CIO, withdrew from that organization in October of 1940, some labor observers actually wondered whether the CIO would collapse or be so weakened that it would try to creep back into the fold. Every time either of the two big blocs seems weakened in any way, observers believe it will seek renewed strength in solidarity. Yet in 1942, when the top leaders, Green, Lewis, and Murray, were asked if they believed organic unity was at all probable, each answered "No." Lewis, the historical key to the whole affair if any man is, made another move in 1945: he rejoined the AFL. In labor circles, unity was again earnestly discussed, but again with no results. In 1947, he again left the AFL.

The enemies of labor may be strong, but some labor leaders are stronger than others. In unity there may be strength, but for the labor leaders, the big question is: Whose will it be?

Two general questions are involved: one has to do with morality or ideology; the other has to do with power. In the first, the rank and file of the unions are considered; in the second, they are not disregarded, but the leader's own position takes precedence. A labor leader in either bloc may or may not believe that healing the breach is in the interests of the laboring people as a whole; and he may or may not believe that the chance for agreement is good.

We asked the leaders a question about each of these points not long after John L. Lewis had gone back to the AFL. The question on morality was worded: "From the standpoint of value to laboring people as a whole, do you think the AFL and the CIO, as nationwide organizations, *should* within the next few years try to: (1) Get together as a unified organization? (2) Remain separate organizations but engage in all joint public activities and policies they can? (3) Remain separate organizations and have little or nothing to do with one another? (4) Fight it out until one or the other loses as an organization?"

The majority of all leaders favor unity. Even though the question is put on an abstract moral level, this majority opinion is an important over-all fact. But the numbers who are opposed to unity, and their reasons, are even more important.

	AFL	CIO
Get together	83%	56%
Co-operate	11	42
Remain independent	3	1
Fight it out	3	1
Total cases	230	178

Eighty-three per cent of the AFL leaders believe that the AFL and the CIO should, for the workers' interests, join forces. Only 56 per cent of the CIO leaders are of this opinion. Yet even if they do not all agree to a unified organization, the leaders of the CIO are for co-operation on public policies. Few leaders are willing to say that the two should "fight it out," or even remain absolutely independent.

Within either bloc, there are no differences by level of leadership. National, state, city leaders within each bloc hold the same views. Both organizations thus appear to be well disciplined on the unity question.

The leaders do not hesitate to voice an opinion. There is no such aloofness from the record as might be revealed by a large "don't know." Apparently they have given the matter much thought, or at least have talked of it a great deal. There is at least moral dissatisfaction and a desire for closer co-operation or unity between the two houses of labor.

What Are the Chances?

It is one thing to believe that solidarity of unions would be good for the laboring people and to want it for that or any other principle; it is quite another to believe that unity is probable within a stated period of time. We asked: "Regardless of what you would like to see happen, how much chance do you see for the AFL and the CIO to become one unified organization within the next few years?" The labor leaders answered:

	AFL	CIO
Good chance	10%	3%
Fair chance	30	13
Slight chance	43	54
No chance	17	30
Total cases	231	176

There is general agreement among the leaders that the chances are slim: 60 per cent in the AFL and 84 per cent in the CIO believe that there is only a slight chance or no chance at all.

The AFL is more optimistic than is the CIO. Just as the AFL men appear to favor unity more as a general moral proposition, so are they more optimistic about its chances.

On the power and on the moral aspects of the question, the labor leader's attitudes are almost entirely determined by his union's affiliation. Neither personal characteristics, political affiliations, nor opinions on other social and economic questions have any bearing on the way the labor leaders view the possibility of unity. The educated and the uneducated, the young and the old, the national, the state, and the city leaders are all agreed—within each of the two blocs.

The Lineup of Opinion

On the question of labor solidarity, most of the leaders in both blocs are morally willing but practically pessimistic; they feel that, "We should get together, but the chances of our doing so are either slim or completely absent." The rest of the AFL leaders are morally willing and practically optimistic; they feel that, "We want unity, and we feel that the chances are pretty high that we can get it." The rest of the CIO are morally skeptical and practically pessimistic; they feel, "We're not at all sure that it would be a good thing, and we don't think the chances are very good anyway."

	AFL	CIO
Want unity and believe it will be achieved	40%	13%
Want unity but believe it will not be achieved	43	44
Do not want unity and do not believe it will be achieved	16	40
Do not want unity but believe it will be achieved	1	3
Total cases	229	176

The split runs deep. Yet a general wish for co-operation of some sort is present in each organization. There is an almost unanimous desire for more harmonious action and organization in the union world. In the AFL, the cry is for organic unity; in the CIO, for increased co-operation short of actual merger.

It is seldom possible to check poll findings by events, as in the prediction of elections. Fortunately, shortly after our questions were asked, the AFL invited the CIO to a talk on getting together. As reported in the press and as carried by the union grapevine, the AFL wanted organic unity whereas the CIO resisted, and argued officially for "increased co-operation as a good beginning." This official CIO line expressed the sentiment of the more conservative CIO leaders, as would be expected in formal talks involving such vital issues.

No personal attribute or attitude of the individual leader correlates with his position on the issue of labor solidarity. The labor leader usually follows the policy line of his organization. His attitudes are disciplined by that policy. Therefore to explain this difference in opinion between AFL and CIO leaders we must look to organization and organizational policy rather than to personal attributes and ideologies of the leaders as individuals. Three considerations are relevant:

1. The labor leader sees the issue of unity not as one of blending or not, but as one of absorbing or being absorbed. Solidarity is an issue of power, and the consequence which interests the

labor leader is who is going to get the power. How much the leader gets depends in large part upon the kind of deal his organization makes. The AFL is, despite various claims to the contrary, the larger of the two organizations. Power in the union world depends a great deal upon size. The AFL leaders believe that their organizations would get most; they would do the absorbing. The CIO fears that it would be absorbed. That is the major reason why more AFL leaders are for accord than CIO leaders.

II. Since the AFL is so much older, and the CIO sprang from it, there is a traditional feeling among AFL leaders that they represent The House of Labor. Many AFL leaders look upon CIO leaders as upstarts, as boys who have done fairly well but who, after all, do not have the experience of the older men in the AFL, the depository of labor wisdom in America. "Look at John L. Lewis," they say. "Well, he is no upstart, but he led the upstarts, and didn't he finally come home? The others will come home, too." Such sentiment lies back of much AFL optimism revealed in our poll.

III. The tradition of the absolute sovereignty of the international union is so strong and untouchable in the higher as well as the lower circles of the AFL that no leader fears strongly that he will be sold out by those above him in the hierarchy. Part of this tradition actually means that those who got there first have the right to most of what is found there. The AFL leaders feel this so strongly that they perhaps impute it to the CIO leaders. However, within the AFL each leader is sure of protection, and between the AFL and the CIO, the AFL leaders see seniority as a strong bargaining point.

As the great jurisdictional battle between the two houses of labor has continued, the vested interests at the top as well as at the bottom have become more firmly entrenched and apparently more obdurate in their demands. The differences and the entrenchments have been cumulative: as both organizations have spread out over the last ten years, the numbers of potential and actual jurisdictional borderlines have grown, increasing the potential and actual encroachments and the mutual hostility.

Unions and leaders of a certain type have not only been true to their type, but a selective process has gone on: the CIO type, as his union has grown, has selected the CIO type, and likewise the AFL.

The AFL and the CIO are united—in two separate blocs. If the young men were more amenable than the older men, if the powerful were more amenable than the less powerful, then such groups in either organization might be employed as levers, but there are no such levers jutting out.

If these organizations were to unify organically, back of the alliance would be the most adroit and complicated political maneuverings ever to occur in our time and place. Only a felt threat of dire proportions from outside the movement could spur such political talent as the unions now possess to such mighty effort.

CHAPTER FIVE

THE SELF-MADE MEN

THE HEIGHTS gained by the American labor leader are elevated in contrast with his humble level of origin. In many ways, the history of his life is an American success story. In the second quarter of the twentieth century, the American labor leaders exemplify this story more than the executives of large American corporations or the officials of government bureaus.

"Those Foreign-Born Agitators"

To the mass public, the American labor leader is frequently not American at all: he is a foreigner. By excluding the labor leader from its stereotype of the American, the mass public can save that stereotype for more conventional types of men.

For example, in a typical Middle Western city of 80,000 we asked a cross-section of women: "Do you think that most, about half, or not so many of the labor leaders in this country are foreign-born?" The important fact that 27 per cent of them would not venture any answer agrees with our general finding of the public's labor illiteracy. Even when asked to make a crude guess, one out of four women were at a loss. However, the remaining three did answer, and two of them believe that at least half of the labor leaders are foreign-born. Here is the distribution of their answers:

Labor leaders foreign-born?	
Most are	19%
About half	28
Not so many	25
Don't know	27
Total cases	992

Although this question calls for a factual answer, these are not matter-of-fact answers; they are expressions of prejudice toward labor leaders in general. This is demonstrated by the close relation between the answers people give to this question and their answers to other questions which directly reveal an anti-labor leader bias.

Those whom we would expect to have more information on the subject do not answer the question any differently than those from whom we would expect less. Formal education, for instance, makes no difference. Moreover, just as many (49 per cent) of the women whose husbands belong to labor unions as those whose husbands do not think that half or more of the labor leaders are foreign-born.

But there is even more direct evidence that this belief is mere bias. The women asked about the nativity of labor leaders were also asked this question: "From the standpoint of the factory workers themselves, do you think unions do a good service job or not?" Now this question does not ask "from the standpoint of the community" or "the public at large"; it emphasizes "the factory workers themselves." Even those opposed to unions from the point of view of their over-all effect on American life might still answer "Yes" from the standpoint of the factory workers. Those who say "No" to this question therefore must be the most confirmed enemies of trade unionism. Some 16 per cent of those who believe the unions do a good job, as compared with 31 per cent of those who believe they do not, think that "most labor leaders" are foreign-born. Those who are most opposed to labor unions are more likely to believe the foreign-born myth than the women who are favorably inclined toward the union's role in the life of the American factory worker. People who cry "foreign-born" at labor leaders are likely to be those who have economic reasons for opposing the practical activities of American labor leaders.

The question of the labor leader's nativity cannot be answered by anecdotes about a handful of leaders. It is, of course, true that William Green was born in Coshocton, Ohio, but that David Dubinsky was born in Russia; that John L. Lewis was born in Lucas, Iowa, but that Harry Bridges was born in Australia. Argument on that level is interminable. There is only one answer to the question—a study of a statistically representative sample of labor leaders, which in each case finds out their place of birth.

The facts discerned by this procedure are that 89 per cent of the labor leaders were born in the United States; 11 per cent were born in some other country.

Place of Birth:	AFL	CIO
Born in U.S.	89%	89%
Foreign-born	11	11
Total cases	228	174

Only one of every ten labor leaders was not born in the United States. Thus, in that middle-sized city, two out of three of those who answered the question on nativity are misinformed. Even many of those who are generally pro-labor, highly educated, and who belong to labor unions are mistaken.

Labor leaders are American-born approximately to the same extent as the population at large. In fact, the bulk of the labor leaders are between 45 and 54 years of age; in 1940, 23 per cent of the white male population in this age group were foreign-born; among labor leaders in the same age group, only 10 per cent in the AFL and 17 per cent in the CIO were foreign-born. This pattern generally holds on all levels of leadership and in all regions of the United States.

In the mind of the mass public, as well as in the calculation of the sociologist, the chances a man has to become Americanized are affected by the length of time his family has been in the United States, and by whether his family was Croat or English, Lithuanian or Australian.

Fathers and sons:	AFL	CIO
Both native-born	61%	62%
Only the son native	28	27
Both foreign-born	11	11
Total cases	226	172

Eleven per cent of the labor leaders are foreign-born, and 27 or 28 per cent of those born in this country had foreign-born fathers. The majority of the labor leaders and their fathers were born in this country. In these respects, there are no differences between AFL and CIO leaders.

Such figures, of course, should be compared with the entire population, but the information required to make an exact comparison is not available. The poll-taker is limited in the number of questions he can ask a group of busy executives; we know the nativity of the fathers of the labor leaders, but we do not know where their mothers were born, and the U.S. Census does not distinguish between the two parents. In addition, age must always be considered in any comparison made.

The best judgment we can make shows that in 1940, 18 per cent of the native white male population between the ages of 45 and 54 were from foreign or mixed parentage, whereas 24 per cent of the native AFL and CIO leaders in this age group have foreign-born fathers. From this it would seem that although fewer labor leaders are foreign-born, somewhat more have foreign fathers than is true of the white male population.

Classifying the foreign-born labor leaders by the region of Europe from which they came, we find that about one-half in each bloc are from Great Britain and Northwest Europe; the remainder of the AFL foreign-born are scattered pretty evenly from Central, Southern, and Eastern Europe, whereas more of the remainder of the CIO are from Eastern Europe.

Origins of fathers:	AFL	CIO
Old migration	25%	15%
New migration	14	23
Total foreign-born	39	38
Total native-born	61	62
Total cases	227	173

The pattern of origin for the fathers of U.S. labor leaders reveals that more of the AFL fathers came from the old immigration (Great Britain and Northeast Europe) than did the CIO fathers, who tend to be part of the new immigration (Central, South, and Eastern Europe). This is, however, an expected implication of age; the CIO men are younger than the AFL men and younger migrants are more apt to be of the new immigration.

Such crude comparison as is possible indicates that more of the foreign-born fathers of native-born labor leaders came from England and the Empire than did the foreign-born parents of the native-born male white population at large.

The Level of Origin

The occupations pursued by the fathers of American labor leaders are perhaps more important as a clue to their early circumstances than their nativity, for they provide a more direct index of the economic milieu in which the leaders grew up. The father's occupation may shift during the boyhood and early manhood of the labor leader, but it is during his pre-adolescent period that an individual's opportunities are most crucially set by the social and economic level of his parents, for at that time it is determined whether he will continue in school or go to work. Therefore we asked: "What was the main occupation of your father when you were ten or twelve years old?"

Occupations of fathers:	AFL	CIO
Free enterprisers . .	33%	32%
New middle class . .	8	7
Wage workers	59	61
Total cases	198	158

The big fact about the occupational origins of the labor leaders is that they are predominantly from labor's own ranks. Six out of ten, in both the AFL and the CIO, derive from fathers who were wage workers, most from the foreman or skilled labor ranks. Three out of ten come from free enterprisers, the old middle class of small farm or business proprietors. The remaining one is of new middle-class or white-collar origin.

The free enterprisers are about equally farmers and smaller businessmen: 15 per cent of the labor leaders are from farmers and 17 per cent from business strata. The farmer fathers were either sizable tenants or owner-operators; the businessmen were primarily small, usually independent craftsmen, in such trades as building, or small retail operators. However, 5 per cent of the AFL leaders and 3 per cent of the CIO leaders derive from fathers of larger executive or business-owner standing; and in the CIO there is a 2 per cent contingent who come from free professional families. These are all classified with the free enterprisers.

In order to compare the occupations of the fathers of the labor leaders with the occupations of the general population, we would have to know the occupational distribution of all men who were fathers during the average census year when the labor leaders were ten or twelve years old. The closest approximation is the occupations of adult males as of 1910. Here is that comparison:

Occupations of fathers:	1910 U.S. MALES	AFL	CIO
Free enterprise	28%	33%	32%
New middle class	13	8	7
Wage worker	59	59	61
Total cases	29,926,007	198	158

These differences are negligible. The occupational origins of the labor leaders appear to be almost identical with the gross occupational distribution of the American male population. Certainly the labor leaders are from the working class in just about the proportions as the population at large. There is, however, a slight tendency for the old middle class to have produced more labor leaders than its quota, and for the new middle class of white-collar people—in 1910, at its beginnings—to have produced less than its quota.

The labor leaders of wage-worker origin are of higher status than the 1910 wage workers at large:

Wage-worker fathers:	1910 U.S. MALES	AFL	CIO
Foremen and skilled	14%	37%	34%
Semi-skilled and unskilled	29	14	18
Rural workers	16	8	9
Total wage workers	59%	59%	61%

The proportion of labor leaders who derive from the foremen and skilled labor level is much greater than that of the male population who held skilled labor jobs in 1910.

In all these respects, the AFL leaders do not differ markedly from the leaders of the CIO. Nor are there great differences in origin among the various levels of leadership within each organization. In view of the great age and educational differences between leaders of the two organizations, this is rather remarkable. The only differences in origin occur within the CIO: slightly more of its national leaders come from the new middle class, especially office and sales workers, and slightly fewer from wage workers, than is true of the state and city leaders.

The labor leaders are of lowly origin, but they do not come from the lowest sector of the population, the rural and the unskilled urban workers. Nor do they come in great proportions from the old middle class. They are the sons of skilled workers and small businessmen and farmers. They are, in an unkindly phrase, "petty bourgeois" in origin.

The only figures available on the occupational origins of businessmen, which might be comparable with these facts, were taken as of the year 1928. In so far as they have changed during the intervening decade and a half, they have undoubtedly changed in the direction of the inference we shall make. Even allowing for substantial errors, they clearly point to wide differences in occupational origin of labor leaders and business leaders.

These businessmen were a top group, and therefore our comparison should be made with the national labor leaders. Such comparison reveals that 56 per cent of the business leaders, but only 21 per cent of the national labor leaders, were from the business classes, and that the businesses of the labor leaders' fathers were smaller. Thirteen per cent of the business leaders but only 1 or 2 per cent of the national labor leaders came from professional homes; and whereas only 11 per cent of the businessmen originated on the wage-worker level, some 58 per cent of the labor leaders did.

Before the Union

The occupational level of an individual's family sets his general life chances; in particular, it strongly conditions whether he continues in school or gets a job; and in the latter case, it sets the level of that first job. The labor leaders, considering their relatively low origins, have a high level of formal schooling. They are better educated than the adult male population of the U.S.: 66 per cent of the AFL and 80 per cent of the CIO, but only 39 per cent of the adult male population in 1910, have had high school or higher education.

The labor leaders of higher origin have more formal schooling than those of lower origin. For example, 52 per cent of the CIO leaders from higher occupational levels completed high school, compared with 22 per cent of the CIO leaders from lower occupational origin.

In some two out of ten cases, national labor leaders attained their education by what appears to be a sharp struggle. Over half of this 20 per cent are high school men, the remainder grammar school graduates. Many of them went to night schools, many took correspondence school courses, mainly in white-collar subjects such as bookkeeping; others attended business colleges of one sort or another where they undoubtedly were exposed to the same type of white-collar skills.

This educational striving does not seem to be immediately reflected in the usual occupations of the labor leaders before they went into the labor unions. Only 18 per cent of the leaders were in white-collar work, divided almost equally between lower salaried professional positions and office and salesmen work. Very few have ever been independent entrepreneurs of farms or businesses. The great bulk—seven or eight out of ten—were wage workers before they became union officials.

Job before union post:	AFL	CIO
Free enterprisers	9%	4%
New middle class	18	18
Wage workers	73	78
Total cases	213	161

The labor leaders were, however, better educated than the men beside them in the shops. Moreover, a good number of them were of higher origin than most wage workers. There are no significant over-all differences between the CIO and the AFL leaders in these respects, but there is a difference in the type of wage work in which the leaders of the two blocs were engaged:

Job before union post:	AFL	CIO
Foremen and skilled	60%	47%
Semi-skilled and unskilled	13	28
Rural workers	..	3
Total wage workers	73%	78%

More of the leaders in the CIO than in the AFL were on the semi-skilled and unskilled levels, and fewer on the foreman and skilled levels. This corresponds to the composition of the unions within each bloc. This organizational fact also explains why more AFL men worked as independent contractors in various trades. Back of the organizational selection lie the differences in age between the two sets of leaders and the changing composition of the U.S. working class as a whole: since the AFL men are older and have been in trade union work longer, their pre-union careers occurred during a period when there was a higher proportion of skilled labor at work, and when trade unions were more likely to be composed of skilled workmen.

Even discounting educational differences, more CIO than AFL leaders followed semi-skilled and unskilled work: thus among high school graduates, 25 per cent of the CIO and 9 per cent of the AFL have a semi-skilled or unskilled job in their pre-union histories.

A better education did not make the labor leaders entrepreneurs or foremen, but it did take them out of the shop into the white-collar world. Thus no more of the higher-educated than of the lower became enterprisers; and among the several grades of workmen, it is the less- rather than the more-educated who attained the level of higher skill.

There are no marked differences in the usual pre-union occupations among the different levels of union leadership. In the

AFL, slightly more of the national and state leaders were foremen and skilled workmen than is the case with the city heads. In the CIO, this is true of the state, but not of the national leaders. More of the CIO national heads worked for a time at professional jobs than did any other group of leaders: 23 per cent, as compared with 7 per cent of the national AFL leaders.

If we combine the level of the pre-union job with the level of origin, we are able to get an over-all picture of the labor leaders' beginnings. The CIO and AFL leaders on all levels of leadership are almost identical in this respect:

Occupational origins:

FATHER	SON	AFL	CIO
Higher	Higher	12%	10%
Higher	Wage worker	24	23
Wage worker	Higher	13	12
Wage worker	Wage worker	51	55
Total cases		189	146

About one-half of the leaders were wage workers themselves before beginning their union careers, and had fathers who were wage workers. Approximately one-tenth of the leaders worked, as did their fathers, in non-wage-worker jobs—white collar, small business, and small farmers.

Between these two extremes of origin, one-tenth of the leaders were born to wage-working fathers but were white-collar employees or small businessmen before their union careers. They seem to have been on their way up before entering the labor union hierarchy.

Finally, the fathers of approximately one-fourth of the leaders had non-wage-working jobs, but their sons' primary pre-union occupation was that of wage worker. These somewhat declassed leaders, as shall be shown later, are likely to be politically insurgent.

As one would expect, these careers correlate with educational chances: 70 per cent of the AFL leaders whose fathers were not wage workers, and who themselves were not wage workers before joining the union, went through high school or beyond, as compared with 32 per cent of those AFL leaders whose fathers were wage workers and who themselves had pre-union wage-working experience. The corresponding figures for the CIO leaders are 87 per cent and 38 per cent.

Most labor leaders held jobs in the trade or industry with which they were later to deal as union officials. They do not appear to have taken these jobs merely to become union members and thus to make their careers in the unions. There is, however, another career pattern: before they became union officials of any kind, some labor leaders held jobs, mostly white-collar, higher in the social scale than those organized by the unions they were later to lead. In both organizations, this white-collar pattern is slightly more frequent among the state officials than among the officers of the internationals, among secretaries than among presidents. The experience is closely associated with educational struggle and with college education: half of the labor leaders on national and state levels who were white-collar workers are college men.

This pre-union career involving white-collar jobs and/or educational struggle may take two formal paths: (1) A man may take a job in a local of some trade union that has organized workers below the level of his occupation. Because of union rules, he will usually take a job in the shop in order to have the employment record necessary to become a union member. This labor link in his white-collar career is ritualistic. Some younger men who were unemployed white-collar workers during the Thirties took laboring jobs from need, and then went into labor union work. (2) A man who has been working as a skilled laborer and has never held any other type of job may struggle to rise from the ranks of labor into a white-collar position. The years during which he struggled for education and better jobs, as well as the character of those experiences and of his occupational origin, do not indicate that he was bent primarily upon a union career. Yet this upward struggle was eventually channeled into a trade union hierarchy.

Beginning Points

The labor leader may begin his union career as a business-like man, a political man, or a disgruntled working man.

Throughout the history of the American labor movement, the third way has been and still is dominant: a man of plain wage-worker origin begins work as a wage worker and rises out of the ranks and up the union hierarchy. He may take this route because of a militancy aroused by frustrated ambition or by an upsurge of indignation. Many of America's older labor leaders, in fact, began their career by being fired for their union ideas. They answered back in the only way open to them during certain economic periods—by fighting for or even by founding local labor unions. But a generalized rebel spirit or an ideological buttress certainly is not necessary to the labor leader's actions. A serviceable ideology can be picked up along the way; often speeches by labor leaders contain much rough-hewn rhetoric and little else.

In the decades before the first World War, and again during the great slump, socialist orientation was an important starting point for many union careers. Ideological adherence to some set of leftward ideas automatically led to a labor leader career; regardless of the brand of political ideas, almost every leftward group has looked upon the unions as instruments of political struggle. In this ideological pattern, a man might enter the shop with the deliberate intention of becoming a leader of its workers; under this impulse, he might either attempt to found a union if none existed or to work his way up in any union already there.

An opposite career-beginning developed perhaps more frequently during the Thirties than previously. Men of some education and background saw the union career as a good proposition. They were white-collar people of various sorts and aspirations, but in the economic squeeze of the Thirties, were forced into shops and factories. Once there, they saw two ways up: the route of the foreman to a management job or the more perilous but in many ways more promising route of the labor leader. Some may also have had ideological convictions, not necessarily more left than those of pure and simple unionism as practiced during the era of the New Deal. There were, in addition, men who raised enough capital to open an office in the union business.

In the reality of given cases, ideological and business motives are always mixed. It is a question of emphasis; in the trade union world there are men who have practical careers in ideology just as there are men who cultivate ambitious convictions. Personal motive and public reason often coincide with opportunity in such a way as to make most difficult any real untangling of the three. David Dubinsky, for instance, or Julius Hochman "went into the shop with the vaguely contradictory ambition of leading the workers toward 'emancipation' while saving enough money to study medicine or law." One thing that Dubinsky didn't want to become—although he had the opportunity—was a small clothing manufacturer.

William Green, whose parents were English miners and followers of Keir Hardie's "Christian Socialism," belonged to the socialist opposition within the AFL before the first World War. He was an organization man, that is, he was part of the miners' organization, which was part of the opposition. His rhetorical talents and this vaguely socialist background undoubtedly increased his motives for becoming a labor leader. After he was in, it has been said, he "rose in the world by standing still." Yet the little motors of ambition are laboring away in the trade union world, as in every other occupational and leadership hierarchy.

Between ideological urge and personal business-like ambition in the career-line of a labor leader, it is not at all unlikely that a shift has occurred, in accordance with the decline of the socialist movement in the United States. Entering the unions out of a belief in some political idea is primarily a nineteenth-century phenomenon, although it carried over into the twentieth. The business-like pattern is probably more typical of the 1932-47 era of union history.

Career-lines

Whatever his original motives, a man may become a leader of some rank by: (1) creating a union himself; (2) being elected by his shopmates to a local union post, either that of shop steward or directly to a local office; or (3) being appointed organizer or business agent by a national or local organization, and from that appointed position climbing up via a series of elections.

The majority of the labor leaders began their union career on the local level, as shop stewards and then local officers, or simply as elected local officers. Only a handful of leaders began their careers in their present offices. Here are the answers to our question, "What was your first job in any trade union organization?" classified by the level of the present job:

	AFL			CIO		
Union careers:	Nat'l	State	City	Nat'l	State	City
Started in present rank	14%	16%	17%	9%	17%	5%
Up from the local	61	57	68	52	51	78
Up from organizer	23	22	8	33	27	11
All others	2	5	7	6	5	6
Total cases	51	37	98	33	41	84

Most of the leaders on all three levels began as heads of locals or as local committeemen. But a second starting point is important, especially among national and state officers: an appointment to the job of organizer.

On the national level of leadership, 14 per cent of the AFL and 9 per cent of the CIO leaders began in their present rank; a great many of these founded the unions they now head. There does not seem to be much movement from the city and the state lineup to the national. The local is the primary starting point for the city, state, and national hierarchies, but once a man enters the city or state organizations, apparently he is less likely to go on to the national headquarters. These figures correspond to the vocational idea current in labor unions that state offices are often places of derailment. The national leaders either begin nationally or rise from the locals without going through state offices.

More CIO leaders on both the national and state levels began as appointed organizers than did the leaders on the same levels in the AFL. The AFL has a slightly more rigid hierarchy of promotion than has the CIO, and the CIO is a good deal more centralized. In both organizations the career begins at the bottom, but in the AFL it is more apt to follow the route up via elections.

This difference between the AFL and CIO, especially in regard to the proportions who began as appointed organizers, not only reflects the fact that success in the CIO rests somewhat more upon organizing skill, but it also reflects and illustrates the rise of the white-collar career.

In the older AFL unions, only 5 per cent of the leaders with entrepreneurial or white-collar backgrounds began as appointed national organizers as compared with some 16 per cent of those with wage-worker background. In the CIO, however, 26 per cent of the leaders with white-collar jobs prior to their union careers began as national organizers as against 16 per cent of those having wage-worker backgrounds. This is not only a difference between the CIO and the AFL; it is a shift in union career-lines as well. The better-educated man with a white-collar background now tends to enter the field as an appointed organizer. Of course, such power as he acquires through elections is gained by his organizing talents, and in this respect he is just like the other dominant career type: the man who begins by being elected as a shop steward or local officer must also organize in order to win elections.

This shift in the beginning point of union careers, and the increased frequency of a white-collar link in the career of the CIO national leaders, point to the growth of bureaucracy in the labor union world.

Twenty or 30 years ago, the organizer came from the ranks, or was drawn by a national organization from among successful local leaders. Sometimes workers who had been discharged for union activity from jobs in the plants were hired as organizers and placed in other locals. What training the organizer had was empirical or handed down to him as a rule-of-thumb. But during the Thirties, when legal frameworks had to be attended to, organizing problems became more technical; an organizer had to have some training. Lore and simple experience were not enough. Business had its training courses for salesmen; during the Thirties, labor unions began to develop training schools for organizers.

The typical organizer is still of the older sort, however, and his career begins in the local. Unions are still more like patronage machines than streamlined bureaucracies. This fact probably affects the organizers or international representatives more than any other category of personnel. In at least one big union in the CIO, there are three types of organizers:

I. Men to whom a job is given as a political pay-off, usually former local officials who were loyal to the national executive but were ousted from their elected post during a political reshuffle. Quite often these men are rather useless as organizers, and they can only do little jobs for the official to whom they are attached. Yet the official feels a moral political obligation to them even when he cannot depend upon them.

II. The inner circle surrounding a national officer, men who are considered wholly dependable and who form the cadre of the machine of the national leader, promoting his security of position. In unions that are split at the top, each of the cliques may have a set of such organizers. They prepare the vote of the locals assigned to them and do the political maneuvering necessary to keep conventions and appointments in line.

III. Organizers who specialize in initiating and maintaining organizations of various kinds within the union world. They see their job as that of a professional, and often they have salaried professional backgrounds. They may deplore the politics in their work or that of their colleagues, but they will play along when it is necessary. Because unions are not strict bureaucracies, but are run by patriarchs according to patronage, there is a strong tendency for the trained organizer also to become a machine politician.

Virtually all routes to trade union leadership start in the locals; regardless of the particular career pattern which he has followed, the trade union leader is a man who has climbed a long way. Considering his occupational origin and the character and extent of his education, he finds the top-flight trade union post a perch of success. And in the American vocabulary, success means money.

Incomes

Money is both the great equalizer and the great differentiator. The national leaders of labor make a good deal more money than do the wage workers they lead but a good deal less than the corporation executives and businessmen with whom they bargain. When the president of the United Automobile Workers sits across the table from the president of General Motors, ten thousand dollars a year is confronting four hundred fifty-nine thousand dollars a year.

The highest salary paid to any CIO official is paid to Murray as president of the Steel Workers: $20,000 per year. The two highest in the AFL are the $30,000 paid to Daniel Tobin, president of the Teamsters, and to his general secretary. It is said that Petrillo of the AFL Musicians now receives $20,000 from the national union and $20,000 from his Chicago local. The lowest salary is probably the $2,400 received by the president of the CIO's Stone Workers Union. But figures showing how many labor leaders receive salaries on the various levels of pay matter more than these random accounts.

Sixty-six per cent of the presidents of 62 international unions, according to a survey made in 1944, received less than $9,500 a year; 50 per cent of these received between $4,500 and $9,499. AFL presidents seem to receive slightly higher salaries than do those in the CIO; 37 per cent of the AFL and 24 per cent of the CIO receive over $9,500.

Of the other general officers of the unions—the secretaries, treasurers, vice-presidents, and general organizers—in 1944 67 per cent received less than $7,500 a year. Among these men there is a great difference in the salaries paid by the AFL and CIO; 41 per cent of the AFL and 22 per cent of the CIO officers received over $7,500 a year.

The officers of local unions are paid very little, considering the magnitude of their jobs. A study of 350 local unions during the latter phase of the recent war revealed that less than half had full-time paid officers. In the 84 cases for which we have information, 35 per cent of the full-time paid officers were paid either the highest regular rate in the trade or the rate of a foreman. Only 18 per cent of the locals paid from $90 to $125 per week, the highest level. Thus, even where the local officers are on full-time salaries, their salaries are not much higher than those of the workers, except that they are paid every week in the year and do not do manual work. The local labor leader is usually ideologically interested in his job or ambitious about the status and influence it affords him among his ex-coworkers.

Yet, as a first rung on a ladder, the local union office does hold out to the wage worker the possibility of higher income. Since the early Thirties, there has often been more chance for a capable man to raise his income by entering the union hierarchy than by struggling for a foremanship. And foremanship is increasingly a dead-end job, while the local union post serves as a channel for further ascent.

The popular impression that union officers are drawing fabulous salaries is erroneous, just as is the idea that only economic interests impel the labor leader to his work.

There is little or no relation between union aggressiveness and rate of pay for labor leaders, nor is there much relation between the size of the union and the rate of pay to officers. Heads of some of the largest unions receive lower salaries than heads of smaller unions. How much the leader gets is often a touchy matter at conventions, and leaders have been known to voluntarily lower their remuneration for political purposes within the union. There is little if any correlation between the salaries paid the top officers of a union and the level of skill the members of the union possess. For instance, the Machinists and Typographers pay their leaders less than the Longshoremen.

Nor is there any doubt about this: the salaries for top men in the AFL are higher than in the CIO; the salaries for local officers are seldom very much above the level of earnings in the trade or industry organized; the typical salaries of the national labor leaders are well above the level of earnings of the union members and well below their counterparts in the management hierarchy.

A study of 264 top corporation executives revealed that even in 1935 the average (median) salary received was $61,200 per year. Note that our union president figures are for 1944, when salaries were generally a good deal higher than in the 1935 depression year.

But this is salary alone: the business executive usually owns some of his company's stock. The 264 top executives who had a median salary of $61,200 held an average of $90,000 worth of stock. The industrial chieftains held an average of $298,700.

The salaries of big business executives are more stable and secure than are stock dividends or factory payrolls. Thus, if 1929 is used to equal 100, executive compensation reached a low of 70 in 1932; the dividends of the year stood at 32, factory payrolls at 36, the average weekly earnings of employed workers at 60; and many of the workers were unemployed.

Styles of Life

In 1925, Mother Jones, one of labor's romantic figures, wrote: "Many of our modern leaders of labor have wandered far from the thorny paths of these early crusaders. Never in the early days of the labor struggle would you find leaders wining and dining with the aristocracy; nor did their wives strut about like diamond-bedecked peacocks; nor were they attended by humiliated, cringing, colored servants. . . .

"The rank and file have let their servants become their masters and dictators. The workers have now to fight not alone their exploiters but likewise their own leaders, who often betray them, who sell them out, who put their own advancement ahead of that of the working masses, who make the rank and file political pawns."

An apologist for one union, wishing to attack the leader of another, says that the older workers "think of him not as a leader of labor, but as a man who has risen to the presidency of the Amalgamated Clothing Workers as one might rise to the presidency of the National City Bank." Or, as an old-time cloak maker is quoted as saying, "Dubinsky grew out of the movement and Hillman was never in it. He worked at pants for a couple of months and then he became right away a statesman."

The cry that the union leader gets to be "too far above us" is constant in any organization of next-to-the-bottom people. Yet there is pretty good evidence that the workers themselves do not mind particularly the style of life of their labor leaders. In fact, in pre-World War I days, several labor racketeers were acclaimed, in part, for parading their new wealth. It is said that official labor circles boasted that John Mitchell, president of the United Mine Workers, was treated as a social equal by Carnegie, Hanna, Belmont, and other robber barons. This, they claimed, gave tone to the labor movement. They did not question how Mitchell had amassed $250,000 in the labor business.

Nevertheless, during these same days or shortly thereafter, Morris Sigman, then president of the ILGWU, lived with his wife in a "furnished room with the barest standards of comfort." And Andrew Furuseth, president of the Seamen's Union, "lived most of his life in dingy hotel rooms and ate in cheap diners." There have been, and there doubtless are, both types; but the typical style of life of the national labor leader today is like that of any middle-class businessman in an urban area.

The national and, to a lesser extent, the state leaders not only make a higher average income than the rank and file, but on the whole their income is more secure and more regular. Long tenure of office means security on a higher level of income, and way of life is related to security and regularity of income.

The national labor leader is a public figure, which means that in his style of living he has both a private life and a public one, and in this public role, he has broad daily contacts. The average wage worker has a limited contact with the world. As David Dubinsky has said: the workers' "existence is all routine and headaches, and it's apt to contribute very little to personal growth. In my job I meet all sorts of people—government officials, labor leaders from every corner of the world, politicians, businessmen, journalists. That is what opportunity is all about—being able to touch the world at many points."

This segregation of the leader from the led continues through every phase of the union organization's life. It is well known that unions in the course of their history generally pass first through a fighting and organizing stage and then through a contract administration phase. In the first phase, the leader is a general; in the second, a contractor and administrator of labor. An effective general must have military powers and be able to give orders; giving orders involves some remoteness from those to whom the orders are given. No matter how many strikes the leader runs, how many mass meetings he organizes, or how often he is put in jail, he is still above the rank and file. He leads the strike, he addresses the mass meeting, he is singled out as the one important enough to be put in jail.

When and if the union passes into the administrative stage, this segregation from the masses of the workers is much more obvious. The leader has left the shop completely; he sits at a desk, he travels and lives in hotels, he generally adopts a quieter manner, commensurate with office life. No matter how often he gets emotional catharsis and political effect from walking on a picket line, by virtue of the tasks his job more or less imposes upon him, he does become personally remote from the rank and file.

Some labor leaders work hard to break down this remoteness; like party politicians, they try to know personally hundreds of people in the organization; they have intimate, informal conversations with local leaders or members. Yet time becomes precious to an administrator, and probably no government, business, or military executive works any harder or carries a bigger load than the labor leader.

Two things begin to happen to the labor leaders: First, they become intimate with their own lieutenants and leaders and depend upon them for contact work. They become enclosed, as it were, by a circle of leaders. This means that they are more and more inaccessible to members of the rank and file. They hire people to be accessible for them. Second, there is a subjective change accompanying this enclosure of the leaders: they become aloof in the sense that people consult them about problems rather than come to them with troubles. Personal intimacy is not possible; they become officials.

This style of life and work has a political meaning closely tied to the personal changes. The labor leaders, having risen from the ranks, are self-made men. Self-made men often tend, even if unconsciously, to look down on those who have not succeeded. Yet to reach at least the first rung, the labor leader usually had to articulate a pro-worker ideology, and he has to keep talking that way. But as a labor leader, he gradually assumes more and more of what is called "sobering responsibility." His contacts, along with the shift in his income and style of life, transform him from the out to the in group.

What he said before his early elections were, after all, said "on his own." Now he faces company officials and labor leaders up the line or on his own level who hold him more or less to account. It is no longer simply the leader and the rank and file; he is now a member of a mature and responsible organization, which is to say, of a vested interest. To the old dialectic of the leader and the ranks there is added the labor *organization* and the business *organization*, and the officials in both hierarchies. The labor leader acquires new mirrors in which to appraise his image from the angle from which others see him, and perhaps to conceive new images of himself.

It takes the young, spontaneous militant only a short time to realize that the rank and file can change its mind about leaders. But a machine can be permanent if a careful watch is kept for everyone in it. To build a machine and to keep it intact and to deliver what the rank and file wants—with that combination a man can be a success in the world of labor and pretty much ignore all the little knots of young militants who know nothing of responsibility.

When the union is big and powerful enough to pay off and the economy is in working order, a machine can hold a union together and keep its leaders at the top. But when something goes wrong in the economy, then new leaders with other ideas are likely to rise.

This cycle of leadership is not a natural history in the sense that every union and every union's leadership must go through it. What disturbs it are general economic conditions. During slumps, especially when the rank and file are militant, leaders of labor must shift to more militant ways or gamble on losing their leadership. Democracy in the unions is like the democracy of some Latin-American countries: it often proceeds by upsurge and revolution rather than by smoothly operating democratic machinery.

The Heights Gained

The labor leader, although typically of native American birth, begins life on a relatively low level of origin. His main pre-union occupation is also low-level: he is a wage worker in the industry with which he later deals as a labor official. His union career—whether he starts his own union, is appointed as an organizer, or is elected by the members—begins in his local at the bottom of the union hierarchy. From thence, there are two fairly segregated routes upward. One leads to the top of an international union, the other to the top of a state federation.

There is a tendency, now, for another type of career pattern to emerge. It involves only a short stop at the local and more back-and-forth movement between the local-to-international and local-to-state federation hierarchies. More crucially, it involves a white-collar link in the pre-union occupational career and an appointive link in the trade union career. The men whose careers embody this pattern tend to be well educated.

This white-collar pattern will become more explicit if the need for a more specialized personnel in a more rationalized and centralized labor union management is to be met. The master trends of the economy also facilitate such a bureaucratic career: the occupational structure is becoming more rigid; statistically speaking, it is becoming increasingly difficult for a bright young man from relatively low circumstances to climb above the position occupied by his father.

The power and success of the leader within the unions depend upon organizing skill and machine politics. Organizing of all kinds is the royal road to power within the American unions. Whether the leader gets his first toe-hold by appointment or, as is more typical, by local elections, he must pass through electoral machines in order to rise. He must be politically sagacious.

The men who now run the American labor unions are the end-products of a long process of American selection. They are the ones who had initiative and persistence. They have occupied one position after another; they have buckled down, climbed to the top, and stayed there. They are self-made men, in the conventional and misleading sense of that term, and they may be expected to display the associated psychological incapacities. In all, the American labor leaders have much in common with the mythical image of the American entrepreneur.

The old-fashioned success story is now less true for business executives, only 10 per cent of whom came up from the bottom, than for labor leaders, 60 per cent of whom came up from the laboring ranks. Curran walked the docks in 1930, and rose to $20,000 a year in 1940. Reuther knocked around the world during the early Thirties—and a few years later was in Washington helping to run the great war.

More than the businessman of comparable power, the national labor leader has built up a business; his commodity is labor, and he bargains for its price. And yet, he personally doesn't make a profit out of his business-like transactions. If he gets 10 cents more an hour for 1,000,000 workers, his salary does not go up accordingly. Indeed, he might even be refused re-election the next year by those same 1,000,000 workers. The labor leader must be as much a politician as an entrepreneur, and sometimes, for short periods, must be much more than either.

Ascent for the bright working-class boy, as well as for the educated middle-class youngster, has been of late more possible within labor union channels than within the hierarchies of business. This is not in respect to the absolute numbers involved, for there are many more business than union positions available, but the proportion of men of lower occupational origin who are at the top of labor unions is much greater than those at the top of business (and governmental) concerns of comparable income and power. The union leaders attain these positions at younger ages and with smaller amounts of formal (expensive) education than do the business and governmental officials.

In many labor unions, even today, a higher education is not seen as an asset for the labor union career. But if present trends continue, the climb to success in unions will require a better education, and more able young men may be expected to follow the trade union route to positions of income in the three big places of power. At the present time, labor's leadership contains a greater proportion of the sons of laborers than any other group of comparable income on which statistical information is available. Although existing information is meager, the CIO seems to have offered young men of working-class parents a faster road to a position of power than any other organization, except the armed forces, during the past decade.

PART THREE

CHAPTER SIX

THE LIBERAL RHETORIC

THE LABOR leader who has gained the heights becomes a labor spokesman; like other spokesmen, following the principle of expediency and searching for the main chance, he needs a language for his contacts with other spokesmen and for his curious relations with the American people. The language he speaks is the rhetoric of liberalism; without it he could not get along in the world of stiff collars and blue suits.

The liberal rhetoric has become the medium of exchange among political, scholarly, business, and labor spokesmen. If all these men on the heights seem to be able to work together, it is partly because they speak the same language and partly because one condition of their success is extensive use of the liberal rhetoric.

Today we are witnessing the Pyrrhic victory of the liberal rhetoric; in the process of its great spread, it is being banalized. Yet for this very reason, the liberal rhetoric is useful: every spokesman can use it for any occasion.

A moment occasionally comes, however, when the spokesman must comment upon some current misunderstanding among legislators and men of affairs. Then he is talking politics rather than chanting liberal formulas, and he must promise action rather than play his customary ritualistic role.

The meaning of these specific stands is usually decently obscured by the liberal rhetoric which surrounds it. In fact, a new expert, the technician of ideology, is now needed in order to make clear what is in the mind of the spokesman. The rhetoric of liberalism is related neither to the specific stands taken nor to what might be happening outside the range of the spokesman's voice. As applied to business-labor relations, the liberal rhetoric is not so much a point of view as a social phenomenon.

Business-Labor Co-operation

The key word in the liberal rhetoric is co-operation. Always there is the urgent and immediate need for increased co-operation between businessmen and labor leaders. There is really no breach between business and labor; there is harmony, although, to be sure, it is sometimes disturbed by agents of bad will who lack the vision of the spokesman.

The idea of natural harmony among the various interests of the economy is, of course, an article of faith drawn from eighteenth-century economics. If everyone works solely for his own interest, his work will be in the interests of all—the poor and the rich, the Southerner and the Northerner, the businessman and the labor leader.

The spokesmen have ceased paying explicit homage to this metaphysical basis of their rhetoric, for no one believes it when it is stated so plainly. But these men have created other assumptions which, like great motifs, seem constantly to reappear in the rhetoric of liberalism. These themes, like that of beneficent self-interest, minimize conflict between business enterprises founded on private property and the propertyless men hired to work in these enterprises.

According to the liberal rhetoric, the most important elements in the entire relationship of business and labor are the spokesmen themselves. Unlike some academic thinkers of the liberal center, the liberal spokesmen split the leaders from the led. Between the led on either side there is assumed to be a great area of constant and natural harmony. "Down at the grass roots," says a labor spokesman before a gathering of the American Legion, "far removed from the mighty sphere of politicians testing each wind, are the men, the laborers and managers, who work together every day, looking toward the same end. . . ."

The cause of all the trouble is a small group of "irresponsible leaders" on each side who force business and labor to wage their imaginary battles rather than allowing them to live as proper neighbors side by side in industrial peace and American prosperity.

The liberal-labor spokesmen, in unguarded moments, are inclined to say that the troublemakers are the selfish, unscrupulous extremists of industry; the liberal business spokesmen say they are the willful, power-seeking extremists of labor. But the more balanced, tolerant, and visionary liberals in both camps emphatically assert that there are extremists in both camps, and everyone agrees that the solution to it all lies with these spokesmen.

On the side of business, the sophisticated conservatives will admit that there are a few extremists among their junior colleagues on the practical right. On the labor side, the men on the heights will admit that there are a few extremists among local organizers entering new industries and among rank-and-file shop stewards. Both sets of higher spokesmen promise to do what they can to discipline such extremists so that the higher spokesmen can get together and solve their mutual problems in the light of harmonious reason.

Their formula for industrial peace is simple. All that is needed is for the spokesmen to be mature and reasonable and above all responsible to their mutual obligations and public trust. For what the men down the line say is not really labor or business talking; it is only some extremists. At this point, the liberal rhetoric frequently works in terms of its "you, too" formula. "Some unions," says a national official of a union to a national organization of pro-business leanings, "have acted in a high-handed and dictatorial manner," but so have some "unscrupulous industrialists." He goes on: "The only successful formula" for industrial peace "is better, closer relationships, confidence and mutual understanding between those who speak for labor and capital." For ". . . peace in industry is based on good will, understanding, and mutual respect." That is the formula for industrial peace.

The liberal rhetoric personalizes and moralizes business-labor relations. It does not talk of any contradiction of interests but of highly placed persons, and of the presence or absence among them of moral traits. Two such traits are stressed: "good will" and "intelligence." If only the spokesmen for both sides were uniformly men of good will and if only they were intelligent, then there would be no breach between the interests of the working people and those of the managers of property. If only the spokesmen had enough intelligence to practice the Golden Rule on one another, there would be harmony.

There is a tendency for the labor spokesmen to stress intelligence over good will, and for the business spokesmen to stress moral good will above intelligence, although the true liberal in either camp stresses each indiscriminately. Thus a management consultant writes, "A faulty system of social and informational intercourse between the two groups emerges as the real villain. Success in the democratic, reasonable solution of group disputes rests on the ability to temporarily view the problem through the other fellow's eyes. Only in this way is it possible to distinguish real disagreement from emotionally biased, prejudice-created, and imaginary battles." And a labor chief explains to a large gathering of union delegates: "I merely say that to prevent strikes should be our goal. . . . There will be strikes from time to time, for there will be instances where nothing but strikes can bring labor and management together and clear the air so understandings can be reached. This is true because we of labor are human and prone to misjudgments, and so are the humans who comprise management, and who own capital." Strikes are instruments of increasing co-operation and are due to the personal failings of "humans."

During wars, the spokesmen find ready at hand the nationalist words with which to clothe their reasons for their co-operation. Patriotism spills over easily into the arena of business-labor co-operation. The spokesmen borrow it to quell trouble in the ranks, and labor becomes part of the great compromised inclusion. But war passes, and with it the alliances it fostered. Then, lest extremists again rise to plague industrial harmony, new goals for business-labor co-operation are created or old ones are refurbished by the spokesmen.

The liberal rhetoric provides both the positive and negative goals. The major positive goals are the retention of the public's confidence in the spokesmen, the maintenance of free private enterprise, and the advancement of American prosperity. Along with these goes the maintenance of the absolute value of industrial stability, not of any particular type of stability but stability in general.

Business and labor must co-operate because of our "mutual interests in the welfare of America" say a dozen spokesmen all at once. More specifically, says one, "because the public is caught in the middle of any struggle we have, and we, as liberals, must co-operate in their behalf." "Democracy," says the president of a progressive union, "is possible only in a society of free enterprise, and trade unionism can live only in a democracy." The labor leader and the businessman are "co-custodians of American prosperity," says the regional head of a union, who is echoed by a prominent business economist, who recently wrote a book subtitled, "How Can Business Leaders Save Private Enterprise?" which includes labor leaders among the business leaders.

For many of the spokesmen, there is an urgent negative reason, as pertinent for the labor leader as for the business leader, both of whom, like all spokesmen, believe in job security: unless there is co-operation, the radicals will take over. Who the radicals are is not usually specified by the fellow-travelers of the Communist Party; but to anti-CP liberals and to businessmen at large, radical means Communist.

No spokesman believes that labor spokesmen and business spokesmen must fight each other; they must co-operate together against both vindictive labor laws and radicals and crackpots. Only the extremists want a fight to the finish, and among the extremists none are so extreme as the radicals. The radicals, as well as the business extremists—those who want to suppress the labor spokesmen—are, as one spokesman says, "frightening new members" into extreme positions "daily by pointing to the other, and if they have their way, we may yet see an entirely unnecessary internal struggle between each man and his neighbor."

In the liberal vision, if the labor leader is not to be an extremist and a radical, he must be responsible to the great American public as well as to his own union members. He must sometimes discipline the members of his own union, even as a businessman must discipline the people who work for him. A scholarly spokesman, writing on autocracy in union government, comments, "We need to bear in mind that undiluted democracy is no answer to the problem, and that where discipline is sacrificed to rank-and-file rule, the union will fail to play its proper role in industrial relations or to maintain adequate discipline." In disciplining radicals and extremists who stir up the rank and file, the labor leader is upholding the liberal goals of labor-management co-operation, his position in the world created by his rhetoric, his job in the union, and the position of the businessman in the American system.

Co-operation, of which the liberal rhetoric makes so much, involves power. There is a great range of possible power relations between business and labor. At one extreme, private business has the power to deal as it will and as the law allows with each individual worker, and each worker has exactly the strength that is in his own back. At the other, organized workers have the power to take full charge of the total productive equipment, ousting the businessman completely as a parasitic growth on the wheels of production.

In the United States today, approximately two-thirds of the business-labor relations exemplify the first extreme: the workers are not organized and they bargain individually with their employers. The other one-third—those in the union—are in between the two positions but closer to the second extreme. Unionized workers are the aristocrats of labor in whose name labor spokesmen co-operate with business spokesmen.

Within this labor aristocracy, there are now two types: the trade aristocracy which during the 50 years prior to the latter

Thirties was dominant, and the industrial aristocracy, which since 1935 has become almost as large as the first.

The Aristocracy of Labor, I

The *trade* aristocracy of labor has, throughout its long history, accepted and practiced the types of co-operation required by business unionism.

There is a basic affinity between business unionism and other forms of business enterprise. If they struggle with one another, it is more like competition between two business enterprises than a clash of basic interest. It is only that both wish to do as well in a business way as they can, which is to say that under the aegis of the AFL, business unionism has been as American as business enterprise itself.

This brand of unionism is not an evangelical movement of classes but a business-like operation, based on a business-like idea, and put into practice by business-like men. These men have simply applied the philosophy of the business community to the restricted skilled-labor market. They have become labor's entrepreneurs.

The older business unionist does not see the relation of business and labor in terms of class, as do the independent and far left, nor in terms of the public, as does the liberal center. He sees the relation in terms of a market for the particular craft he represents, just as a businessman selling bricks sees the market as oriented around the price of his bricks.

The aim of the business unionist has been pure and simple: to force the employer to pay dearly for his members' labor by organizing a union having monopolistic control of a particular skill. He does not assume any responsibility for efficient production. Like the old-style competitive businessman, whose historical shadow he is, the business unionist pursues his particular narrow interests with no thought for the interests of society or even for his own industry, much less for workers as a class. He has always been ready and willing to co-operate with some businessmen against other businessmen, other workers, and the community.

The kind of solidarity of workmen needed by the business unionists is that of a craft within a local labor market. Yet even in the simplest craft union situation, the scope of co-operation which business needs to secure monopoly tends to enlarge the basis of the solidarity. The typical union becomes an amalgamation of crafts within a local area. Each union leader, as it were, becomes a vice-president in an amalgamated company which works for the bread-and-butter interests of all its craftsmen. Co-operation is no longer with individual enterprises, but with the trade association of employers.

In 1897, the Carpenters Union in Chicago made a business-like agreement with the employers' association of that city whereby the union, in return for a closed shop and other standard union goals, agreed to prevent its craftsmen from working for non-members of the employers' association. This was called collusion and a business-labor racket. Today such agreements do not exclude any employers who will meet union terms; the co-operation is now on a larger scale and is acclaimed as an example of business-labor statesmanship by the President of the United States.

The sun of business unionism did not set in 1929 along with the market capitalism it expressed. Its animus continues on a larger scale. For now, like the business community, labor must think in broader social terms, relating itself to society and the state in a co-operative way.

The Aristocracy of Labor, II

Co-operation between business and labor is not entirely due to the dominance of the liberal rhetoric or to human relations among the spokesmen. With the upsurge of a new aristocracy of labor—the industrial workers in the CIO—the type of co-operation has changed.

By the middle Thirties, the world of business and labor was different in many respects from what it was in 1900. The businesses of America had come together in huge empires of money and power, and, at a slower rate, the unions had also finally moved into the areas of mass industrial monopoly. The unions grew big, not nearly so big as businesses, but five times their size at the beginning of the depression.

This new industrial aristocracy now needed a new ideology, which had to be in line with the liberal rhetoric. This was not difficult: the liberal rhetoric is highly adaptable. Like their older colleagues, the new unionists believe that class struggles and all other forms of bitterness are wholly due to a simple failure of intelligence on one side or both. They do not want to be responsible for such eccentricities so they draw up highly intelligent plans. Being younger and better educated than *trade* unionists, they can spell out the rhetoric into a more explicit ideology.

To the view that the interests of labor and business are complementary rather than contradictory, the industrial unionists add that labor and business must co-operate in the actual process of production and in the conduct of the political economy as a whole. To insure peaceful plants and profitable enterprises in a stable economy, the leaders of labor will deliver a responsible, which is to say, a well-disciplined, union of contented workers in return for a junior partnership in the productive process, security for the union, and higher wages for the workers of the industry.

In the economy as a whole, they believe that "The principal groups in our free society should get together and solve their mutually dependent problems." Not only are the workers and the bosses in each plant conceived as partners, but the working class as a whole is to be considered the partner of the business community.

The employers should not be led, says Philip Murray, by "men stupefied by class dogma," but rather by "economic statesmen. Similarly, we need labor organizations that will not merely advance the interests of particular groups of labor, but will regard the interests of the industry as a whole, including the workers, and of the economy." So runs the liberal rhetoric of the new industrial union spokesman.

As the old citywide business-labor pacts were aimed at securing an effective monopoly over the labor supply and the services or commodities market of the city, so today, union-management co-operation is aimed at securing an effective stabilization of the productive relations of the entire industry within the national economy. Craft selfishness on a local basis is replaced by industrial solidarity on a regional or national basis. The co-operative aristocracy of industry would rationalize production without socializing it. Their unionization promises, according to their ideology, to be a further agent of the private bureaucratization that is the main trend among business corporations themselves.

If the corporations can achieve a stable bureaucratic basis without labor unions they will certainly do so. But if labor unions are here to stay, or even if they are troublesomely persistent, then it may be more statesmanlike, and cheaper, to include them within the industrywide, cartel-like arrangement. Often that is what the fight is all about: will the union be included?

From the side of business managers, the drive for industrial peace is a drive for the stabilization of existing arrangements, including their running balance of profits. Above all, they do not want the basic relations between property and workmen considered in the negotiation process; if they are smart, they see unions as political sidetrackers as well as agents of plant discipline. From the side of the established union leaders, the drive for co-operative stabilization is a drive for security of union tenure. They, too, want peace rather than trouble; and if the industries' profits are not large enough to allow them peaceful inclusion, then why should not the union leaders help the industry increase its profits?

If the old unionists have at times become condottieri leading roughneck bands for local robber barons, the new unionists might in time become administrators of disciplined and contented workers for monopoly corporations.

But there are many hitches in union-management co-operation. If the CIO ideologists are not careful, the managers of corporate property will select only the reasonable concessions that are offered—that labor will not strike, that labor will help with the wars, that labor will be responsible; but they will reject labor's pretensions to a voice in production within the plants and in planning for the U.S. political economy.

As the area of co-operation expands, from citywide craft to nationwide industry, the topics covered in the agreements and demands from both sides come to include national economic matters. The unit of co-operation moves from craft to industry, and the aristocracy of industrial labor will try to stabilize its position by collaborating with nationwide trade associations. In the middle of the perils of the modern economy in its slump-war-boom cycle, and the insecurity of the anxious middle class, this collaboration will be made more orderly and just under governmental auspices. Such a development toward the corporate state will be hailed by the rhetoricians of liberalism as great national statesmanship.

CHAPTER SEVEN

THE RACKETEER BUSINESS

THE LABOR racketeers have been participants in the closest co-operation yet achieved between businessmen and labor leaders anywhere in the capitalist world. Labor rackets represent a co-operation between some businessmen and some labor leaders on a local basis; they have excluded benefits to other businessmen, to other labor leaders, and to most workers. Yet like all co-operation between business leaders and union leaders, the rackets have often involved the more astute businessmen and the more business-like labor leaders. Like other successful business ventures, they have involved a high degree of determination, which is to say, ruthlessness, toward competitors.

Labor rackets have been seized upon by right-wing spokesmen as isolated from the normal stream of American life and yet as inherent in labor unionism. These are precisely the two things that the labor rackets are not. Labor racketeering is neither isolated from the standard business and political life of American cities nor divorced from those ambiguities that now make up American liberalism. And although labor racketeering is not inherent in any type of unionism, both it and business unionism are products of the economic mechanics of American society, with its many opportunities for the enterprising individual who is earnest about its capitalist ethos.

Business Unionism and Labor Racketeering

A union accumulates power. It may do so only to increase the income of its members within the existing rules of the game and/or to improve the business position of its leaders.

Throughout their history, the unions have used such power as they have accumulated to improve the immediate conditions of work and pay for their members and to modify the rules of work within the plant and on the labor markets.

In labor racketeering, however, the power of the union has also been used to improve the business position of the labor leaders. In this respect, the leaders have merely adapted themselves to the prevailing circumstances and practices of American economic life. Labor racketeering has been one of the most American features of labor unionism.

Some of the best and most successful members of the American business community were robber barons. It is not surprising that, in the process of their adaptation, some labor leaders also become robber barons in their own small domains. Of course none of them has approached the kind of financial success enjoyed by the leading robber barons of business, but some of them have tried hard and some of them have not done badly.

Men who go to the trouble of initiating and then running a sucessful business expect to get their share of the proceeds. Such is the standard incentive for business activity. The labor racketeer runs a business. He is a successful marketer of labor, a logical product and a sharp practitioner of pure and simple business unionism in America. He is what is commonly admired as "a smart operator"; his sagacity and pluck are esteemed by many people, including some of those whom he is said to have exploited.

Co-operation implies a definite objective mutually agreed upon. Money is the most easily agreed-upon object of such co-operation as might be expected to prevail between businessmen and labor leaders and, for that matter, politicians. Business unionists and businessmen involved in racketeering have found it easiest to agree in those terms.

In the Nineties, business was rough with labor organizations. If a committee of working men approached an employer, the men were as likely to be fired as given an audience. If unions of any sort were to exist, there had to be an intermediary who could represent labor and who was not dependent upon the employers for his job. In those days he had to be as hard as the employers were likely to be, and he had to have power backing him. The solicitor who filled this job was the walking delegate or the business agent. He was a salaried man usually appointed by a local or a citywide federation.

His power might overshadow the authority of the elected officer of his union, because his was a full-time union job, while in most cases the elected official stayed at his trade. Their sharp rise to almost absolute dominion over a labor force sometimes made many of these business agents anxious to exercise their power; often they could call strikes without the formality of a vote.

The job was loaded with opportunity, and they were businessmen full of personal initiative. For those who had no socialistic ideas of merely serving the workers' interests, unions were a new kind of business. The business unionists tried to make a bigger business out of them, in the same way other men were making bigger businesses in the America of the Nineties.

If the business agents of various unions within a city formed a board of business agents, they might then have an almost unbreakable hold over the labor market of the trades they represented. As the appointed business agents accumulated power, the power of the elected officers of the unions declined; the elected officer might eventually be replaced by the business agent, or the elected officialdom of the union itself become corrupt in the new business-like way.

The crudest form of corruption was absconding with the union treasury, but more often it was rationalized and long-term. The officer of a union might rent union cards to a contractor or businessman who was employing non-union labor; in return for a bribe, he might admit ineligible members to restricted trade unions or for due consideration, he might allow a probation period to a non-union contractor, and so on.

The more important forms of labor racketeering, however, involved the businessman more directly: the union officer would co-operate with one businessman, or one organized set of businessmen, against other competing businessmen; he might call strikes against the competitors and provide strike insurance for the members of the local business cartel. Hold-up strikes were thus used as weapons to enforce a profit-sharing plan whereby the profits from higher prices were shared between the employer and the manager of the labor market.

To understand the labor racket we must understand its three parts: the local machine politician, the local business cartel, and the labor racketeer. All three were part of the same network of business-like graft.

Business, Politics, and Labor

To the extent that he was successful, the labor racketeer was a partner of the machine politician. For instance, P. H. McCarthy of San Francisco rose in one decade (1898-1909) from the presidency of the Building Trades Council to the mayoralty of the city. If a powerful boss can control an entire American city, it is not surprising that labor union locals also are bossed. Frank Hague of Jersey City and Daniel Tobin of the Teamsters Union are brothers under the skin.

As the machine politician operates within the city, so the labor racketeer operates within the union. Both reward their friends and rebuke their enemies, and in neither case does the rank and file often protest. Both are big shots, successful men who have, practically single-handed and by major force of will, made their own way. Furthermore, both are usually good fellows: they don't seem to forget their local or home town; now they have made good, they spend their new money freely.

Co-operation is mutually beneficial: the political boss provides legal protection; the union boss provides necessary money from the treasury and jobs for the political machine members. Money, protection, and jobs are the life blood of any political machine. When the businessman is added, as a willing member of the triangle, he provides more money for the union boss and for the political boss. In return, from the politician he gets protection from city laws and the favor of city contracts; from the union boss he gets workers at cheaper prices than he could otherwise obtain them, often more cheaply than his competitors outside the three-cornered cartel. Sometimes he engineers a strike against these competitors, while his own men continue to work for his continued profit. This local business-labor-political cartel is the backbone of sound labor racketeering.

Businessmen caught in one of two kinds of business squeeze are most likely to be involved. First, there are the businessmen operating in small-scale competitive industries who are unable in other ways to establish anything approaching the aim of all successful business—monopoly. The racketeer of labor and of politics may be able to help such a racketeer of business organize the industry and thus eliminate cutthroat competition. Second, there are the businessmen for whom it is cheaper to pay off a labor racketeer than it is to pay off the union members in the higher wages which honest and alert union officials might obtain. Some businessmen of this type are shoestring operators or marginal producers who, if they had to meet union-shop conditions, could not continue in business.

Given these facts, and the advantages derived from local monopolies, it is not surprising that in the building trades "behind every crooked business agent there is a crooked contractor," nor that, especially around the time of the first World War, such contractors often financed the campaigns of trustworthy union officers in order to retain their services.

Ethics are clearly outside the domain of business-like decision; the businessman has only had to transfer his own ideology into the labor leader's sphere of action in order to excuse him. A trade association lawyer told Harold Seidman, an expert on labor racketeering, "These fellows are really all right when you get to know them. After all, they are just out for themselves, like you and I. You couldn't expect them to act differently."

The Gangster

For a full understanding of the racketeer business, we must add to the city politician, the labor racketeer, and the business baron one more actor: the American gangster. The gangster is a man who uses violence for personal business ends without permission from the formal authorities. In the business-labor sphere, he began as a simple thug hired by legitimate business enterprises. In certain cities, he has ended as the power behind the government, large areas of business enterprise, and many labor unions.

As early as the Sixties, American businessmen employed little armies of thug-like men to fight unrest among the workers. Until the big strikes of 1909, the unions got their fighting men from their own ranks. But after that period until the Thirties, professional thugs, appointed by each side, fought many a business-labor battle.

In accordance with the general division of labor, violence thus became a specialty. The craftsman-as-worker ceased to use his fists; the craftsman-as-thug was hired to operate within this jurisdiction. In fact, the professional thug was one of the first professionals hired by the unions.

In the earlier phases, after the battle for which they were hired was finished, the thugs could be fired; they would go elsewhere to practice their trade. But there came a time when the professionals were harder to dismiss. Gangsters did not like the insecurity of such temporary work. They moved into the domains of their employers and established themselves on a more business-like and continuous basis. Competing groups of gangsters amalgamated, controlling the entire labor market for thugs. It is known that in some instances they became storm troops within a union, guarding the thrones of certain local labor officials.

Before World War I, the gangsters worked for the businessmen and the labor leaders. By the time the war was over, several unions were working for the gangsters; and a little later, the gangster had usurped the creative role of the businessman within citywide industries.

With prohibition, the gangster became a national figure controlling several American cities and the labor unions in them. When Al Capone ruled Chicago, businessmen, labor leaders, and politicians went to him "to have things straightened out."

For instance, he ran the cleaning and dyeing industry of the city by means of a trade association; discipline was provided by unionized truck drivers who smashed competitors. The officials of the AFL admitted that 28 of their Chicago affiliates were in the hands of Al Capone and company.

Small-scale businessmen in highly competitive fields such as the service trades seemed to welcome a solution to the problems of price-cutting and cutthroat competition, even in the form of gangster control. The gangster solved the classic problems of competition. Some businessmen actually invited gangsters to organize their industries in order to raise prices and stabilize profit-making. The difference between the pre-gangster and the gangster era is that the gangster put teeth in the business-labor cartels.

There is no way of knowing how widespread labor racketeering has been for given years or for certain eras of business-labor relations. An appropriate figure for estimating its scope would be the percentage, for definite periods of time, of all union members involved in local unions where racketeering of various types flourished. Such figures are not available and probably never will be. We are at the stage of understanding where we can say such things as, "Between 1912 and 1921 in Chicago hardly one building was erected which did not pay its toll to the labor racketeer," but no statement is possible for the country as a whole. However, labor racketeering has been confined to certain cities and more or less to certain industries.

A labor racket has never worked on a nationwide scale for any period of time, with one exception: the capital-labor cartel in electrical work which H. H. Broach devised between electrical contractors and union leaders in many cities. The idea was to boost and stabilize the bids made on city and private building work. But essentially the kind of lucrative tie-ups with the political and the business spheres needed for successful labor racketeering are available only through local monopolies.

Labor racketeering has flourished in small-scale industries

where intense competition has prevailed, business not yet having grown large enough for an effective cartel arrangement which would insure some degree of monopoly and intelligent control over the competition. Furthermore, racketeering has been most prevalent in industries handling perishable goods and in those with a local market. In the main, these have been the building trades, cleaning and dyeing, restaurants, the garment trades, furriers, trucking, theaters, produce and live poultry markets. Most is known about the building trades.

Construction work, because of the archaic way it is carried on, has always involved speculation. Usually the contractor has to tie up money which is returned to him only after the building is completed. The interest on this money is often large; time becomes money. The business agent has been able to take advantage of these conditions. Bribes might speed up the job; otherwise the job might be struck. Theater owners provide another example: their commodity is, in its way, just as perishable as fresh vegetables. Both must be sold on the spot, and rapidly. In addition, movie houses are vulnerable to sabotage of the crudest sort, like stink-bombs; and the theater operator, unlike the factory manager, must admit anyone who buys a ticket.

The Role of the AFL

Labor racketeering is not known to have occurred in big unions of the mass industrial type. Partly this is historical; when racketeering really flourished, around the time of the first World War, the AFL was the only large labor organization existing. But part of the reason goes deeper and tells us something about the AFL type of labor leader and union. The rackets flourished in the locals of these unions; internationals have seldom if ever been directly involved. Why, then, have not the heads of the internationals, or the AFL Executive Council, suspended these racketeering local unions or taken steps to clean them up?

Locals infested by racketeering have often been part of the political machine of the international officer and part of the machine network that sustained the key powers in the AFL

Council. "We can't do anything about it," Matthew Woll once explained to a City Commissioner investigating a poultry racket. "You see, we got to look to the votes of the boys down the line to hold our own jobs."

By 1930, not less than half of the voting strength of the top of the AFL hierarchy was concentrated in building and in transportation unions, and these were the unions where the rackets had been and were most evident. Certainly Gompers and Green never practiced a labor racket of the sort under discussion. They adhered to the jurisdictional sovereignty of each international: their strength rested upon their upholding that rule. In 1932 Green felt so strongly about the absolute sovereignty of the international that he protested violently when the courts unseated a corrupt official; to the man involved he wrote: "The laws of your international should be respected," and should not be "set aside by the courts."

So the higher leaders of the AFL, although not engaged in the rackets themselves, have nevertheless tacitly accepted them by virtue of a do-nothing policy, because the machines upon which their jobs and powers rest have included racket-infested locals.

However, there is nothing in the ideology and outlook of these AFL leaders which would cause them to become indignant about the pure and simple, business-like tactics of the racketeers. When the international is an absolute domain with vested rights given its leader, the racketeer is merely taking that view and expanding it for his own benefit.

With its guiding philosophy and its expedient pragmatic course of action, the AFL has often been caught between socialist ideas on the one hand and labor-business racketeering on the other. In several known cases the racketeering has been given preferential support. In 1918, when the central body of New York City was taken over by unionists with ideas about a labor party, trade with Russia, and making housing a public utility, Samuel Gompers joined the notorious racketeer, Robert Brindell, in the attempt to oust the radicals and regain control of New York.

The simple business unionist usually believes in a natural harmony of interests between business and labor; the racketeering business unionist goes a step further, believing in a natural harmony between business and labor and himself. In its developed forms, labor racketeering carries to its logical conclusion the idea of business monopoly in the area of capitalist adventurism and individualism.

The business unionist believes in carrying into his sphere of operations the set of ideas that make up the basic, unexpressed ideology of the political machine. He will reward his friends and rebuke his enemies. The racketeering business unionist makes the arrangement less formal and more immediately effective: he will reward his personal friends in a personal pecuniary way, and he will punish his individual enemies in an individual way, by withholding from them the monetary fruits of business-labor co-operation.

Adventure capitalism produces robber barons; and in a somewhat delayed fashion, on a much smaller scale, labor unionism produces its labor racketeers. There is a Commodore Vanderbilt and there is a Robert Brindell. Industrial capitalism, at one point in its evolution, produces the sober, bourgeois entrepreneur, afraid of the encroachments of government upon his liberty and of the idea of joining other businesses. Correspondingly, labor unionism produces its sober bourgeois labor leader, believing in voluntarism, afraid of government encroachments, not interested in labor solidarity, but working for independent and sovereign craft unions. There is the early Henry Ford and there is Samuel Gompers. Many American unions are still in the Gompers and Ford stage, and there are still spotty areas in the local union world which call to mind Brindell and Vanderbilt.

Now there is a new type of correspondence between business and labor, and new types of leaders on each side. The mass industries have produced in the world of giant corporations the engineering, managerial type of leader; the unionization of these mass industries by the new business unionism is slowly beginning to produce an engineering, managerial type of labor leader.

The liberal-labor view of this development in labor is generally favorable. It is, fundamentally, one more adaptation of union leadership to the various phases through which business enterprise has gone. David Dubinsky and Walter Reuther are perhaps the best-known examples of the type, although Philip Murray and, in a curious but clear way, John L. Lewis fit into the pattern.

We should not be misled because this newer type of union leader has been more militant in organizing tactics than older types of union leaders. Conditions have changed in 20 years, and his organization is of a different type. Yet in so far as he can be, he is a business unionist. He is not so different as he sometimes looks.

Before the first World War, business unionism, the liberal idea of business-labor co-operation, and the notion of trade unions as primarily economic and not political devices were sometimes sidetracked locally into labor-business racketeering. We have seen how these elements have been connected.

Today, under the changes in the total social structure, the liberal idea of business-labor co-operation and the notion of trade unions as primarily economic devices within a governmental framework *could* be sidetracked into a corporate type of political economy, or into an arrangement that would pave the way for one.

The gangster of the Twenties and early Thirties was able to take over certain industries because he was a stabilizing force in a highly competitive situation. The NRA cut the ground from under the gangster by organizing business and, in an odd way, labor. The teeth were now provided by government.

In the sphere of ideology, the liberal ideas which now prevail so widely are capable of leading those who take them seriously into a perilous adventure. Liberalism today often looks like a mantrap whose victims might well be collected in the hunting trips of the sophisticated conservatives.

Whether or not the unwary will be so misled, and whether or not the structure of business-labor relations within the governmental framework will shift in the direction of a corporate state, depends a good deal upon the images of business which American labor leaders hold and upon what their outlook and character will allow them to try to do.

CHAPTER EIGHT

LABOR'S IMAGE OF BUSINESS

THE POLICIES and strategies of the labor leader are heavily influenced by his appraisal of his own strength and that of his opponents. All co-operation involves such initial appraisals before relations can be established. Therefore we asked the labor leaders: "Do you think that such business organizations as the National Association of Manufacturers and Chamber of Commerce have more influence or less influence over national affairs than trade union organizations such as the AFL and the CIO?"

The Power

A substantial majority of the leaders of American labor believe that business organizations carry more weight in national affairs than do labor organizations.

Three-fifths of the AFL and four-fifths of the CIO leaders impute greater influence to business organizations. Only 5 to 11 per cent believe that labor has more power, and less than one-fourth believe that the power of business and labor is balanced. The positions of the leaders do not make any marked difference in their estimations of the relative influence of business and labor.

Which Is Stronger?	AFL	CIO
Business	61%	79%
Equal	23	14
Labor	11	5
Total cases	221	175

These findings suggest two questions: Why do the leaders in both union blocs feel overwhelmingly that business organizations are so influential? And why are the AFL leaders less positive about it than those of the CIO?

Historically, labor organizations and their leaders have been in a minority position. Their strategy has been shaped in an environment of continuous hostility. Their official tribulations have been many, and unofficial animosity toward them has been widespread. "Labor," says one leader, "has to overcome certain traditions. . . . Labor in America has not acquired emotional equality. . . . The public is more incensed about abuses by labor than it is about abuses by business." The labor leaders' understanding of their hostile environment explains a great deal about their thinking, and it is reflected in their answers to our general questions.

There is an ebb and flow of attack between business and labor organizations. During the decade preceding the late war, the labor unions were generally on the offensive; during the war, they continued to get more than they gave; after the war's end, a period of attempted consolidation of gains began. (It was at this point that our poll was taken.) Since the war's end, they have been afraid of an attack from business, which did come through in the legislation of 1947. Historically, their major fight has been for the very life of their organizations; this is again true in their current time of trouble.

The union officer is an elected official, dependent upon the loyalty of fellow leaders and upon the rank and file of his organization. The great organizing upsurge of the Thirties showed that officers who were too unresponsive to the desires and needs of the mass of industrial workers could lose power. The corporation manager on the other hand is not an elected official in the same sense. His power does not depend upon the loyalty of the men who work for him and he does not usually lose his job if a union successfully invades his plants. The upsurges of the Thirties did not oust the managers from their positions of power. Their responsibilities are not to the workers whom they employ but to themselves and to their scattered stockholders.

This difference in power basis means that the power of the business leader is likely to be more continuous and more assured than that of the labor leader. The labor leader is more likely to be insecure in his job if he fails to "deliver the goods."

There are several general reasons why more CIO than AFL leaders are convinced of the greater national influence of business.

The CIO leaders are better educated, as we have seen, and education affects the answers to this question:

	AFL		CIO	
Which is stronger?	High School Graduate and More	Some High School or Less	High School Graduate and More	Some High School or Less
Business	74%	59%	79%	83%
Equal	17	29	14	14
Labor	9	12	7	3
Total cases	88	129	94	76

The more highly educated leaders in the AFL feel very much like their equals in the CIO. But a rather curious pattern of belief occurs within the two organizations. Educational level does not make much difference in the CIO answers, but more of the less-educated leaders in the AFL believe that labor has as much or more power than business. These leaders are the old-timers of the labor hierarchy who, in general, run older unions well entrenched in their crafts and trades and are more concerned with local balances of power than with national influence. They are more secure within their unions, and they feel their unions are more secure within the economic framework of the nation.

In the recent memory of its leaders, the CIO has fought business harder than has the AFL and also has been under attack more. Businessmen have often fought off the militant CIO in any way open to them: during the latter Thirties certain AFL unions were able to secure contracts with business firms before organizing a single worker.

The CIO has entered the most powerful industries and those having the most aggressive anti-union policies: the mass industries of steel, rubber, automobiles, which for decades the AFL failed or did not try to organize. The leaders of the CIO had more opportunity to measure the enemy in his strongholds.

The CIO has been more politically active on the national scene and its unions have been thrown in contact with the politically alert sectors of big national business. The industries with which they deal not only have plants across the nation, but the distribution of their products is both national and international. These unions have had business with the national trade associations, which translate economic power into political influence.

Why do labor leaders feel as they do about the relative influences of business and labor? Their spontaneous answers fall almost uniformly into a simple straightforward formula: Regardless of whether they think business or labor is the stronger, they believe that labor is strong because of the people it involves and that business is strong because of the money it possesses. These are the pillars of power as the labor leader sees them.

Why Labor Is Strong

Virtually the only source of superiority claimed for labor organizations is the democratic power of having more votes. Those labor leaders who believe that labor is stronger than business, or just as strong, often answer conditionally; there is a wish in their estimates: "Labor carries more weight because it has the votes. *When properly organized,* this voting strength has great influence on the national and state governments."

All the leaders, regardless of their estimations, see their role in the struggle of power as one connecting that potential force to the point of national decision. "There are more votes behind organized labor. *When* elected officials know, they are careful about votes against labor." And another man says: "Labor can, if they desire, elect practically anyone in certain districts of our nation."

Some leaders say that labor is strong among different sectors of the population: "The unions generally have influence in industrial areas," says a labor leader who believes they are on a par, "where employers exercise control in the rural districts." And again: "The NAM influences manufacturers and the labor organizations influence the working people and families."

✦

Both AFL and CIO leaders see the question in terms of the political strength of numbers, but there is a revealing difference in the way the two groups reason. More of the AFL see labor's strength in terms of pressure: they talk in terms of "power over politicians" and apparently they see the power of organized labor primarily as that of a lobbying machine. Some CIO leaders talk in the same terms, but more of them talk directly in terms of "more votes," "more people," "the masses." Their view of labor's democratic strength is that of a political party.

One CIO leader gave a thoughtful, full explanation for his answer, which contains most of the elements brought out in the answers as a whole: "I have answered 'about the same,'" he says, "for this reason: Labor organizations numerically are much stronger than trade organizations and possibly could swing any election, providing the membership of the unions go en masse to the polls and vote for candidates recommended by the leadership of their unions. However, this is not the case and, therefore, labor strength is weakened. Trade organizations financially are stronger than labor organizations and are able to control the finances of both political parties thus offsetting the numerical strength of labor organizations."

Why Business Is Stronger

The labor leaders who believe that business outweighs labor in national affairs give many more detailed reasons for their belief. Feeling themselves surrounded by hostile forces, these leaders are apparently more alert to the sources of their opponents' strength than to their own.

Power is relative: the weakness of labor is the strength of business, and vice versa. Yet in explaining why business is more effective, hardly one labor leader examines the weaknesses of labor. The labor leaders' view is the hard-boiled view of men who have mixed in politics as a going concern in America. Most of them think business is more influential in national affairs for one basic reason: money talks, and business has the money.

Yet money must be transformed before it becomes influence.

The medium most frequently mentioned by the labor leaders is the direct money channel between business and politics. About one-third say that business has a more direct financial hold over the political order than does labor. In their reasoning they focus upon every aspect of the political process, and everywhere they see the money link between business and power.

Some point to the politician and say flatly that he can be and often is bought by business money. "Money controls political representatives." "Campaign funds for the elections of the representatives come from these organizations." "The large trusts have more money and there are men in our Congress who would sell out their constituents for the 30 pieces of silver."

Other labor leaders see the money tie as a more formal one: it is the whole party machine that is bought by business. Money is the open sesame to control of politics: in "the entrenched political machines . . . financial assistance made by business organizations has paid large dividends in the form of legislation that works in their interests." And many of the labor leaders see the matter from the lobbying standpoint: business has more power than labor "because their finances can maintain many lobbyists in Washington." The lobbying tactics of big business and of their trade associations are "almost perfect," and "they have more money to pay lobbyists than labor."

A few labor leaders see a direct link between business and politics in personal terms of a status equality between the representatives of each: businessmen have "more often the same background and outside interests as the legislators and governmental officials . . ." and "many members of Congress come from this group. They have no sympathy with and very little understanding of the aims and objectives of the organized labor movement."

The content and control of the mass media as an influence in the power struggle, mentioned by only a few labor leaders who feel that labor is stronger, was pointed to by one-fourth of those who think business is stronger. This link with mass media, like that with politics, is seen as financial.

The labor leaders see the mass media as part of big business. "Both the press and radio are big businesses and they have exactly the same viewpoint, as do other big businesses." "They own the media which form public opinion." "Their concentration of power and wealth based on their control of the means of production also includes their control over the most effective means of expression." According to these leaders, if big businesses do not own the media outright, they control them indirectly by money: "They have the finances to promote their ideas through the press and radio." "They control the press and radio of the country through advertising." "They can and do spend greater sums of money on propaganda. They have full access to radio, which is denied to labor."

In a few of the answers given to this question, the old animosities between CIO and AFL leaders crop up. Labor would be stronger, say a few of the CIO leaders, if the AFL were not so full of racketeers and if we could get together with them. Labor would be stronger and we could get together, say a few of the AFL leaders, if only there weren't so many Communists in the CIO.

Yet the important fact seems to be this: labor leaders, even as other men, are not inclined—at least in public—to pay attention to their own weaknesses; they look more closely at the enemies' sources of strength. They are, in general, men on the defensive. They seem to understand well the standard American ways of power. The minority, who somewhat hopefully acclaim the power of labor, see the potentiality in terms of the democracy of numbers.

The American labor leaders seem less like leaders of a mass struggle, which indeed most of them are not, than like poor men dealing with rich enemies in a conflict where money is the key to victory.

Not only the labor leader's view of the businessman's power, but also what the labor leader thinks business is going to do with this power is important. Power is not a threat unless there is intent to use it.

The Intent

The labor leader's estimates of business policy are both more objective and more personal than those of a disinterested observer: he knows many objective facts not available to the public, and he is personally involved in the meaning of these facts. His attitudes are important in so far as they reveal something of his psychological structure, for while the objective situation changes, the psychology of a power elite does not change so rapidly.

The policy makers of larger businesses, according to the question we put to the labor leaders, can take one of three stances toward the labor unions and their leaders: (1) They can accept the principle of collective bargaining and deal with the unions in good faith; (2) they can tolerate the unions and deal with them as far as they have to but no further; (3) they can try to break the power of the unions in business-labor relations.

The second and third alternatives are not mutually exclusive: a business executive can tolerate a union now because he feels he has to, but can plan for any future opportunity to break the union. In such cases, the difference between the second and the third posture is a difference in timing.

The sharp opinions expressed by labor leaders on the intent of business reveal a great and watchful tension. Almost 90 per cent of them can be said to be distrustful of the intent of business. Only 14 per cent of the AFL and only 6 per cent of the CIO leaders believe that big business has accepted the principle of collective bargaining and is dealing with the unions in good faith.

Business intent:	AFL	CIO
Accepts unions	14%	6%
Tolerates them	57	53
Out to break	29	41
Total cases	225	177

In each bloc a majority feels that the unions are merely being tolerated. The dominant view of the labor leaders of America at the end of the war went like this: "The men who run big business may put up with what they call 'all this union business' now, just as they did during the war, but that is only because the law makes them; they have by no means really accepted the new status of our unions and the principle of collective bargaining; they don't deal in good faith with us, and they don't intend to."

A sizable group of leaders go further. They believe that business intends to fight to the finish, that the policy makers of the larger businesses are working to break the unions altogether. At least 41 per cent of the CIO and 29 per cent of the AFL leaders feel this way.

More CIO than AFL leaders think business wants to break unions, just as more CIO leaders believe that business is more influential than labor in national affairs. The reasons for the different power-images held by the AFL and CIO also hold for this difference in their evaluations of intent. On the question of intent, however, there are variations of belief among the leaders according to their positions in the union world, the time they joined the labor movement, their educational levels, and their political party affiliations.

The national leaders of the CIO and the AFL agree on the toughness of business's intention toward labor. In both union blocs about one-quarter of the national leaders think business is out to break labor and about 66 per cent believe that the unions are merely being tolerated for the time being. Within each bloc, the city officials are more distrustful of the intent of business policy. But the CIO men of the state and city levels of leadership are more distrustful of business than AFL men.

Business	AFL			CIO		
intent:	Nat'l	State	City	Nat'l	State	City
Accept	13%	17%	14%	8%	9%	4%
Tolerate	66	66	49	65	52	48
Break	21	17	37	27	39	48
Total cases	61	41	123	37	44	96

In their everyday work, state leaders deal with politicians and with the political representatives of business. The anti-union drive, which the 1946 Congress inaugurated on a national level, had been going on in many states for a long time. Thus, before the national leaders, these state leaders had daily worries about the intentions of business.

The city leaders are in closest contact with the rank and file, who in turn are close to the sharp edge of any unpleasantness between business and labor. The city leaders of labor are also in immediate and continual contact with the workday representatives of business.

By comparison, the national leaders' contacts with business representatives are more intermittent. Their role is frequently that of the troubleshooter. Moreover, in their eminent positions, many of them are beholden to the myth, if such it is, of the practicality of business-labor co-operation.

There is evidence that the state representatives of the CIO, fewer of whom are tied in with Republican machines, tend to be more aggressive in pushing labor's interests and therefore are more likely to encounter resistance from business. The CIO city men are part of relatively new unions, in newly organized industries with long histories of stern anti-unionism. Again, they are more likely than the AFL city men to feel the tensing muscles of business.

Within the AFL, however, there is one particular group that is more skeptical of the intentions of business than any other—the men who joined the labor movement after 1935.

	AFL		CIO	
Business intent:	Before 1935	1935 and After	Before 1935	1935 and After
Accept	15%	14%	4%	8%
Tolerate	64	41	62	48
Break	21	45	34	44
Total cases	137	76	52	114

In the AFL, about 45 per cent of the recent joiners as against 21 per cent of the old-timers, and in the CIO, 44 per cent of the recent joiners as against 34 per cent of the old-timers have the most pessimistic view of business's intentions. It must be remembered that the CIO leaders who joined before 1935 were at one time members of AFL or of independent unions.

As in the estimations of power, so in the judgments of intent, the difference between the AFL and the CIO leadership is partly an educational difference. Among the better-educated leaders of both blocs, there is little or no difference; but between the lower educated in each bloc there is a sharp divergence:

	High School Graduate or More		*Some High School or Less*	
Business intent:	AFL	CIO	AFL	CIO
Accept	10%	5%	17%	8%
Tolerate	57	57	57	47
Break	33	38	26	45
Total cases	88	96	132	75

Twenty-six per cent of the AFL leaders of lower educational level, as compared with 45 per cent of the CIO, think business wants to break labor.

The determining factor in the labor leader's estimation of business intent is union affiliation rather than such factors as political party membership. There is of course a tendency in the AFL, and to a lesser extent in the CIO, for Republicans to be slightly more trustful of the good faith of business than Democrats or bi-partisans. These Republicans are also more inclined to believe that labor is as strong or stronger than business. In short, the Republicans are slightly more at ease about the power and the policy of business.

Among the CIO Democrats, there are as many who think business is trying to break the unions as there are those who believe that business is merely tolerating them, and there are many who think that business is trying to destroy the unions altogether. The Democratic Party chieftains have that to worry about when they arrange the constellations of their support.

The Power and the Intent

Judgments of the intention of big business in the United States are closely related to estimations of the relative power of business and of labor. Those labor leaders who think business is more powerful than labor are more inclined to believe that business is out to break labor, and those who believe that labor is just as strong or stronger than business tend more frequently to believe that business accepts or tolerates labor unionism:

	Relative Strength			
Business	AFL		CIO	
intent:	Business	Labor	Business	Labor
Break	35%	21%	43%	32%
Tolerate	56	57	53	53
Accept	9	22	4	15
Total cases	140	77	140	34

But not all labor leaders fall into the extreme patterns of the most afraid (business is stronger and wants to break us) or the least afraid (we are just as strong, and business accepts, or at least, tolerates us). There are also the most trustful (business is stronger, but does not want to break us) and there are those who expect a showdown fight (we are just as strong or stronger, and business is out to break us).

The labor leaders can be ranked in terms of how much they fear the power and the intent of business. The man most afraid is the one who believes the enemy is stronger than he and is intent on breaking him. The man least afraid is the one who feels his organization is as strong or stronger and the enemy does not, at least immediately, intend to break him.

Image of business:	AFL	CIO
Most afraid	23%	35%
Intermediate	49	52
Least afraid	28	13
Total cases	217	174

Approximately half of each bloc falls into the intermediate position: trustfulness is greater than the direct feeling of their own power. About a third of the CIO and about a fourth of the AFL leaders are in the most anxious group. Some 28 per cent of the AFL, and 13 per cent of the CIO leaders, however, are not at all anxious about current business-labor cooperation: they feel labor is as strong as business or stronger, and they take a happy view of the intention of business.

On all levels of leadership within the two organizations, the CIO leaders take a more suspicious view of business-labor relations, but the reasons of various levels differ. Both CIO and AFL national commands are anxious about business-labor relations because they estimate the power of business in national affairs to be greater than that of labor, whereas in the lower echelons of the CIO, the state and city leaders are more anxious than their AFL counterparts because they believe that business is out to break labor.

There is thus little difference between the AFL and the CIO national leaders' image of business. One out of five national leaders believes that business is more powerful and means to use its superior power to break unions. But among local leaders, and among those with less education, differences between the CIO and the AFL occur: of those with less education, four out of ten in the CIO but two out of ten in the AFL are the most fearful; of the leaders on the lower levels, four out of ten in the CIO compare with three out of ten in the AFL.

The biggest knot of pessimism is in the less-educated, lower ranks of CIO leaders. They are more recently up from labor's ranks and are in closer daily contact with the workers in the big industries. Events have already indicated that the watchful anxiety of such leaders is not without foundation.

The "Fascist" Threat

Probing further into the fears and anxieties of the labor leaders, we asked: "Do you think that there is a threat to American Democracy by a 'fascist' totalitarian movement in this country within the next five years?" The choices given were: (1) There is a definite and serious threat; (2) there is some threat and it is likely to become more serious; (3) there is some threat but it is not likely to become serious; (4) there is no threat at all. Among the labor leaders who answered, there is a divergence in the meaning of "fascist": the question is only *a crude sponge* with which to sop up reactions to a current symbol of economic and political doom, yet it is valuable when analyzed in conjunction with other questions. Here is the over-all pattern of response to this direct question:

	AFL	CIO
Fascism: a serious threat	20%	30%
Some threat: likely to become serious	35	39
Some threat: not likely to be serious	35	25
No threat at all	10	6
Total cases	225	172

Not more than one out of ten labor leaders in either bloc is willing to say there is no threat at all. Fifty-five per cent of the AFL, and 69 per cent of the CIO, feel that the threat of fascism in America is serious or is likely to become so in the near future. But there is a more pronounced difference between the two organizations on the various levels of leadership, the difference being greater within the AFL. Here are the proportions of leaders on each level who believe that the menace is or will become more serious:

	AFL	CIO
National	40%	78%
State	60%	66%
City	59%	67%

The state and the city leaders of the two blocs are not very different in their reactions. It is the AFL high command that is least alarmed (four out of ten), the CIO top command that is most alarmed (eight out of ten).

What makes this alarm important is the context in which it is expressed. The general fear of fascism among the labor leaders is associated with the specific fear of the power and intentions of big business. Divided according to the degree they fear the power and intent of big business, here are the proportions of the labor leaders who believe that the threat of fascism is serious: In the CIO, fascism is seen as a serious threat by 80 per cent of those who are most afraid of big business as against only 50 per cent of those who are least afraid. In the AFL, the fear of fascism drops from 67 to 44 per cent as the leaders become less afraid or more trustful of big business.

Image of business:	AFL	CIO
Most afraid	67%	80%
Intermediate	56%	67%
Least afraid	44%	50%

Why Labor Leaders View Businessmen as They Do

The judgments which the labor leader makes of the power and the intention of business rest upon: (1) his expedient view of current negotiations; (2) such ideological convictions as he may have; (3) his personal feelings about businessmen in general and those with whom he has particular contact.

The view of the labor leader is decided primarily in terms of what business has just done or what he thinks it is about to do. He makes up his mind as he watches businessmen around the negotiation table or across a picket line or in a grievance session. The angle, however, from which he views the current activities of the business community is that of a man who heads an organization of workers and is watchful of their interests.

The atmosphere of conversational circles in which labor leaders move (as well as in those where businessmen feel at home) are rich with invective. In their private circles, there are conventions which exact from labor leaders an occasional name-calling blast against businessmen. This atmosphere, plus expedient watchfulness along the lines of business unionism, is almost the complete content of many labor leaders' ideology of business-labor relations, and given the ideology held by many businessmen, the labor leader is often well-enough-equipped to do his job.

Labor leader invective is often directed less against business as a system of power than against the personal and moral attributes of businessmen. To overlook this personal element in his lack of esteem is to overlook an important feature of the labor leader as a type of man and, consequently, an important human element in business-labor relations.

The American labor leader often feels socially inferior to the businessman with whom he negotiates. This feeling arises from his low social origin, his more rapid ascent, and his knowledge that the businessman is more likely to be esteemed by the public and the community.

In the arena of power, the labor leaders are newly risen men; no matter how much bluster some of them may employ, they feel the social gap. They reveal their feelings in their general tendency to imitate the standard middle-class, business-like mode of living, and by the resentment they show when they talk about business's lack of respect for labor. This craving for status and respect is often a strong undercurrent of their lives.

Thirty years ago many labor leaders were willing to sacrifice such social esteem as they might have felt due them in return for the power and income they enjoyed. Today, many of the newer leaders want social esteem because they already have an income that is generally respectable and a power which is not to be scorned. In their long struggle to win a more secure position for unions and more respect for the workers, the labor leaders in America have also been waging a fight for more security and respect for themselves.

Now, when the union as a huge bureaucracy is attempting to integrate its interests with those of the corporate bureaucracy in business-labor co-operation, the labor leader gets all the more annoyed by frequent disrespect from businessmen. He too is an executive. His income does not approach that of the business executive, but he has climbed up the American ladder and he is morally respectable and, moreover, a man of power. He feels that he is entitled to respect, in the name of his union and in the name of his own hard-won, conscientious career.

The labor leaders, who as a group come from the laboring class, most of whom have worked for wages in the normal course of their careers, are susceptible to personal irritations of this sort which are no doubt reflected in the images they are prone to have of businessmen. The epithet used by businessmen against labor leaders is irresponsibility; that used by labor leaders against businessmen is arrogance.

Personal aspirations and frustrations are entangled with going institutional policies: the businessman who makes plans for employee relations that exclude the union is also excluding the labor leader. The labor leader who tries to integrate his union with the corporate bureaucracy is also including himself in the bureaucracy: the integration of the two bureaucracies requires some integration of the two types of bureaucrats. The feeling of a status of inequality is an index of the separation of the interests of the two worlds.

In the long run, of course, prestige will be gained if power and income are securely held. In a few unions there is a shuttle from union to corporation, and vice versa to a lesser extent. This is not seen as a sell-out by the official biographer nor by the president of at least one large and progressive union. At present there is only a slight tendency in this direction. Where it occurs, it is viewed as evidence that the union is the biggest thing in the industry and that men can gain prestige from working in it. This development does raise a personnel problem for unions: they have continually to recruit more bright young men. Yet, with increased business-labor co-operation, why should there not be an exchange of personnel, even as there is between government and business? Personal careers are involved in the struggle between the giant bureaucracies of business, labor, and government. Career maneuvers within and between them are now justified by bright cloaks of new kinds of liberal, business-like honor.

PART FOUR

CHAPTER NINE

PROGRAMS AND EXPEDIENCES

MOST OF the labor leaders accept at all times the American political system, which sometimes tolerates the labor leaders. In their interplay of acceptance and rejection, both the system and the leaders are altered, but, in the course of their individual careers and in the "natural" history of their unions, the leaders are changed most. It has been said of British labor, and it may truly be said of American labor too, that "each reform achieved gives the reformer one more stake in the existing system."

Excited revolutionary socialists have fought for and expected to realize broad goals in short periods of time; others have had broad goals and the will to pursue them for generations; reformers of various sorts have worked for long periods in energetic pursuit of narrow goals. The American labor leader in politics as elsewhere works for narrow goals in short order.

The environment in which the labor leader acts is full of strange new perils and well-known headaches, and he moves across it with some guile and much expediency but little vision. He is in government up to his neck; within the political parties he is down on his knees. He has been and he is now a political opportunist.

The Short End of the Long Run

It is said that the opportunist lacks principle: his activity is along short lines to narrow goals. He is a creature of drift and circumstance rather than a master of independent action; the result of his expediences is more a product of the main drift than of his own will and vision. The opportunist is thus a sometimes troublesome but not usually serious obstacle to the masters of the main drift.

There is nothing inherently evil about opportunism. For those who want to reach small goals in a little while, opportunism is just the thing. It would be foolish to take the time to build enduring means to immediate ends. The labor leader does not want to wait; he wants the pay-off of his policy to be visible to men of limited memory and high expectation. Four years can be a long time in the life of the trade union leader: think of 1934-38; or 1920-24.

The corporate executive is also a practical man and an opportunist, but enduring means, developed for other purposes, are available to him for the conduct of his political as well as his labor affairs. The corporation itself is now a very stable thing; in fact it is more stable and more important for the continuance of the American arrangement than the lifetime family. The corporation gives the executive a stable base for durable expectations, and the executive can also rely upon it in the pursuit of his short-term, opportunistic goals.

Unlike the corporation, the union is usually in a state of protest; it is on the defensive in a sometimes actually and always potentially hostile society. And there are no enduring means which are ready-made and at the labor leader's disposal. If he wants such means, even for his little goals, he must build them himself.

History is not merely the realization of the will of social actors. It moves by itself, even while it is being pushed by willful actors. Things go on behind men's backs. In the field of industrial relations, strong forces are moving toward what can already be seen as the portent of a corporate-like system. Caught in the drive for stability, labor leaders, even in their short-run demands, need a full vision of the business-labor relationship and its consequences.

If demands are consciously worked out, and their consequences responsibly taken into account, they become goals. If, for instance, in the 1946 GM strike the consequences of the demand to set up a public relation between wages, prices, and profits had been traced out, the demand would have had to be made not on one corporation but on the political economy as a whole. If that had been done, and goals worked out for each union, the GM program would have been very different from what it came to be when used simply as a short-time tactic against one corporation.

The entire relationship between the political and economic orders must be thought through by union strategists, for unions do not now live in an economic order on the one side and a political order on the other. Many leaders have been and are now acting as if they were in an economic world only, but more alert leaders know that they live and must act in a political economy. Both the means which they use and the ends they pursue are as much, if not more, political than economic. The short-run pursuit of economic goals by economic means is coming to have long-run political consequences which may be ignored only at the risk of destruction. In the meantime, what long-term program do the labor leaders have with which they hope to meet the intricate perils of their enlarged sphere of operations?

On Wanting and on Having a Program

When the leaders of any organization are asked whether or not that organization should or should not have a long-range program, the answer normally expected is an overwhelming "Yes." For with experience in public acting, men become spokesmen, and spokesmen must always have programs.

Having a program, or feeling that one should have a program, does not, of course, imply anything about the content of that program. In fact, an answer either way does not indicate what other beliefs the labor leader may hold, much less the concrete actions of his daily work. It is so easy to say, "Yes, we should have a program," that it is not surprising that well over 90 per cent of the AFL and CIO labor leaders say so.

But there are certain sets of labor leaders who reply, "No, labor should not have a long-range economic and political program." Two per cent of the CIO leaders but 10 per cent of the AFL leaders replied in this way. Moreover, these AFL leaders are concentrated at the top. Twenty-one per cent of the national, 12 per cent of the state, and 4 per cent of the city AFL leaders believe that labor should not have any long-range program.

This AFL group is composed of the same men we have already described as the gerontocrats of American trade unionism: they are relatively old; most of them have been in unions since before 1919. They are more likely to believe that labor's position is strong and that business now accepts and bargains in good faith with unions. Such wisdom as the AFL older men have stored up does not include the sophistication required to answer "Yes" to this general question.

We followed up our general question with one of estimation: "Over and above the basic concern with such problems as wages, hours, and union security, do you believe that most U.S. unions have or have not any long-range economic and political program?"

Three-quarters of the CIO leaders and about half the AFL leaders are of the opinion that most labor unions do have long-range political and economic programs. The difference is to be expected: not only has the CIO put out more pamphlets and literature concerning larger issues than those typically posed by simple unionism, but its participation in politics has had a broader and more noticeable character than that of the AFL. These answers do reflect actual differences between the activities of the two organizations.

Within both organizations, the closer a leader is to the rank and file the more likely he is to maintain that most unions do support a long-run program aimed at political and economic objectives. It is the national leaders, who presumably would have the most to do with any such program, who do not believe that long-run plans exist.

Within the AFL, 56 per cent of the city leaders as compared with 34 per cent of the national leaders, and within the CIO, 80 per cent of the city as compared with 62 per cent of the national, support

Most unions do have a program:	AFL	CIO
National	34%	62%
State	41%	77%
City	56%	80%
All leaders	49%	79%

this view. And in both organizations the state executives have an intermediate position.

Not only the leaders close to the rank and file in the union hierarchy but also the less-educated leaders are more prone to believe that most unions have a long-range program. In both union blocs, on each educational level, the relatively less-educated leaders believe in the existence of a program more than do the more-educated; and on every leadership level, the less-educated believe it more than the more-educated. Here are the proportions of those who so believe by position and educational level:

	AFL		CIO	
Most unions do have a program:	High School Grad. and Over	Some High School and Less	High School Grad. and Over	Some High School and Less
National	24%	41%	52%	73%
State	21%	50%	77%	82%
City	48%	62%	76%	87%

If we want to consider these answers indicative of the actual situation, it would be safest to accept what the national leaders say since they are in the best position to know. They are the least willing to assert that long-term purpose exists in most unions. The answers of leaders further down the hierarchy and closer to the rank and file probably contain less accurate information but reflect more hope, expectation, and trust. They are the men who must sell the union to the workers. In close and continual contact with the rank and file, these leaders know what it takes to organize them and keep them organized, and perhaps their answers reflect an element of that wishful thinking which pervades most salesmen. Many of these lower leaders lack experience in the ways of unions and the careful wisdom which such experience bestows.

If we combine general expectations about a program with beliefs about its existence, an over-all view of how the leaders of

American labor stand is obtained. Two dominant positions account for 95 per cent of all the leaders. They feel unions should have a program and think that they *do* (75 per cent of the CIO; 46 per cent of the AFL), or they feel unions should have programs but think they *do not* (22 per cent of the CIO; 45 per cent of the AFL). In the AFL, however, there is a small group who believe the unions should not have any program and that most of them do not. These are undoubtedly the most contented men of the union world. Most are heads of international craft unions who have been in the movement for several decades.

The Goals of Labor

Those leaders who believe labor has a program were asked what its main points are. Their answers can be classified in terms of the range of social attention they display. Some focus on the union members only; some include the wage workers as a whole, in unions or not; some see all classes within the nation as the object of the program; some envision the international community. The scope of the groups to be benefited by the union's program thus runs from union members, wage workers, nation, to world.

Here are the proportions of leaders in each union bloc who said their programs should benefit each of these groups; more than one target group was sometimes named by a respondent. Only 16 per cent of the AFL, as compared with 43 per cent of the CIO leaders, think that unions have a program and name the nation as the object of that program. Over half of those in the AFL who specify labor's program conceive of it in rather narrow terms, whereas well over half the CIO leaders think of it more broadly.

	AFL	CIO
Have program	49%	79%
Aimed for:		
Union members	15	10
Wage worker	9	12
Nation	16	43
World	2	7
No answer	9	12
Have no program	51	21
Total cases	225	172

The programs mentioned differ not only in terms of the groups of people whom they are designed to benefit but also in the types of gain or benefit intended. There are three types of goals mentioned: (1) primarily economic with no political means specified; (2) general social and welfare activities and labor legislation; and (3) goals involving increased political freedom and participation, without specification of the exact means to be employed. The CIO leader is more program-conscious than the AFL leader, and more frequently he means social welfare and political reformism as well as merely economic goals.

	AFL	CIO
Have program	49%	79%
Type of goal: *		
Economic	24	31
Social	20	39
Political	16	45
No answer	8	11
Have no program	51	21
Total cases	225	172

* Some respondents named more than one goal.

If we combine the two previous classifications of program content named by the labor leaders, we get this table:

	AFL	CIO
Broad political	17%	45%
Narrow political	18	15
Broad non-political	29	26
Narrow non-political	36	14
Total cases	89	113

At one extreme is the leader whose goals embrace the nation or the international scene in political terms. At the other extreme is the leader for whom the program benefits union members, or perhaps wage workers at large, in the social welfare or economic spheres. Between these two extremes are leaders seeking political goals for narrow groups and leaders seeking economic and social goals for the national or international community.

Regardless of whether or not the labor leader includes political aims in his descriptions, and whether his program embraces union members or the people of the whole world, specific comments show clearly that the leaders are not describing *programs* at all: they are describing either short-term *demands,* or generalized *principles.*

These comments are typical: "Full employment, a veteran's program, passage of all legislation favorable to labor, passage of the Wagner-Murray-Dingel Health bill . . . better standard of living for the working people . . . election to office of men sympathetic to labor's views . . . thirty-hour week, better dental care, economic education of trade union members . . . civilian control of atomic energy, building a just and lasting peace . . . extending social security . . . better wages, better hours, more and more of everything good . . . to remake the world by abolishing poverty."

The impression left on the reader by hundreds of such slogans can be summed up like this: The labor leaders display the type of political mentality characteristic of the practical right and the liberal center: they demand a great many things in an agitated manner; they ask not the next steps in any program they might be following but a sequence of excited or bored demands on current legislatures, or a defense against specific bills and items the other side may propose. Occasionally a few principles, so general as to be politically meaningless, may be proclaimed amid these short-run, shifting, defensive gestures. Such piecemeal agitation is now the political substance of American liberalism. Like liberals in general, the labor leaders do not connect specific demands with general images of the kind of society they want, nor do they integrate immediate demands and general principles into programs.

Bi-partisan Politics

The overwhelmingly economic goals and methods of labor have been at the historical center of the movement in the U.S. In 1902, Gompers asserted that "it is the economic life that is to be remedied" and that this "should be done through the economic life and through no other medium." All "political intervention in industrial affairs" was to him either political juggling or the bungling of politicians. With the New Deal period, however, political means began to be used to gain traditional economic ends, these political means being well within the prevailing two-party system.

There are several available types of political means even for the pursuit of economic objectives: (1) lobbying and pressuring without an independent party, which oddly enough is known as the non-partisan tactic and which has always been the major strategy of the U.S. labor unions; (2) the independent electoral party, founded by or consistently backed by labor and representing the interests of labor. These are the only two tactics U.S. labor has considered, even momentarily. There is a third possibility: (3) the independent revolutionary party.

The lobbyist, in general, wants to secure his position; the electoral party wants to reform specific features of the society; the revolutionary party would transform the structure of society. Each of these three orientations tends to see one or both of the others as subordinate means.

The revolutionist will be for reform in order to strengthen his chances, but not by way of compromise. He will work for temporary guarantees if they do not hamper his independence of action, but he does not believe that his long-run interests can be guaranteed short of the transformation of society. Occasionally the electoral party man may talk vaguely of such a transformation, but often he finds the consolidation and protection of his position necessary for the reform of the existing social structure. The lobbyist wants nothing of any transformation of social structure, but when it will guarantee his interests, he is for reform.

When the independent party and the lobbyist act for the same ends, the reform is generally also a guarantee. For instance, the reform of the public school system may improve the educational level of the worker, but presumably it also improves the union's chances of maintaining its position. A minimum wage law wins the esteem of the worker while buttressing his image of the union. Reforms and guarantees differ in that reforms generally run over a longer period of time and affect power positions only indirectly.

✦

American labor has confined itself primarily to the role of mugwump and lobbyist, pressuring within and between the two major parties and upon the administrative process to guarantee its gains and secure more economic reform: the liberal economic perspective of business-labor co-operation has thus been paralleled in the political arena.

No matter at what point the pressure is exerted, its content is always the promise of labor votes and sometimes direct or indirect donation. The non-partisan lobbying machine invariably bargains for men and programs that it thinks might be favorable toward labor. This approach to the political arena is typically American. It assumes that politicians are opportunistic creatures who, if they need labor support, will become effective political instruments of labor.

The constitution of the AFL states flatly: "Party politics, whether they be Democratic, Republican, Socialistic, Populistic," and so on, "shall have no place in the Conventions of the American Federation of Labor." In the late Eighties an AFL convention again denounced "political programs." By the turn of the century, it was finally recognized officially that members of the AFL, along with the rest of the citizens, did have the right to use the ballot as they saw fit, and that it would be a good idea to elect friends and not enemies, regardless of party. This could have two legitimate purposes: (1) to push along the legislative demands of the AFL, and (2) "to secure an impartial judiciary that will not govern us by arbitrary injunctions of the courts nor act as the plain tools of corporate wealth."

Since it first appointed a legislative representative to Washington in 1895, the AFL has lobbied. But during the first decades of the twentieth century, when business organizations, such as the NAM, were killing many of labor's demands, it had little success.

The 1906 campaign was the first in which the AFL participated on a national scale. The city and state units of the AFL have exerted most of the continuous pressure. Here, there is the same tactic: labor leaders attempt to deliver the labor vote in return for concessions and favors from the local machines. In some large cities, labor unions are part of the very belt-lines and cogwheels of these machines.

These political views are part of the business unionism that has prevailed; they stick to economics and stay out of political government. Even in the New Deal period, the AFL leaders feared that government intervention and reforms might weaken the need for labor unions and might, moreover, encroach upon the standard American liberties. The business unionist thus borrows from the ideology of the nineteenth-century entrepreneur and the present-day practical right: government should be a *fair* policeman of a fair struggle fought by economic means over economic ends. However, under nineteenth-century conditions the entrepreneur, indirectly subsidized by government, didn't need to play politics.

The business unionist says: "Reward your friends and punish your enemies: that is all the politics we need." He borrows this perspective from the boss of the American political machine.

More progressive union leaders may present such views in the guise of social work. David Dubinsky, who took his union out of the socialist tradition into the New Deal constellation, says: "Labor should be a social pressure group, pushing its views on great social questions, lobbying for progressive legislation, keeping our society in balance. Labor must be in social politics, not in party politics." Such views generalize for society the arrangements by which a union keeps a small-scale industry in balance and away from cutthroat competition. That is why one garment leader, wise to the shape of big business, has commented: "The future of the American workers does not rest with the garment unions."

Consciously or unconsciously, underlying the strategies and ideas of many labor leaders, is an image of political reality as a pluralist system of interests which balance each other in shifting compromise. It is the idea of natural harmony carried from the economic into the political sphere—like so many other liberal images, reflecting the idealized version of late eighteenth- and nineteenth-century economic society.

In full flower, such a pluralist vision would by-pass the state; each big organized interest bloc would make its own deals with the other blocs. Each is acknowledged to have its rights and its just share of authority. If the distribution of authority and rights is explicitly and tolerantly recognized by all the entrenched interests, and somehow cemented by good will, everything will be all right. An elaborate net of giant deals, made outside the jurisdiction of the state, underpins the social and political structure. And the interests involved in these deals, especially corporate business and corporate labor, are not voluntary but sovereign groups. They regulate themselves, they regulate the society as an economic and political whole; their leaders run the show.

The pluralist view is the lobbying, non-partisan view expanded. The spokesmen for U.S. unions are now using its techniques in only a small way, and with them they are busy losing out.

From Ideas to Politics

Having no explicit ideology, the American labor leaders borrow convenient fragments of various brands of liberal ideologies. Not only their action but their reasoning is opportunistic. Therefore unions as organizations, with their present position in the flow of history and the constellation of power, pursue such ends as are immediately desired with such means as are immediately available. The leader will work for pure and simple unionism, for better wages and conditions, and the security of his union, since it is an organization living perilously in a hostile environment. This line of explanation—the character and the position of the organization—is the most adequate one with which to understand the labor leader.

But the other level of explanation—the personal plane—should not be by-passed, even though, from the standpoint of sociological determinism, it seems romantic. The personal explanation supplements the organizational. With it the expedient and fragmentary conduct of the labor leader is explained in terms of his career and the type of man he becomes by virtue of his life and leadership in the American trade union.

The main thread of this psychological explanation is that, in the career of the labor leader, there is a shift from political ideas to practical politics, both in connection with the program the leader may fight for within the union and the program for which he may attempt to have the union fight. The case of the older generation of labor leaders differs from that of the younger just as their careers differ. But eventually both find themselves in the necessarily compromising situation of the practical politician.

His political coloration and the changes which the U.S. labor leader undergoes are most clear-cut in those careers that began between 1900 and 1920, when socialist ideas and ideals were much in the air, when New Dealism had not yet sidetracked socialist political goals and obfuscated the strategies designed for realizing them.

To prove that many trade union leaders of the older generation began as men of radical ideas, we can name names and quote from documents, but only one statistical point is known: as late as the middle Twenties, during the La Follette campaign, some 42 per cent of the labor leaders were affiliated with third parties of one sort or another. This compares with less than 10 per cent of the labor leaders in the middle Forties.

To belong to a "third party" is not necessarily to have political ideas, but it does mean exposure to ideas, for third parties are usually built more on ideology than patronage.

The drift from radical ideas to practical politics is also apparent in the careers of the newer generation of leaders, a great many of whom have never known minority party life. In 1924, when four out of ten labor leaders were in some minority party, the younger men were still in high school or grammar school. Yet many of the men who came into the union world out of the upheavals of the Thirties began as grass roots militants. Their images of what they were working for may not have been well thought out or very systematic but they were urgent about what they were doing. In all this, they reflected the mood and capacity of sections of the hard-pressed rank and file whom they organized.

For a time, in their careers, the best of the older generation possessed both strong will and organized vision, but the best of the younger generation has always had more of the first than of the second. Few of them had an ideology; they simply saw things in terms of what they were called upon to do as militant labor leaders in Flint, Akron, and Detroit and in the steel and coal hamlets, but for this little time they acted as if they saw things whole.

Fewer of these younger men have foreign-born backgrounds, so fewer are likely to have a tradition of clearly formulated radical ideas. They were motivated by indignation; and they drew support from, and in turn led, rank-and-file militants. But such militancy is not of enduring character. It wears out the leader; and if it does not quickly win through to security, it peters out among the rank and file, who become indifferent or passively resigned.

Three mechanisms facilitate the movement of a labor leader from ideas to politics. These affect all who make that move, the older as well as the newer generation.

I. If a man with ideas rises to the head of a union, he almost invariably comes up against both factional fights among leaders and mass passivity among members.

Caucuses are formed and his attention becomes focused mainly upon the opposition within the union. In order to do anything, he reasons, he must somehow gain control of the caucuses. This, in reality, is identical with strengthening his own position within the union. He must make deals with various locals and intra-union factions. More often than not, such deals involve compromising whatever program he would like to pursue. Thus, in order to hold his own within a union that began democratically, the labor leader must evolve from man of ideas to practical politician. According to those who kept their ideas and now have no power, he becomes a careerist and a "union politician trying to hold on to his job."

Not all unions experience factional fights; such fights *may* be signs of rank-and-file vigor. Yet in the historical balance sheet, mass passivity probably outweighs the need for compromise in factional deals in the labor leader's transit from ideas to politics. The failure of left political movements in America is an important factor in the de-radicalization of the labor leader.

II. By the very weight of its success in organizing, and of its need for security, the labor union tends to go through an adaptive process which directly affects the kind of leader who succeeds in keeping his power. This process, with business unionism in general, represents the main line of development in the union world—adaptation to American society.

Many a union has grown, as one proud labor historian says of an older union, from "a small union, bounded by its own little labor and radical world, into a great institution of labor, which is an integral part of the American community." This process is even more dramatic in the case of recent unions, such as steel. Men, such as Golden and Ruttenberg, who participated in the great steel drives, apparently had to adapt quickly to the changes in the union after it secured a number of contracts:

"John Witherspoon and Bud Barton, unlike many other belligerent local union leaders, have become able contract administrators. Bud is more comfortable now in a suit coat and vest. John still likes his chew of tobacco, but he now wears hats that fit him, and his appearance inspires confidence. The union has made them substantial citizens in their community. Both found it hard to change over from fighting management at every step to co-operating on the basis of equality. They did so slowly and carefully, lest in so doing they lose the confidence of their following. For several months they floundered until they learned how to be constructive leaders of men. They found that acting as the spokesmen for the hates and grievances of a group of workers is easy. All they had to do, then, was to give vocal expression to the popular attitudes of the group. The job of giving the same group constructive guidance, often entailing unpopular acts, they found to be much more trying. It is a mark of distinction that Barton and Witherspoon made this transition, because most militant local union leaders, who rise to the surface in the organization stage of unions, fall by the side when the union moves into the stage of constructive relations with management." The union has found it necessary to implement this transition by organizing the selection of leaders, by sending special instructors from headquarters to train leaders for the locals.

As within the union, so between the union and the business world, success also requires adaptation to the stability of contracts and deals. If the original program was radical, there must be compromise. Deals, sometimes in the form of contracts, sometimes in other forms, must be made with other leaders within the union and outside it rather than continuously rallying the people in the union around the leader by the assertion of a program.

III. His success and retention of power in the union carry direct implications for the role of the labor leader in the community at large. Becoming "contract administrators," the steel workers stated, made the local leaders "substantial citizens of their community." This is typical, for as the union grows and becomes more firmly knit into community life, that is to say, the middle-class life of the small businessman, local officers "in various parts of the country serve with business, church, and social leaders on boards of philanthropic and educational institutions, and are active in civic bodies of all sorts," including the Chamber of Commerce and the Masons. In short, the union leader becomes a big shot and acts with the responsibility required of such standard types of spokesmen.

These mechanisms often work slowly. Life in the union seems to gnaw at the radicals' defenses, a little at a time; the leader is beaten without having known that a battle was going on. This is not merely an American phenomenon. It is also typical of the political course of the German labor movement and of its leaders, right up to the Hitler debacle; it came to its German climax on May 2, 1933, when storm troopers occupied trade union headquarters. It is true also of the union movement in Britain. At twenty-six, Bevin organized the unemployed of Bristol; at fifty-six, he organized the labor force of Britain for war, for the cabinet of Mr. Churchill.

If this political line of development is typical, and will continue, then the labor leader's shift from political ideas and the will to carry them out to the fumbling confusion and false security of practical politics carries a great freight of meaning for the future shape of American society. The unions, as agencies of protest for the worker, absorb the leaders of that protest, the only men who could give it the focus, force, and continuity that is needed to accomplish a durable and bearable situation. In acquiring this economic agency, the workers lose the men among them who might make political protest effective.

The labor leaders are lured into power, and once there, plied with troubles and insecurity. The radical man who enters the labor movement loses his political virginity; that is to be expected of those who traffic with basic relations, no matter how lightly. Yet in losing his political virginity, the labor leader, like Dreiser's country girl in the great city, often becomes the whore of power.

There is nothing spectacular in all this: it is the cumulative effect of little things. And there is nothing peculiarly labor-leaderish about it. All insurgents who become spokesmen thereby lose their insurgency. Yet it is somehow easier to excuse in the others: they are not leaders of a protest of such proportion; they follow the main drift with a certain fitness and pleasure, feeling there is something to gain from it, which there often is. But the labor leader represents the only potentially liberating mass force; and as he becomes a man in politics, like the rest, he forgets about political ideas. Politics as he comes to know it has to do with big power relations that pay off small potatoes in short runs of time. Genuine political ideas are programs uniting principles with step-by-step demands. Programs take time; of the long meantime, the labor leader is afraid; he crawls again into politics-as-usual.

CHAPTER TEN

PARTY TIES

THE BI-PARTISAN policy of the unions is official, which means that for many labor leaders it has become mythical. Despite their liberal rhetoric, as men on the heights, the leaders of American labor are neither political teetotalers nor non-partisan. "There are enough labor bodies and union officials about the premises," it has been said, "so that every candidate can boast of a number of endorsements and of a coterie of labor officials in his retinue." In recent national political campaigns, the Teamsters' Tobin was sitting in with the Democrats, the Carpenters' Hutcheson and the Plumbers' Coefield sat in with the Republicans. These labor leaders belong to various committees and perform errands for the national party high commands; as political partisans, they serve partisan party interests.

The Lineup

Officially, in accordance with the ideas of Samuel Gompers, the labor leader as the head of his union may endorse any candidate who is, or who is expected to be, a friend of labor. If this were carried out strictly, no labor leader would answer our question about the party to which he belongs by naming the Republicans, the Democrats, or some third party. He would answer "Independent" or "Gompers' policy" or "any candidate supporting labor"; we shall term it the bi-partisan line.

Yet, when we asked the leaders of the AFL and the CIO about their party affiliations, only about one-fourth said they had no party; three-quarters named specific parties to which they belonged. Here is the party lineup of the labor leaders:

In both the AFL and CIO, the bulk of the leaders are registered Democrats. There are, however, differences: there are more Democrats and slightly more third-party members in the CIO, and there are more Republicans and followers of the bi-partisan line in the AFL.

	AFL	CIO
Democratic	51%	65%
Bi-partisan	26	19
Republican	19	7
Third party	4	9
Total cases	222	175

The labor leaders are not aligned politically as is the general population. In the last five presidential elections, neither the Democrats nor the Republicans have been able to gain more than a 5 per cent lead over the other party, and the third-party vote has remained less than 1 per cent. But among the labor leaders, the Democrats have a rather heavy majority over the Republicans; and, relatively speaking, and in view of the possibilities that prevail, there is a sizable "third-party" vote.

This general pattern of political party differences between the AFL and the CIO leaders holds on each level of leadership. There are more Republicans and generally more bi-partisans in the AFL and more Democrats and third-party members in the CIO. But within each bloc there are interesting variations among third-party members and those following the bi-partisan policy.

	AFL			CIO		
	Nat'l	State	City	Nat'l	State	City
Democratic ...	36%	55%	56%	54%	70%	67%
Bi-partisan	41	17	23	20	18	19
Republican ...	16	26	19	6	7	8
Third party ...	7	2	2	20	5	6
Total cases ...	56	42	124	35	44	96

In the AFL there are more bi-partisans among the national than among the state and city leaders. In the CIO on the national level there are more third-party members than on the lower CIO levels.

These tendencies seem strongest among the most powerful men in the American labor world, the presidents of the internationals:

In the CIO 24 per cent of these top leaders belong to third parties compared to only 7 per cent in the AFL. In the AFL presidential group over half of the leaders are ghosts of Gompers as compared to 24 per cent of the CIO presidents.

	AFL	CIO
Democratic	19%	52%
Bi-partisan	52	24
Republican	22	..
Third party	7	24
Total cases	27	21

The Gompers men are more often found at the tops of the union hierarchies than on the lower levels. Whereas only 24 per cent of all AFL leaders are bi-partisan, 52 per cent of the presidents of the AFL internationals are; and in the CIO, where the over-all figure is 17 per cent, that for the presidents is 24 per cent. This points up one function that the non-partisan policy serves within the union: since the affiliations of the lower leaders, not to mention members, are mixed, it is often more advisable for the top leaders, who have the task of holding the union together, to be non-partisan. In this way they can mediate between local endorsements and the complex and protective tie-ins of the various organizations.

There is a traditional feeling among these ghosts of Gompers. They are the older men, in the movement for a much longer time than those who willingly express party affiliation. Considering this, and their politically perilous position in the union world, it is not difficult to understand why they cling to the position which over the years has seemed the safest for labor leaders. Certainly there is no evidence that they are model independent citizens who make up their own minds on the merits of each case. Such people are likely to be highly educated, but the ghosts of Gompers are among those labor leaders with the least formal schooling.

The political lineup makes plain the basic character of the split between the CIO and the AFL leaders. The difference in union affiliation is the most important we have found in determining the labor leaders' political ties. Specific opinions do not seem to be closely associated with membership in given parties. There are, for instance, no strong differences among Republicans, Democrats, bi-partisans, or third-party members over the threat of fascism or over the relative estimates of the power of business and labor in national affairs. Of course, more of the present third-party members believe that third parties are best for the interests of labor, both now and in the years to come. In the CIO, third-party members show a tendency to feel that the threat of fascism is stronger; yet, in the AFL, the Republicans are the most fearful of fascism. The existing parties are not ideological in character and the labor leader's party affiliations do not form any consistent ideological pattern.

The most determining factor of the labor leader's affiliation, when he has one, is whether he belongs to the AFL or to the CIO. Yet it might be expected that some of the differences in party affiliation within each bloc, as well as between them, might be due to the same causes known to operate among the mass population, such as age, education, and social standing. Not one of these traits seems to influence the party affiliations of the American labor leader. Once we take into account whether the leader belongs to the AFL or to the CIO, other factors become less important. However, three factors do seem to affect party affiliations within the general influence exerted by the union blocs.

1. The peculiar regionalism of American political institutions is reflected in the lineup of the labor leaders, just as it is in the general population and doubtless in other elite groups. The Northeast is the only geographical area where any sizable third-party bloc exists. About one-fifth of the CIO leaders on all levels in the Northeast belonged to the A.L.P. in 1946. The concentration of Democratic Party loyalty appears in the South and the West where about seven out of ten of the labor leaders in both blocs are affiliated Democrats. The remaining three are either Republicans or follow Gompers.

In the Middle West, mainly in and around Colonel McCormick's Chicago, despite the Democratic inclinations of that city, the proportion of non-partisan labor leaders is greatest. Here almost four out of ten AFL leaders and three out of ten CIO leaders claim to have no party. In part this undoubtedly reflects their attempt to straddle the local-national party issues.

II. The nativity of the labor leaders is a factor in their politics. Those who have foreign-born fathers or who are themselves foreign-born appear to be more politically liberal. Thirteen per cent of the foreign-born AFL leaders are in a third party as against 2 per cent of native birth; in the CIO, 42 per cent of foreign extraction are third-party members as against 3 per cent of native birth.

Nativity does not seem to make much difference in the Gompers policy, held more or less intact for many years by early foreign-born U.S. labor leaders. But among those who do affiliate, the closer they are by birth to European tradition, the more likely they are to be members of third parties and the less likely they are to be Republicans.

III. A third factor in political party affiliation is the occupation of the father. These differences are slight but suggestive. Within the AFL, 60 per cent of the leaders whose fathers were white-collar employees or small businessmen are Democrats, as compared with 44 per cent of those whose fathers were workers. Eighteen per cent of the leaders of white-collar extraction are bi-partisan as against 36 per cent of those from wage-working families.

In the CIO, higher class extraction seems to push the individual toward more liberal or radical political affiliation: 12 per cent of those from white-collar families, as against 6 per cent of those from wage-workers are members of third parties. We shall consider this again when we take up the third-party issue itself.

Regardless of political adaptation to regional politics, differences caused by nativity, or the possibility that the leaders of relatively higher occupational origin are more liberal or radical, the outstanding fact remains: the basic split on party affiliation is between the AFL and the CIO leaders.

Standard personal and social causes do not uniformly determine the political affiliation of the labor leader nor explain the fact that seven out of ten labor leaders belong to one or the other of the major parties. Nor does the party affiliation of the labor leader determine his ideology. Both party affiliation and ideology are determined by machine-like adherence to the political pattern of each union bloc. Apparently there is more political discipline within each bloc than one might gather from inspection of formal organizational charts or from listening to anecdotes of cliques and struggles. The present-day leader of American labor is overwhelmingly machine-minded and patronage-minded; he is utterly American in his politics. To him politics usually means just about what it means to an American political machine boss in Chicago or Memphis. It is, nevertheless, interesting to know what the labor leaders as a strategic elite think about the two major political parties today—in particular, if they see any differences in party labor policies.

Views of the Major Parties

"Of course, there are individual exceptions in both parties," we said to the labor leaders, "but taking the Republican and the Democratic Party leadership as a whole, do you feel that nationally, the two parties stand for about the same labor policies, or for different labor policies?" They could answer: "about the same," "much the same but with real differences," or "quite different."

This question is of course quite formal: it cannot be directly answered in such a way as to tell us which of the parties the labor leader thinks is good and which bad in its labor policies, or whether both are either bad or good. Furthermore, as analysis of the answers showed, the question does not permit the kind of qualified answer many men prefer. For instance, many labor leaders feel the Democratic Party is different and better except for its Southern wing, which they feel is as bad as the Republicans. A man who feels that way might answer: "much the same but with real differences," or "quite different." The value of the question is therefore limited.

The two parties are:	AFL	CIO
About the same	32%	28%
Much the same, but with real differences	26	26
Quite different	42	46
Total cases	227	174

The answers given do not differ between AFL and CIO leaders or between the various levels of leadership in each organization. Four out of ten labor leaders think the two major parties are quite different in their labor policies, almost three out of ten are on the fence, another three out of ten think they are about the same.

The leaders who think the two parties differ in labor policies are more likely to be Democrats; those who believe the two parties have the same labor policies are more inclined to be bipartisan or AFL Republicans. These differences might be expected, however, and none of them are very large.

By examining the detailed comments made by the labor leaders in their answers, we can gain more insight into the motivations and methods of their reasoning. The most frequent comment made is that "after all, the policies of the Democrats are more favorable to labor than those of the Republicans." In the 146 detailed comments examined, only three labor leaders said that the Republican labor policy was better. These three used the roundabout argument that a Republican administration would make business better and thus benefit the labor unions.

A great deal of pro-Democrat sentiment rests on memory: "The labor unions grew under the Democratic Party leadership . . . and," the comments hopefully project into the future, "are continuing to grow."

The Republicans are seen as "working for the manufacturers . . . ," "they definitely represent capital," and as having "never sincerely approved or adopted a beneficial labor policy." The interesting point about such comments is that Republicans, as well as bi-partisans, make them.

The Democratic Party is often supported as the lesser of two evils, but more by CIO than AFL leaders: "The forces of reaction are working in both parties . . . but at the present time, such forces predominate in the Republican Party." They see the Republican Party as "reactionary and anti-labor," while the Democratic is "expediently pro-labor." "The two parties," says another labor leader, "are much alike. I have seen them exchange platform planks, but the Republicans are more frequently against labor."

There are two further groups of commenting labor leaders. One is intolerant of both parties and thinks both are bad. The other is tolerant of both parties, thinks there is good and bad in each, and has faith that, in the end, the two-party system will bring more good than bad.

The intolerant ones say, "Both parties represent big business and would delight in being able to establish the open shop." "The Democratic Party," comments another, "is the war party: it is used by big business to profess a mild liberalism so as to gain popular support when a new war is planned." "The differences are far too microscopic to matter." The tolerant ones say, "In both parties there are men with social vision and understanding of the needs of the nation. Personal attitudes rather than party declarations control."

The most striking impression is the lack of ideological consistency displayed by so many labor leaders. Many Republicans feel quite strongly that the Democratic Party has a more pro-labor line; many bi-partisans are bitterly partisan; many Republicans, Democrats, and bi-partisans believe both parties are very bad indeed for labor's interests, that labor desperately needs a labor party, yet continue to be what they have been.

The Labor Vote

The mugwumps and lobbyists of labor cling to their political ways for practical and expedient reasons, often consciously sacrificing their beliefs. The immediate advisability of their course thus rests heavily upon the reliability of their deals.

Often labor's hold over its candidate is weak. The primary loyalties of the politician are to his party; any interest group must be a very strong factor in the success of that party to share in those loyalties. In general, given the structure of party loyalties, the more labor is continuously *in* the higher councils and machines of the party, the more it can count on stable support from politicians. That support is a largely expedient matter; it depends upon whether the politician believes labor's power is a major factor in his election and whether he needs the labor leaders' endorsement to win. The reliability of the deals thus depends upon whether labor leaders can deliver the labor vote.

We only have scattered anecdotal evidence: the few statistical findings are hard to interpret because they pertain to the Roosevelt era. Until the early Forties, Roosevelt was so strong among wage workers that it was not clear whether the unions delivered the vote or whether wage workers would vote Democratic in any case. A Democratic politician's hold on the labor vote did not then depend upon his endorsement by labor leaders.

The most severe test of any labor leader's ability to deliver the vote occurred in 1940, when John L. Lewis repudiated Roosevelt and called for the election of Willkie. "If Roosevelt is re-elected," said Lewis, "it will mean that the members of the Congress of Industrial Organizations have rejected my advice and recommendation." The national vote for Roosevelt dropped 7.5 per cent from the 1936 figure. But in 63 carefully selected counties and 14 towns where CIO members predominated among the voters, it dropped only 6.2 per cent. As a matter of fact, Roosevelt ran well ahead of his national percentage in CIO industrial regions and cities. John L. Lewis resigned his presidency of the CIO. Again in the 1946 elections, only 5 per cent of the Congressmen whom the CIO was determined to defeat lost; but 40 per cent of those whom the CIO tried to re-elect were defeated.

Even the most potent labor leader cannot necessarily count on union members to follow his decisions about political candidates. Unions are not now set up that way; motives for joining and being good members are not primarily political. It would seem, however, that more union than non-union wage workers consistently vote for a Democratic Party candidate. Here are the proportions of wage workers who voted Democratic out of the total major party vote cast in three presidential years:

Year	*Non-Union*	*Union Members*		
		TOTAL	AFL	CIO
1944	56%	72%	69%	78%
1940	64%	72%	71%	79%
1936	72%	80%	80%	85%

The Democratic vote among wage workers declines over the period; but in all three elections, more of the union members, especially within the CIO, voted the Democratic ticket than did non-union wage workers. Belonging to a union has the same effect on white-collar workers where, in fact, it makes an even bigger difference.

A more direct question has been asked the public: "As you know, the CIO unions through their Political Action Committee are trying to elect a lot of Congressmen. If you knew that a candidate for Congress was backed by the CIO, would you be more likely to vote for him or less likely?" The question is ambiguous. One does not know whether it is the CIO or the PAC that is being reacted to more, nor what the reaction would be to an AFL man. Here are the results:

	Non-Union	*Union Members*	
		AFL	CIO
More likely	12%	20%	47%
Uncertain	24	25	25
Less likely	64	55	28
Total	100%	100%	100%

About 25 per cent of each of the groups are uncertain, and this proportion is large enough to swing an election. Even among the CIO, less than half were willing to say that such support would make them more likely to vote for the proposed candidate. The AFL reaction is, of course, a further reflection of the split between the two organizations. Only one-fifth would back a CIO candidate, which means that they are almost as politically anti-CIO as the general non-union public. Union membership is not synonymous with political belief. The split in labor's ranks is a serious obstacle to its bargaining power with knowing politicians on the national level and probably in many localities.

Effects of the New Deal

Recent labor politics have not been bi-partisan but strongly pro-Democratic. Third-party politics have been weak and scattered. These are two parts of the same development: both are largely explained by the New Deal's effect upon the politics of labor.

The New Deal picked up and modified many old radical, third-party ideas and put them into a halting kind of practice. Minority party ideas often have that fate and as a consequence the minority parties themselves tend to decline or disappear. The New Deal destroyed any reason-for-being of a national third party. That administration, and in particular Roosevelt himself, side-tracked independent labor organization in politics on an immense scale. Of all the spokesmen, Roosevelt—so far the major party politician of the twentieth century—was the most expert with the liberal rhetoric.

In the early Thirties, when the slump began to go deep, labor unions found, as they always have during depressions, that economic strategies alone are not enough. In several cities labor parties emerged out of lost strikes, but after the New Deal successes, their chance was gone. During the Thirties, independent labor parties were supported in only two states, in each case functioning primarily as Roosevelt adjuncts.

The Minnesota Farmer-Labor Party was able to persuade the Democrats to withdraw a 1936 state ticket in return for their support of the Democratic national slate. A Non-Partisan League was founded to help the Democrats with the 1936 election. But by 1938 the AFL had left and it was a CIO instrument, a prototype of the later PAC. The New York branch of the League grew up into the American Labor Party, which helped elect both Roosevelt and Governor Lehman.

The story of one large international of socialist background is especially revelatory. Throughout its history, both leaders and rank and file of the ILGWU had supported the Socialist Party. Few leaders in this union were without strong political and ideological conviction. Schlesinger, Hochman, and Dubinsky had been Socialist Party members, Sigman and L. Levy had been Anarchists, and Communists had been prominent in the union.

During the later Thirties under Dubinsky, the top leadership of the ILGWU was de-politicized. Dubinsky showed the way by resigning from his life-long membership in the Socialist Party in 1936. With his great "resourcefulness as a tactician," says a quasi-official biographer, he realized "the best way to liquidate the remnants of factionalism was to set the example of disaffiliation from the old-line radical movements. He became a presidential elector in the Democratic Party of New York, which is a very different thing from belonging to a political faction within the labor movement. Most of the other leaders of the International followed suit.

"All the leaders of the International became politically New Dealers," this labor historian continues, "and in New York virtually all of them joined the American Labor Party, which was not a party but a tactical device of the New Deal to promote its own political fortunes in New York." The American Labor Party, founded in New York State, "was just the thing the International had been looking for. Being nothing but a political instrument of the New Deal, it gave the International a chance of combining all-out support of the Roosevelt Administration with its own traditional belief in 'independent' political action. Everybody in the union—conservatives, centrists, radicals—hailed the ALP as the promise of an American counterpart of the British Labor Party."

The socialist background of the ILGWU makes this case most striking, but the shift was made everywhere. The labor leaders' uncritical devotion to the New Deal is accounted for by their organizing successes during its life. They are enthusiastic about any administration under which their unions grow five- or six-fold in almost as many years. Politically, the New Deal just suited the labor leaders, especially those who did not know what they wanted to do politically but felt they ought to do something. Roosevelt offered them a chance to be safe, respectable, and yet politically active.

Nineteen-twenty-four was the peak year for labor's third party; in a later chapter we shall examine this campaign in detail. But between 1924 and 1946 something happened:

	AFL		IND.	CIO
	1924	1946	1924	1946
Democratic	21%	51%	7%	65%
Republican	16	19	7	7
Bi-partisan	26	26	14	19
Third parties	37	4	72	9
Total cases	320	222	43	175

The composition and types of the third parties are, of course, quite different for the two years. In 1924 "third parties" meant, for all the leaders combined, 17 per cent Progressives and 25 per cent various labor parties. By 1946, the third parties to which the labor leaders belonged were merely appendages and labor fronts of the Democratic Party rather than independent political organizations of labor. Most were in the American Labor and Liberal Parties of New York, a few were old-line socialists, and one admitted Communist Party membership.*

In these crucial years, the shift from third parties to the Democratic Party is decisive. Even in the AFL, there is twice as high

* *See* Chapter Eleven: Communists and Labor Leaders.

a proportion, 51 against 21 per cent, of Democrats in 1946 than in 1924. Third-party members drop seven-fold: from 37 to 4 per cent. In 1924, there was no CIO; the only comparable organizations are independents. This is a possible historical basis of comparison, for it too reveals the change in political coloration that comes with movement from smaller into larger, more successful unions. The proportion of Democrats increases nine-fold: from 7 per cent to 65 per cent; the proportion of third-party members drops from 72 to 9 per cent.

In AFL, CIO and independent unions, the proportions of leaders who are bi-partisan or Republican remains much the same: the main shift is from third party to Democratic.

The New Deal made no changes in the composition of the Democratic Party. In most states, localities, and in Washington, the Democratic Party leaders are either the same or comparable men. The best of the liberals now recognize that the relation of the New Deal to labor, like its relation to the problems of American life in general, was essentially opportunistic.

It has left no durable instrument for liberal, much less radical, activity; it was never radical, of course, in any sense of the word. Its effect has been to strengthen further the boss habits among labor leaders and to destroy the chances over a long time for independent political action by labor. The Democratic Party, as A. A. Berle, Jr., has recently indicated, is "not a party but a national aggregation of local blocs and machines, each reflecting and exploiting local situations, and mainly interested in local offices which have no bearing on national policy. . . . They agree chiefly on the Democratic label, on mutual respect for each other's patronage, and on presidential nominations."

On the other hand, the New Deal made labor big and more successful in the conventional pattern accepted by labor leaders and by political publics from liberal center to right wing. It helped create the new industrial aristocracy of labor. But its effect on the political development of labor in America was essentially to put it aside.

The New Deal's effects on the ideological atmosphere in which the labor leader as well as other social actors must behave were in the liberal direction, in a sense forming part of the main drift to a managed economy. Many Americans have abandoned their naïve faith in the politics of laissez-faire.

The liberal and leftward forces ebb and flow from centralization to decentralization. By the early Forties these forces had been so centralized that no leftward man, wanting to bring pressure on the hub, could push any spokes leading to it. Liberalism itself, not to speak of the labor leaders, had acquired habits of dependency. Leftward forces would have to be built up all over again from the bottom, and as men began the faltering attempt to do this they found the heritage of New Deal ideas confusing. For a little time liberalism had been almost official.

No one can make even passing comments on the political effects of the New Deal without mentioning how it ended. These, after all, are the decisive comments on it: it never solved the structural problems of the great slump, but in alleviating them here and there, acted as a shock absorber and a huge deflector of more vigorous action; it ended in war, and after the war was done with, things were in no better shape; they were worse and more complicated.

There is one point about the labor leader's political affiliations and problems which must be examined in detail before going further. It would be naïve to believe that all the leaders who are members or close followers of the Communist Party stated their political affiliation as such. Nor do we believe that the influence of the Communist Party within American labor unions can be adequately revealed by answers, even if completely accurate, on party affiliation. More indirect methods of investigation need to be employed.

CHAPTER ELEVEN

COMMUNISTS AND LABOR LEADERS

IT IS said there are racketeers in the AFL and that the CIO has Communists. Both statements are true. And there is no point in saying them if they are immediately followed by the standard liberal qualifications that have been worked out for the confusion and defense of both cases. There are racketeers among the leaders of AFL unions and there are Communists among the leaders of CIO unions. There are also a few Communists scattered in the AFL, although so far as we know, there are no conventional labor racketeers in the CIO.

We have already examined the labor racketeer. We wish here to answer three sets of questions about the Communists: (1) What images of the Communists prevail among the mass public and among the several political publics? What are the major relations between the Communists and these publics? (2) What are the facts within the unions: How did Communists get into them? What types of relations do Communists have with labor leaders? And—the most crucial question of all—just how many labor leaders and labor unions are involved in any way with Communists and the Communist Party? (3) What have been the major lines and tactics of the Communists in the union world? What have they sought?

In short, what has been and what is the political character and the relevance of the CP within the world of the U.S. labor unions?

Images

The mass public forms a huge backdrop before which the political publics now argue about the devious and intricate issues of the Communist Party. The mass public, which knows little or nothing about the Communists, is against them in the same way that it is against any radical or "un-American" idea, movement, or institution. On the whole, however, it does not take the threat of Communism in this country very seriously. Between 1937 and 1946 the mass public was asked at four different intervals whether or not it thought the United States was on the way to Communism. Only from 12 to 21 per cent said "Yes."

The greatest success of the Communist Party in the United States has been accomplished with the active aid and support of conservatives and reactionaries. Together they have made the mass public think that "Communist" is a synonym for "left" in general and "radical" in particular. Among the political publics, only the practical conservatives and the conscious and unconscious fellow travelers among the liberal center use this tactic. But it is widely enough believed to be put down as a successful accomplishment.

The images of Communists held by the mass public are obtained largely from the practical conservatives. In this, as in many other such matters, these small bourgeois are the respectable opinion leaders of the mass public. To them, as to the public at large, the word "Communist" is a generalized smear word, identical with other words, like radical, red, and even liberal. It is quite probable that a typical member of the practical right could not describe what it means to be a Communist, but if anyone speaks of public affairs in liberal ways, he is immediately tagged.

On the Communist issue, as on so many others, the sophisticated conservative sees the practical right as a militant shock troop, is glad that it is there so that he himself may be free to use other methods. The most sophisticated spokesmen of the right take this position: First, they stress, above anything else, the foreign policy implications and dangers of Communism. That is, of course, in line with their stress on the foreign dangers to their American way of life. Second, and more important in the present context, they believe that if the labor movement is ferociously attacked and indiscriminately smeared with red paint, labor leaders may be forced to heed the cries of the Communists for unity with labor against the capitalist enemy. The point, they continue, is to help the anti-Communist labor leaders in their resolute struggle against the Communists. Every ill-directed and foolish charge against the unions and the leaders, say the most sophisticated conservatives, is a rock thrown at the chief bulwark against Communism: straight, non-political, American labor unions.

This sophisticated line is directed at the practical right, sometimes sincerely, sometimes not; it is also aimed at the liberals whom the sophisticated conservatives strive to use as ideological shock troops, just as they try to use the practical right as practical shock troops.

In the liberal center some are for and some are against the Communists. Among those who are for, we find three types: Some simply are dupes: people who do not know what is involved in what others are getting them to do. These innocents blend imperceptibly into the two other types: the tolerant and the homeless ideological opportunists. All three, and especially the latter two, are repelled by the terrible word, red-baiter. The tolerant says: "After all, the Communists have worked hard for many good causes; many of our best friends are Communists." They usually are not deeply involved, but they act as transmission belts and as fronts for the Communist network of organizations that come and go in the curious kaleidoscopic world of voluntary associations.

Many liberals today are opportunists on the CP issue: they are caught between a lack of political ideas and a fear of big business. They become fellow travelers, by default as it were, and in a passive way. Given their dearth of political ideas, they think that to criticize the Communists or even to fail to go along with them is to play ball with the NAM. But they are not merely opportunists, nor are they, despite their being caught in the collapse of liberal ideas, naïve ideologically. They feel lost and homeless and are reduced to becoming ideological opportunists. Probably the shrill voice of the anti-CP liberal helps to keep them on this line.

Among the anti-CP liberals there is one type who, like the

practical rightist, expresses his distaste in a loud, petty manner. It has been observed by members of the independent left that the practical right, the liberal center, and the Communists themselves share this type of political mentality and temperament. Many anti-Communist liberals have simply carried over habits acquired during a previous stage, for many were Communists during the Twenties and Thirties. Having seen the error of their ways, they would atone in the shrillest possible voice. Not only do they occasionally boast about being red-baiters, but they inform on Communists to Congressional and other official committees. In the end, the kind of verbal warfare they carry on against the Communists exploits all the prevailing strong tendencies against all forms of radical activity. Nor do they hesitate to use and to strengthen the official agencies of reaction. They may believe they play their little bugles for the benefit of the tolerant or homeless liberal, but right wingers of all degrees are the ones who listen most attentively and are most pleased with the anti-CP tactics of the liberal center.

The independent left is in principle anti-Communist, but today, apparently, it is all principle and does not act in the battle. The far left, however, struggles with the Communists. Its warfare is conducted primarily within the unions, and its fight is the least noisy of any public. It never draws upon conservative forces for ideological or active aid. Some of its best friends are or have been among the duped rank and file of the Communist Party; the more opposition-minded these party members are, the more friendly is the far left to them.

The left's tactic aims to out-compete the Communist Party in the political and economic spheres of the worker's life. It would approach the worker and explain to him, in the full context of its consistently radical program, why it is against the Communists, and why the worker will be misled by following the Communist dispensation. In its two-front war against Communist and Capitalist, the left walks an extremely difficult path.

All the political publics and large sections of the mass public understand that the labor unions are the major arena for the

Communist battle. The other chief field of combat and intrigue is the culture and propaganda world, especially those forms of culture which are, or might become, popular or mass in distribution. But at present there is as much active opposition to the Communists from the labor movement as from any other single source.

Relations with Communists

The majority of the American labor leaders actively or passively fight Communists. Their motives for this fight, within as well as outside their unions, are mainly of three kinds; often, the motives of a single labor leader combine all three elements, or any combination of them.

I. First, the labor leader may be against the CP ideologically. We have seen in detail that the opinions of the majority of labor leaders are not Communist in any sense of that word. A very great many of them are as anti-Communist as any businessman; and most of them, we believe, are more vigorously against the Communists and more consciously alert to them than the majority of liberals.

Ideology is not a strong point of American labor leaders, yet in the collapse of liberalism as a set of live ideas, they may be caught between pure and simple unionism on the one hand and half-heartedly Communist ideas on the other. In this they share something of the homelessness and nervelessness of many liberals, but unlike such liberals, labor leaders do not live by ideology.

II. The animus of the labor leader against the Communists is most likely to be the same sort of feeling he has against any faction which is a danger to his rule of the union. In fact, he is likely to be more upset about the Communists than about other cliques because, with experience, he knows that Communists, usually skilled machine politicians, are hard to beat in any all-out factional fight. The labor leader fights Communists as he would any other rival faction within his union.

III. There is another motive impelling the labor leader to fight Communists within the unions which combines parts of the first two: Communists are bad for public relations in general, and in particular with the businessmen with whom the labor leader negotiates, the workers whom he organizes, and the federal government upon which he may be dependent.

The concerted CIO drive against the Communists at the end of the war, intensified during 1947 and 1948, is said by responsible sources to have been undertaken, in part, at the behest of the war-worried government. During the late war, when Russia and the U.S. were officially friendly and the American Communist helped hold down wildcat strikes and enforce no-strike pledges, neither the government nor the union heads molested the Communists within the unions. But when the war ended and the tensions mounted between Russia and the U.S., the Communists again began to talk of "imperialist wars." Then, like all burghers loyal to their government and hostile to dubious radicals, the CIO began its drive to oust the Communists from its unions.

In his pursuit of bigger and better contracts, the business unionist does not want to be stigmatized as Communist by his co-negotiators. Moreover, and especially if there is basis for such a smear, it definitely hurts organizing attempts. The case of Lewis Merrill, late president of the Office and Professional Workers (UOPWA), is in point: Communist talk definitely deterred the union's attempt to organize Wall Street financial workers. Merrill resigned from his several important Communist-front posts and attempted to swing the union out of the Communist zone of influence.

The fight waged by the labor leaders may thus serve several purposes at once: it makes them feel better ideologically; it is an attempt to kill off troublesome factions within their unions; it strengthens their relations with the federal administration; it improves their negotiation chances with business; and at least as a safeguard if not an outright help in their general public relations, it may ease resistance to their organizing efforts.

The labor leader who wants to fight the CP, for any of these motives, faces first the Communists themselves, who immediately smear him as a red-baiter, even if he is further left than they, or rather, especially if that is so. The CP labels all its critics red-baiters, whether they are to the right or to the left of the current Communist line. The Communists would appeal to the large liberal center in such a way as to intimidate all their critics to silence. They want two kinds of people: those who are for the CP and those who are silent. Second, the cries raised by his attack or defense will throw against the labor leader all union-busters who call everything left of practical right "squabbles among Communists." Often the anti-CP labor leader is squeezed in a rhetorical vise between fellow-traveling liberals and practical conservatives.

The independent and the far left, as well as the sophisticated conservative, understand this predicament perhaps better than other publics. But the first two are too powerless to help, and so far they have not brought forward any tactical ideas that the union leader will accept. The sophisticated conservatives, however, are in a position to help him and from time to time they do. If the squeeze tightens, business unionists, having no ideology of their own, will find the sophisticated conservatives' program an inviting salvation.

This consideration of the major motives impelling the labor leader to fight the Communists and the political context of this fight serves as an introduction to the positive relations now existing between labor leaders and Communists. In this aspect, more than in any other, numbers are crucial; for the key questions are: What is the character of the relations? How many of each type exist? We shall try to answer these questions as accurately as possible from the union files and Communist papers at our disposal and from interviews made in the last several years with union personnel of every shade of political opinion.

Although, in the labor leader's relations with Communists, ideological convictions are ordinarily irrelevant, the closest relation that can exist between the two occurs when the leaders of the union are convinced party members and when the union's official voice supports the party's views. There is to our knowledge only one such U.S. labor union, the International Union of Fur and Leather Workers. Founded in 1913, this union was invaded during the Twenties by the Communists, who have since run it. Some of its leading officers have been openly Communist; an unknown but probably appreciable number of its members are. In 1937, it left the AFL and entered the CIO, procuring a charter which included leather as well as fur workers. In 1947, this union had enrolled around 75,000 fur and leather workers: 1.2 per cent of the total CIO membership and 0.5 per cent of the total union members in the United States.

Even in this clear case, the success of the Communists involves not only political belief but also opportunism. The fur industry is dependent to some extent upon import-export houses which deal with Russia. It is, therefore, useful for a furrier here to be on good terms with the business representatives of Russia, who have probably urged employers to attach themselves to the Communist union. Some of the business-like employers, in line with their close and convenient relations with Communist labor leaders in the union, have joined and contributed money to CP fronts.

The more typical relation of labor leaders and Communists is openly expedient. The labor leader may be dependent upon Communist factions within the union for his power, although this may have come about without the labor leader knowing what was happening. Once in that position, he may have to play ball to keep his union post. On the other hand, the labor leader may actively court a CP faction by supporting its resolutions or patronage. In this way he hopes to use the zeal and energy of the Communists to advance his own career, or even one of his programs. John L. Lewis formed such a relation with the Communists during the beginnings of the CIO; on a smaller scale, R. J. Thomas apparently followed suit after being unseated by Walter Reuther from the presidency of the Auto Workers. Lewis was first Republican, then Democrat, but primarily he was a man who wanted a certain program and certain tactics of organization; and in furthering them, he used anyone who would help him. R. J. Thomas's motives were equally clear: he is a back-slapping, compromising man who wanted his presidency back; he knows little about CP ideology.

The labor leader carrying on opportunistically with Communists may head a union which is by no means Communist, but contains a small, efficiently organized CP faction. Such a labor leader may well be annoyed, but he plays along at least passively to insure his own position. Varying degrees of this kind of dependency apparently exist today in about a dozen CIO internationals.

The leader highest in the union world who is in such a relation is Philip Murray, chief of the CIO. Philip Murray is no more a Communist than is Herbert Hoover. Furthermore, his union, the Steel Workers, is not only non-Communist but has been actively fighting against the CP. But as head of the CIO and of the Steel Workers, Murray's power is based on organized voting strength, including the strength of Communists. Murray fears that too strong a move against the Communists would lose him the support of the United Electrical, Radio, and Machine Workers of America.

The Electrical Union, third largest in the CIO, numbering upwards of half a million members, is the base of Communist power in the CIO. Many of its leaders are either party-liners or are under pressure from party-liners. The president of the union, Albert Fitzgerald, is a figurehead; both Julius Emspak, the secretary-treasurer, and James Matles, the director of organization, who run the union, are party-liners, and with them are at least twelve more top leaders. In all districts of the union, the Communists are in fairly firm control, although everywhere there is active, often organized opposition. The opposition is led by James Carey, secretary-treasurer of the CIO, and president of the Electrical Union until 1941, when he lost the post after breaking with the Communists.

The three largest CIO unions are in the steel, electrical equipment, and automotive industries. Steel contains an unimportant number of scattered party-liners who are well under the administration's control. In the Auto Workers Union, the Communist faction has been of more serious proportions, although never comparable to the Electrical Workers. The president of the Auto Workers, Walter Reuther, is strongly anti-Communist; but George Addes, the secretary-treasurer until November, 1947, and R. J. Thomas, a vice-president until 1947, received support from Communist factions within the union. Both these men lost out in the 1947 convention, and the UAW is now one of the most outspoken anti-Communist unions in the country.

All CIO unions, classified with respect to Communist factions or control, lined up as follows in January and December, 1947:

	JAN., 1947	DEC., 1947
Against the CP and actively engaged in fighting it	41%	62%
Troubled by, but not under threat of CP control	35	15
Controlled by CP factions	24	23
Total membership	100%	100%

During 1947, the CP was isolated in certain unions; its strength in the middle zone was demolished. It was during this year that Communists were under official attack by Congressional and other committees; this atmosphere was helpful to the union men who were trying to get rid of the Communists for their own reasons. Yet in most cases, it was not merely a struggle of cliques that occurred; it was also a rank-and-file uprising. The outstanding case was in the UAW, which made a clean sweep of the CP faction. The character of the campaign and victory destroyed the notion that the CPers always form a super-efficient machine. By 1947, a selective process, operating with each turn and twist of the party line, had weeded out most of the really effective men the CP once had in the union.

From the standpoint of the labor leaders, the Communist problem is inconsequential in the AFL. No AFL international contains a CP clique that is a threat to the uniformly non-CP administration of these unions. Such Communists and fellow travelers as exist are confined to two or three big city locals or districts of internationals. Altogether they do not amount to a sizable percentage of either AFL leaders or members.

It is, of course, easier to compile a list of unions containing CP cliques than a list of union personnel who are Communists. Although the general and labor press report factional fights and resolutions which reveal the Communist hand, they seldom give names and almost never complete listings. It is possible to identify as party-liners or members approximately 30 out of the 260 general officers of internationals, or 12 per cent. This figure is by no means conclusive, for CPers are less likely to be in general offices than in more hidden positions—business agents, legislative representatives, or appointed organizers. One favorite spot that appears from our listing is that of the district or regional director, who is sometimes appointed and sometimes elected.

The figures given, as well as the crude classifications upon which they rest, are only approximate. Moreover, union personnel in the CP border-land is now subject to a high turnover, as the two numerical snapshots at the beginning and the end of 1947 make clear.

Lines

To ask why there are Communists in the CIO and not in the AFL is also to ask how the Communists got into the CIO. There were three ways in: First, John L. Lewis let everyone in during the great organization drives of the Thirties. Second, once in, the Communists worked hard and zealously to maintain their union cliques. Third, during the late war the U.S. government and its unions were on officially friendly terms with Soviet Russia, and the Communists profited from this wartime unity.

They won positions of power and trust in the CIO by the standard method of gaining power in U.S. labor unions: by being the organizers. They rode into power within the CIO just as the

CIO rode into power within the union world: by taking advantage of the organizing opportunity of the middle and later Thirties.

In the AFL that chance never existed, which is primarily why there are so few Communists within AFL unions. Not only were organizing tactics employed by AFL unions less dependent upon new ideas, but their drives did not enter the mass-production industries in which, quite intelligently, the Communists were most interested. But crucially, during the Thirties the CIO was building its machine whereas AFL machines were already built and fenced in before any organizing campaigns were undertaken.

The policies of the Communist Party within U.S. unions have gone through several phases. In 1920, the U.S. branch of the Communist Party was ordered to "establish Communist nuclei" in all labor unions and from within them to work in the direction of Communist policies. From 1920 until 1928, the policy of "participating in reactionary trade unions," of boring from within, was unsuccessful.

In 1928 the international line changed, and the American Communists were ordered to establish rival unions, which they immediately began to do. Their success was fragmentary. They set up a rival to John L. Lewis's miners but got nowhere. In the needle trades they were rather more successful, winning control of the important Joint Board of Cloakmakers in the ILGWU. They also tried hard, but unsuccessfully, in the Southern textile field. At its peak, the Trade Union Unity League, the name of the holding company for the unions which the Communists attempted to build, never included more than 57,000 unionists. In 1935, it was dissolved.

This was the time of the Litvinov collaboration with capitalist democracies. The American Communists promptly called for a united front with existing unions; that is to say, they readopted the bore-from-within policy. In 1934 the CP press saw Roosevelt as a Wall Street stooge and "Social Fascist"; the next year, he was the beloved leader of a sacred mission. In 1934 the

AFL unions were reactionary tools designed to sell out the worker; the next year they were the very instruments by which the entire working class could be liberated.

In the same year that dual unions were abolished by the Communists, the CIO was brought into being, and the personnel of the Communist unions was offered to John L. Lewis. This was experienced personnel, and Lewis was hard-pressed. He had beaten the CP when it tried to enter his Mine Workers, so he thought he could safely use it in his big drive. He accepted, and by 1937 or 1938, Communists were occupying important posts within newly arisen mass unions.

The historical facts and the present reality about AFL and CIO differences in regard to Communist factions have from the beginning been used against the CIO by the AFL. Employers have been warned by AFL organizers, and the press of the country has eagerly picked up the AFL cries of Communist. At a meeting of its organizers on April 29, 1946, William Green flatly asserted that the difference between the CIO and the AFL was a difference between "a foreign-controlled organization and an American organization," and that this was the issue that would be drawn in the organizing campaigns of the two union blocs in the South.

The Communists tend to fear unity between the AFL and CIO, for one of its results, anticipated by majority leaders in both blocs, would be the elimination of Communist factions from power in the labor union world.

Like many non-CPers, Communist union leaders have retained by intrigue the power won by organizing efforts. Many union leaders as well as members of liberal and left political publics, however, accuse the Communists of intrigue that prefers wrecking a union to losing control of it. In the histories of several unions there is ample evidence to support this charge. Once, in the earlier days of the UAW, when president Martin refused to name the Communists' candidates to central office positions, they called some 200 wildcat strikes to make him look too weak and irresponsible to handle the union. The same kind of tactic was used in at least a dozen other young CIO unions in an attempt to capture the whole CIO during the 1937-38 business recession. Hillman, Murray, and Lewis, each in his own union, quietly and effectively rid themselves of Communist factions. But even so they were afraid, and the top CIO leadership, which is anti-Communist, is still afraid to risk its own position and disrupt the whole CIO by a concerted and wholehearted drive.

The revolt against the CP gained impetus when on August 23, 1939, the Nazi-Communist pact was announced. The CPers within the CIO were able to stick, however, and there were few recantations. With the about-face in June, 1941, and the wartime unity of America and Russia, the Communists were again able to entrench themselves. The anti-CP drive, begun after the war, is still under way; as tension increases, the CIO leaders attempt to oust the Communist factions, within the cautious limits they deem necessary for the security of their own positions.

The charges made against the Communists by liberal and left-wing opponents are primarily:

First, the turns of these U.S. Stalinists from leftward to rightward, and back again, have been determined not by their judgment of the changing needs of the working people, or by pressure from these people, but by the changing needs of the ruling group in Russia.

Second, the ways for maintaining power which are habitual with the U.S. Stalinists include personal defamation and intrigue, carried, if need be, to the point of wrecking a man or a labor union. "They have resorted," Harold Laski writes, "to splitting tactics without any hesitation. . . . Organized as a conspiracy, their major desire is not to select the best possible leadership in ability and character for the end socialism desires; it is to get those upon whom they can count for uncritical and devoted obedience to their orders into the key positions of a movement or party they enter to use for their own purposes."

Third, Communist rule within the U.S. unions they control is dictatorial: although they talk the language of democracy, they do not believe or practice democratic principles. "They require from their own members," Mr. Laski continues, "the complete and unquestioning sacrifice of their consciences to the decisions their inner leadership makes. A refusal to make that sacrifice is the proof of a dangerous and rebellious personality for whom excommunication from the body of the faithful is the only possible remedy."

Fourth, the existence of the Communist factions, and their lack of independence, is a strong deterrent to the formation of a new party for labor, which might be acceptable under certain conditions to a considerable number of labor leaders, and which might have a chance to increase the power and the participation of the U.S. working people in American political life. It is even feared by some that the activities of the CP, such as its promotion of the Wallace presidential candidacy, will weaken any genuine leftward tendencies of labor in America, and that the resulting confusions will demoralize the movement and make it that much easier to defeat.

CHAPTER TWELVE

OLD PARTIES, NEW PARTIES

THE POLITICAL choice for labor unions in America has never been limited to the two-party system or the Communists. Intermittently throughout their history they have attempted independent political action. As each attempt failed, American labor unions have slipped back into the bi-partisan tactics that have formed their main political tradition.

But today the unions are bigger than ever before. No longer are they weak either in numbers or in economic power. Furthermore, since the New Deal is dead and the swing is against labor in national politics, many labor leaders are persuaded that they will have to fight politically harder and in new ways. Again they have been talking about a party for labor.

There is no talk of a new party among the practical or the sophisticated conservatives; only if the two standard parties were to fail them, or if the mass public was to become politically alerted, would they need one.

In November, 1946, 50 per cent of the politically passive people, despite their general approval of the institution of labor unions, believed that unions should keep out of politics altogether. Twenty-one per cent thought labor should support one or the other of the major party candidates; only 11 per cent favored the unions' forming their own labor party, although 18 per cent were undecided. Again in December, 1946, only 10 per cent of the mass public said that they would vote for a new labor party. Even during 1936-38, the maximum proportion in favor was 16 per cent.

In general, professionals and union members show the most interest in an independent labor party. In 1945, and again in 1946, for example, some 24 per cent of the country's unionized workers said they would join "a new national party . . . organized by labor"; and an additional 20 per cent were undecided.

A labor party is not a debatable question among members of the extreme left; one of their continuous aims has been to help form a party of farm and factory labor, perhaps including reliable militant runaways from the middle class. Such a party would provide an arena for socialist agitation in which the various splinters of the left might exert influence. The independent left in its present contemplative state does little but watch closely.

Talk of a new labor party has been most intense since the war's end among the liberals, especially those under CP influence. By now they have emerged from the New Deal episode, although they have no new ideas that go beyond its so-called left wing. Such pro-third-party liberals would include in their party all the progressive elements in the population: labor, little businessmen, small farmers, and all the rest of the little creatures of capitalism. Much of their talk eventuates in plans to capture the Democratic Party and recompose it as a liberal organization.

In the meanwhile, the winter of 1947-48 saw Henry Wallace lead the formation of a third party. It is not, however, a labor party, but is widely held to be a Communist front, designed, in the CP view, to fight the anti-Soviet policy of the United States, and supported by party-line union leaders only.

The histories of attempted independent labor actions are not known to the mass public, but they do affect the decisions of the politically alerted publics, and the labor leaders are variously involved with these publics. It is useful, therefore, to understand something of what independent labor action there has been in the recent course of United States political history.

A History of Failures

From the Jacksonian era to the Nineties, various attempts were made by labor and by socialist intellectuals to engage the unions in independent party action. Occasionally subtle exponents of a new party parade these attempts, apparently in an effort to show the experience labor has had with independent forms of political action, yet none of them seem relevant today. Labor then bears little resemblance to labor now. Furthermore, labor leaders have not learned much from political experience, nor from any of it have they built a serviceable, historically grounded view.

Independent electoral action has taken three forms in the United States: (1) *third* parties, similar to the two major parties, backed by similar kinds of people, with little ideological content; (2) *Progressive* parties, ideologically centered on capitalist reforms, opposed to the major parties, and supported by the little creatures of capitalism, especially its agrarian contingent; (3) *labor* parties, working in the interests of labor, backed by labor, and with a labor ideology. Types two and three may occur within the same organization, but only type three can be considered independent labor action.

Here is the minority party vote for each presidential election since 1896:

Minority party vote:	
1896	1.2%
1900	1.3
1904	4.2
1908	3.7
1912	6.3
1916	3.5
1920	4.5
1924	16.9
1928	1.0
1932	3.0
1936	3.0
1940	0.4
1944	0.7

These figures are percentages of all votes cast in each of the years, minus the Prohibitionist and the Bull Moose vote of 1912. Were we to include the Bull Moose vote in the minority party figure for that year, the percentage would be 33 instead of 6.3, but such an inclusion would not be congruous with our purpose in calculating the series. Theodore Roosevelt's campaign was in no sense a labor effort; it was merely a third party built along the same lines as the other two, definitely Republican in its essential beliefs. Financed by men like George Perkins, and utilizing many Republican state and local bosses and machines, it was a temporary bolt, serving in some part to head off La Follette's nomination. After polling 4,100,000 votes—27 per cent of the total cast (to Wilson's 6,300,000 and Taft's 3,500,000), it fell apart. Roosevelt remarked that such a party could not be held together because "there are no loaves and fishes." The 1912 Progressive Party was "neither more permanent nor more enduring than Teddy Roosevelt's high resolve to fight the bosses of the Republican Party."

The 1912 figure of 6.3 per cent represents the historical climax of the socialist movement. Eugene Debs polled 900,000 votes in 1912, when membership stood at its high of 118,045. By 1922 the party had melted to 11,019. Yet it revived once more, as a hard-working member of the farmer-labor-intellectual coalition in the 1924 Progressive campaign of La Follette.

American Progressives have insisted that special interests and corrupt influences be removed from government, popular control broadened, and the welfare functions of government enlarged. Other demands have been made, but these are the common denominators of the various campaigns. In the Progressive image of American society, the people's lobby is the successful one. Progressivism has rarely exceeded the bounds of the liberal rhetoric, although at times it has seriously meant what it said.

The Progressive strain has been predominately agrarian, not industrial, and certainly not Marxian. "More than political buncombe accounts for the reference to Jefferson in the Progressive platform." This is to be expected in a country industrialized as late as the United States. The "grass roots" of the American left have grown from agrarian areas because much of the class exploitation has assumed a regional form.

In its few broad political attempts, labor has tried to tie in with these agrarian impulses, seldom demanding more than what would be acceptable to Progressives. In their biggest effort, that of 1924, the unions did indeed carry the backwash of populism, as a regional analysis of the vote makes clear. In this attempt, as in others, the unions did not envision any outcome beyond a triumphant people's lobby. But for five years before 1924, AFL organizations not only participated in but often led the struggles of farmer, labor, and intellectual organizations to launch political action in various states and larger cities.

Back of these attempts was, first and foremost, the growth of the unions during the war. By 1920, union membership had reached what was then its historical peak: some 5,000,000, or 20 per cent, of the wage and salaried workers were organized. Since this growth had come about under government auspices in return, as it were, for labor's contribution to wartime unity, political activity was all the more enticing. Wartime unity in America, as everywhere, placed a shackle on the unions; but with the war over, they tried to translate some of their increased economic strength into political power. This effort was strengthened by the dislocation of wages and the cost of living, in which labor got the short end. An ungrateful insult given to Gompers by General Pershing at a postwar dinner was symbolic: the forces of reaction were on the offensive and a hunt was under way. Every lost strike and every injunction was an invitation to independent political action by labor.

In 1919, independent political activity surged. The Non-Partisan League of North Dakota, primarily a farmer organization, supported the current coal strike. In Minnesota, the League and the State Federation of Labor supported a farmer-labor party; The Chicago Federation of Labor organized the Labor Party of Cook County; the Labor Party of Illinois was founded; unionists in New York formed an American Labor Party, resolved to fight for government ownership of all utilities. The railway unions set forth the Plumb plan, which provided for government ownership and operation of the railroads. Although by 1920 the plan was defeated, the stand of such craft-like unions for government ownership contributed not a little to the political excitement that gripped labor. In 1919, a thousand delegates, from various union groups and city and state parties from 37 states, met in Chicago to form the national American Labor Party. Despite Gompers' explicit opposition, certain city, state, and national bodies of the AFL supplied the nerve of the endeavor.

By 1920, when the ALP, renamed the Farmer-Labor Party, convened in Chicago, there were parties in no less than 15 states. In 1922, the railroad unions, in collaboration with AFL city, state, and national units, formed the labor wing of the Conference for Progressive Political Action. Some 18 internationals were represented by AFL officials or delegates. With the unions were the Socialist Party, the Non-Partisan League, and the Committee of Forty-Eight.

Nineteen-twenty-four was the "nearest American workers have ever come to a farmer-labor alliance independent of the major parties." For the first time in their history, Socialists collaborated nationally with liberal and other political groups.

There was no one-party organization, however, back of the La Follette candidacy, except for the slender units the Socialists had in several states. La Follette and his running mate, Burton K. Wheeler, ran as independents with the endorsement and aid of the CPPA and other organizations. Their names were on the ballots under Progressive, Farmer-Labor, Independent, and Socialist endorsement.

In keeping with its usual practice, the AFL in 1924 presented its political suggestions to both major parties. These mild economic and legislative demands were rejected by the Republicans and ignored by the Democrats. Only then did the top AFL leadership reluctantly endorse the candidacy of La Follette and Wheeler. "It looks as if," Gompers said sadly, "we are forced to turn to La Follette." It was the first time in its history that the AFL endorsed the candidacy of men not running on the major party tickets. Between 1885 and 1924, the AFL had 12 times refused to entertain resolutions in favor of third parties. And now, in 1924, they did not endorse, much less create a labor party; they hesitantly endorsed only the independent and personal candidacies of La Follette and Wheeler.

Throughout, the trade unionists played a conservative and cautious part: they were obviously "reluctant to sever . . . ties with the major parties." They took the Socialists' support for granted and did not yield in the least to their demands for a third-party organization. By no means did all the unions endorse even verbally the candidacies of the Progressives: the Pressmen supported Davis; the Carpenters and the Mine Workers supported

Coolidge. Even among the railroad unions, the Trainmen withheld their endorsement of La Follette. Often-promised union funds did not arrive; organizations were planned but not developed; and even before the vote was cast, "scores of labor leaders had abandoned ship." The city central of New York shifted to the Democrat, Davis, five days before the election. This central was too entangled in strategy and obligations with the old parties to make a clean break, and it was too impressed with the need for immediate success to chance the sacrifices required to get a new party going. They wanted, says one contemporary observer, a "larger cut of the capitalist swag." In their fear of hurting their connections with the two standard parties, the labor unions defaulted the leadership of an independent movement.

The labor leaders supported La Follette in exactly the same way as any candidate of the old parties: their enthusiasm was in proportion to their estimate of his chances of winning. In that kind of defensive political strategy the labor leaders had been trained and in that way they thought. They continually feared that their bargaining power within the standard parties was being dangerously weakened. They seemed to be acting explicitly upon the AFL policy formulated in 1910 and reaffirmed in 1920: to trust the "ballot only so far as results are foreseen to be a positive certainty."

The official return to the bi-partisan principle—if it can be said that the AFL abandoned it in 1924—was made in 1925. The socialist Hillquit said to the labor men who withdrew, "If five million voters were not enough, will you wait until we have swept the country? . . . Did you start your trade unions on that practice? . . . Did you wait until the workers in the different industries clamored to be organized?"

By 1924, American prosperity, the great ally of Republicans, was under way. There was virtually no newspaper support of the La Follette ticket, and the total campaign fund amounted to less than $240,000. Given these facts, the showing made is one of the most remarkable in U.S. political history. The Progressives received 16.9 per cent of the presidential vote. Almost

5,000,000 votes were cast for La Follette, close to 16,000,000 for Coolidge, and about 8,000,000 for the Democrat, Davis. La Follette had tapped the old populist sources. The votes he received indicated quite clearly a national sentiment, except in the South, for some kind of progressive political movement. But there was no movement, and this campaign did not constitute one. It was built around the personality of one man, not around the structure of a new political party; the coalition behind it fell apart after the election. The AFL continued its bi-partisan policy, and the various brands of third-party thought and tactics went their own ways into oblivion. By 1930, not one state labor party of the great 1924 surge was left.

During the Thirties independent political effort was drained off into the New Deal. Indirectly at the same time, the New Deal created the conditions for such an independent party attempt by fostering the growth of labor organizations.

The Democratic coalition achieved by Roosevelt began to crumble in 1938, but the exigencies of war gave it longer life. In 1943, after the passage of the Smith-Connally Act, the PAC was formed under the auspices of the CIO to be a streamlined bi-partisan group for labor. If it differed at all from the time-honored AFL tactic, the difference was in its increased vigor; its attempts to use the organizations of the unions to get out the vote was half-hearted. It was formed mainly because of the loss suffered by the Democrats in the 1942 elections. In that year the CIO began to worry again about the labor vote: it wasn't "coming out." By 1943, the PAC was a going concern. During the 1944 campaign it did good work for the Democratic Party, and within the party, it pressured heavily against James Byrnes as the running mate for Roosevelt.

When the war ended and after Roosevelt was dead, the coalition of the South and labor, held together by the big Democratic city machines of the North, rapidly and obviously started going to pieces. Shortly after the 1944 election, power passed into the hands of Harry Truman, the choice of the big-city machine mediators, who had supported him against the South's Byrnes and labor's Wallace. Since then, the Democratic Party has disintegrated further into a "mob of aspirants for local jobs."

Labor has been alternately estranged from and happy with the Truman administration. The President's bungling intervention in the GM strike, which gained him much unpopularity with the unionized public, and his explicit strikebreaking role in the railroad strike indicated that he was, in labor as in other matters, an opportunist who would readily bear rightward if that seemed to be the way to go. Since then, his veto of the Taft-Hartley Act and similar tactics make it seem that he is trying to win back labor's sympathy.

The 1946 failure of the PAC came home strongly to labor circles. The organization had ridden the coattails of Roosevelt for one national campaign and had been held together by the master strategy of Sidney Hillman. In 1946, both men were dead, and for the first time in 14 years labor votes were split. The Congressional defeat of the Democrats in 1946 was a stunning blow for the PAC, yet after the defeat, talk of a third party was officially denounced: PAC was to continue working within the Democratic Party. By the summer of 1947, committees were working busily to develop machines for effective service in city campaigns, as foundation stones for a strong national bargaining agency in 1948. The board of the PAC had been enlarged to include Reuther, Murray, and three other international heads. There is even reason to believe that PAC was in part designed, and is now maintained, to head off an independent political attempt on the part of discontented labor leaders. Like the ALP of New York State, it acts primarily as an appendage of the Democrats, presumably because the latter includes more of labor's friends and fewer of labor's enemies.

In 1947-48 any independent labor party attempt was further deterred by Henry Wallace's candidacy on a third-party ticket. The character of his support was not that of, and could not lead to, a labor party. Although appealing to many scattered people of good will, Wallace responded primarily to the call of the Communists, whose tactics were to further the foreign policy line of the Soviet Union, which in the spring of 1948 meant primarily to fight the Marshall plan.

Members of the organizations supporting Wallace who would not go along with the Communists made this plain when they resigned from the effort. Frank Kingdom, for instance, said: "The call to Wallace came from the Communist Party and the only progressive organization admitting Communists to its membership. . . . He is named by them to serve their ends."

Only those unions which followed the Communist Party line supported Wallace in defiance of the official policies of both the AFL and CIO. There was no labor base for any labor party, "but rather a mugwump movement hothouse-forced by the Stalinists."

Liberals against Wallace's candidacy thought the tragedy lay in his detracting from the Democrats' chance to win and helping the Republicans'. The leftists, focusing more on the petty-bourgeois Stalinist character of the Wallace support than on the bourgeois party fight, saw the tragedy in terms of the confusion it caused among the workers.

The tenuous quality of Wallace's leadership of any independent movement was revealed by his indication that, if President Truman were to take a friendlier attitude toward Russia, he would withdraw his candidacy. By running as the CP's front, Wallace strengthened the Stalinists in this country and abroad, and he set back rather than furthered the attempt to turn American foreign policy from its war orientation.

Although the democratic left was of the opinion that something was to be gained by any political group that tries to detach people from the old parties, that was only a formal criterion. The independent and far left, for once, agreed with a union leader, who "repudiated the Wallace drive as inimical to the best interests of American workers." Actually, the left felt, Wallace and his political chaperons set back the attempt to form a new labor party in the United States. Those American labor leaders who honestly desired a new labor party saw this, too, and were disheartened.

What Labor Leaders Think of a New Labor Party

Unlike the intellectual members of the various political publics, the labor leaders are political *actors;* they head organizations whose policies are politically relevant. They consider irrelevant much that is said in discussion of independent political action.

This is reflected in the division of opinion within the liberal center, the ideological home of the labor leaders. Often liberal discussion of a new party seems to cluster, on the one hand, around those who advance the organizational practicality of the trade union leader, and on the other hand, around those who want to go along with those few labor leaders who publicly or privately support the idea of a labor party.

The labor leaders are deeply involved in the argument; presumably they would be the ones to act on any serious proposal. Many are now men with much to lose. Their reasons for and against a labor party are, therefore, of a different order and weight from those advanced by the liberal journalist and the political lecturer.

We asked the leaders of American labor: "As far as national politics are concerned, would you during the next two or three years prefer to work for labor's viewpoint within one or both of the major parties, or would you prefer to set up a new labor party entirely separate from either of them?" Here are the proportions favoring a new labor party: *

	AFL	CIO
National	8%	8%
State	5%	19%
City	18%	31%
All leaders	13%	23%

The CIO leaders favor a new labor party more than the AFL leaders, but only on the lower levels. Thirty-one per cent of the city leaders in the CIO favor a new party,

* These figures on a new labor party indicate nothing about labor's reaction to Wallace's "third party." Our questions were answered during the summer of 1946, and although there was Wallace talk then, his candidacy did not become certain until the winter of 1947.

compared to 18 per cent of the AFL city leaders. In the CIO, the lower the level of leadership, the more likely the leader is to be for a new party, while in the AFL the city leaders are most, and the state leaders least, in favor if it. City leaders in general are more apt to agree with the rank and file, some 24 per cent of whom generally favor a labor party.

The issue of a new labor party involves a question of timing. The labor leaders might well be against an independent labor party during the next two or three years, but believe in its practicality for ten years hence. In order to get closer to these longer-run feelings we asked: "Do you think that eventually (say, within the next ten years) gains for labor will best be made by working within one or both of the major parties, *or* through a new labor party entirely separate from either of them?"

Twenty-three per cent of the AFL and 52 per cent of the CIO leaders declare for a new labor party when the question is put in these terms; about twice as many are for a new party when the longer time-span is specified.

The ten-year question also gets a different reaction on the various levels. Here are the proportions who believe that labor in America is going to need a party of its own sometime in the next ten years:

	AFL	CIO
National	18%	65%
State	15%	33%
City	28%	56%
All leaders	23%	52%

In the AFL, the pattern found in the first question holds: the city leaders are most in favor, the state, least. In the CIO, however, the national leaders are as much or more in favor as city leaders. In both blocs the state men are the least enthusiastic. They are the lobbying and bi-partisan type of labor leader, and no one wishing to push a new party could count strongly on them for support. The leaders closest to the rank and file, the city leaders, most frequently support a new labor party. The national heads are thus caught between state and city forces. Their position is especially clear-cut among the presidents and secretaries of the CIO internationals, where more who want to wait are found than in any other leader group: only 8 per cent are for a new labor party now, but over half of them favor it in ten years.

Why They Think as They Do

To ask what determines the mind of the labor leader on the advisability of a new labor party is to ask which types of leader are most for it and which are least for it. We already have the outlines of the answer, for we know which levels of leadership are most and which are least enthusiastic. It is possible, however, to refine this answer, and to summarize the leading arguments involved.

1. The bi-partisan tradition within the American unions is of respectable weight; labor's attempts to create an independent political party have failed, and the entrenched parties put many practical obstacles in the way of any labor leader who would try again. The leader who would earnestly come out for a labor party therefore has to be less an opportunist and more a man with a program. He must be willing to go against the immediate facts of power in a two-party state; he must be willing to risk immediate defeats in the hope of long-run victories.

That is not to say the more intelligent or the better-educated will be for the new party. Education makes no difference in the answers to the above questions. But whether a labor leader is an opportunist or a programmer makes a difference; it is the latter who talk most frequently and earnestly of a new labor party. In the AFL, all of those who are against the idea of unions having a program are also against the idea of a new labor party, both now and in the future; but 25 per cent of those who favor a program also favor a new party now or in the future. So few of the CIO are against a long-run program that it is impossible to correlate their replies on the two questions. The problem of a new labor party is by no means identical with the question of a long-range program for labor, but the way things now stand both in the political situation and in the mind of the labor leader, they are closely associated. However, it is not programs or ideologies that govern the decisions of the leaders of American labor; it is expediency. Among the most expedient considerations are the labor leader's current opinions of the two-party system.

II. New-party sentiment is based upon dissatisfaction with present political parties. Those who believe that the present two-party system is the true representative of the democratic American way, or that it is effectively representing labor, are against any independent labor party.

The dominant view is that the two major parties are themselves opportunistic and may be made to do the will of anyone or any interest which can exert power over them. This belief makes it seem unnecessary to go to the enormous trouble of setting up a new party. If something must be done politically, the existing means of political action are quite good enough. "Labor's votes," thus comments one labor leader, "can be used as a balance of power which will tend to make present parties nominate more liberal candidates." There are pro-labor elements in both parties who will work for labor there rather than join a new party: "There are more liberals in both parties that are more apt to align themselves with the labor viewpoint within their parties than to affiliate themselves with labor parties."

III. The labor leader's expedient and cautious resistance to a new party varies directly with his expedient estimate of the chances for a new party to win. Since Gompers, most labor leaders have believed that any labor party would of necessity remain a minority mugwump, running with no real chance to win. To such men labor means 2,000,000 or 3,000,000 skilled workmen, rather than 15,000,000 or 25,000,000 organized workers. But their view dominates, conditioning the beliefs of even those labor leaders who no longer explicitly think of labor as a minority.

This fear of failure is displayed in the widespread insistence that any new party must include not only labor but farmers and white collar and, above all, little business. In other words, labor's party must collaborate with the practical right to form another party just like those already existing.

Anxieties are increased by the fact that a national labor party would require immense effort, not in one state but in 48 separate states. On those scattered rocks many an attempt has foundered. The grass roots, as a system rather than a sentiment, sets a most difficult task for the political organizer of any independent party.

Any third party would have the least chance of succeeding in the South where, since the Civil War, a one-party system has been dominant. Among the AFL leaders there are no regional differences in labor party sentiment, possibly because the issue is not so important to them as to the CIO. However, CIO leaders from the South are as disillusioned with the present political party system as those from other regions, but with two significant differences: First, 73 per cent of the Southerners are against the idea of a new party, as compared with 51 per cent of those from the Northeast and 24 per cent of those from the West. Second, only 7 per cent are in favor of a party eventually but are opposed now, as compared to 29 per cent of those from the Northeast and 32 per cent of those from the West. It is in the South that we find illustrated in sharp detail the principal reason for the labor leaders' general opposition to a new labor party: they don't think that it has a chance to win.

IV. Fear of flat failure deters labor leaders from forming a new party of their own, but they also fear even the consequences of setting one up. Those consequences are seen in the area of labor organizations, the political sphere, the realm of business, and the American public.

Taking a risk in a hostile environment, when beleaguered by enemies, is a different proposition from taking a risk in well-known territory with one's friends as witnesses. The key slogan of labor politics is: reward your friends and punish your enemies. To set up an organizational rival to the two major political machines is to arm your enemies and divide your friends. But if one is friendly enough, and gains strength by friendship, one can surely win over somebody: "A new labor party would lose our influence with both old parties," says one labor leader, "and we couldn't hope to elect in the next ten years. If labor becomes strong enough, one party or the other will become the labor party by another name." Both for the unions and for the leaders it is better, some think, to be in with some power than to have all established powers against you.

The consequences of setting up a new party, regardless of possible long-run success, ramify into the question of labor's unity. "A new party would tend to break down our unity." One meaning of this is that an independent labor party might require a clearly stated program. The workers and the various union chieftains would not be as unified as they are now, when they are not sure where the others stand. Programs are not good unifiers of politically heterogeneous people held together by leaders constantly looking for the main chance. A party might well require labor leaders to take stands on all sorts of national issues in which only the glittering rhetoric of liberalism is permissible in U.S. political life.

In addition, "one labor party begets another, and several labor parties would be inevitable in the United States." This reason ties in with the idea frequently promoted by liberal journalists that no labor party could avoid "disruptive entanglements with the Communists." Therefore, the conclusion runs, let's stay out of all that. In extreme form, the argument goes: A new labor party would atomize American political life and the labor movement as well, which is what happened in Czarist Russia before the Bolsheviks, and in the Weimar Republic before Hitler. "In a great society," says one liberal labor spokesman, "the scales of political freedom can be balanced only by two great parties. . . . The progressive task is to work within this system and not to break it."

For those labor leaders who cannot understand such obtuse political reasoning, the fearful consequences lie closer to the operation of pure and simple unionism: to set up a labor party would infuriate many employers with whom the business unionist has to deal in a practical way. Those employers would be less tolerant during the course of negotiation, and thus the main business of the business unions would be disrupted by unbusiness-like political conduct.

To come out for a labor party would also be a tactless piece of public relations. It would put labor in the spotlight, a target for the whole community of opinion, indeed a slow-moving target for high-powered verbal rifles. Events are moving too rapidly, some labor leaders believe, for labor to take the center of the stage with a slowly building independent political weapon.

v. The explicit arguments for and against a new labor party are wholly on the plane of the unions' good and the unions' security. But back of these arguments there are personalities. The labor leader's view depends in some part upon the image he has of his own role in any new party.

A new party for labor would mean either that the present labor leaders take on new tasks or that new men assume them. In either case, there is opposition from present leaders. Some labor leaders assume that "the same leadership would have double duties," and that "labor needs its leaders where they are; a labor party would take from the labor union many of its leaders. Labor's strength would be dissipated, weakened, and undermined." Such men apparently do not think anyone but the present labor leaders could operate the new party.

Yet any new party would undoubtedly require and create new leaders. Many present leaders are fully aware of this: it is behind their traditional denunciation of intellectuals, who in fact have consistently supported independent political parties.

Some labor leaders, however, look with personal enthusiasm at the new jobs a new party would create. The major tendency in the career of the union leader has been to move from political ideas to practical politics. Although the older men are more likely to use their time and energy for measures of personal and union security within existing organizations, there is a countertendency among the young men who have had swift success. If a young man is already at or near the top of the union world, he may be looking ambitiously for new outlets. He is more energetic in organizing new unions or extending the unions that exist, and he takes more readily to political channels of ascent. He is less likely to be satisfied with the prestige he rates in existing political organizations, and more likely to hold an image of his success in terms of other power hierarchies.

The younger lieutenants in the union world are more inclined to participate, even if unofficially, in new political attempts. Within their own unions they may have to run errands, but in small political groupings anxious for labor support, they represent labor. Some of these young Turks, it is said, were not very alarmed about the labor legislation of summer, 1947, for they saw this as a possible way to rid themselves of the many riders of the union movement and as increasing the chances of the labor leader who works in new political ways, as well as in the old manner, for the people he represents.

Social origin, age, and position in the union may influence the amount and type of political activity in which a labor leader engages. Once having identified themselves with the purposes of labor unions, men coming from higher occupational, educational, and social levels tend to be more assertive than the sons of laboring men and capable of a peculiar kind of middle-class indignation.

If such middle-class zeal is channeled politically, given the higher educational levels that accompany it, we might expect more labor party action from labor leaders of middle-class extraction than from the sons of the proletariat. Among leaders of the CIO, 54 per cent of the men with non-wage-worker origins as against 41 per cent with wage-worker origins favor a new party in the next ten years. The corresponding figures for the AFL—25 to 21 per cent—are not significantly different.

The fear of the failure of a new party and of the dire consequences of organizing one dampens the independent political energies of the labor leader. But fear also impels the labor leader to proceed with the task. In the end, how a man stands on this issue rests upon what he fears the most, and why.

Among the fearful are, first, those who believe that business is stronger than labor and is out to break the unions; second, those who fear fascism as a serious threat in the United States; and third, those who are fearful of the disunity of labor, and feel that labor organizations should, but will not, get together against the enemies that confront them. The leaders who are most fearful in these respects are generally also the most enthusiastic about a new labor party. Here are the proportions in favor of a new labor party, now or eventually:

	AFL	CIO
Most fearful	37%	59%
Intermediate	22%	58%
Least fearful	16%	27%

In the AFL, 37 per cent of the most fearful are for a new labor party, whereas only 16 per cent of the least fearful are for it; but in the CIO, it is 59 to 27 per cent. Among American labor leaders, it is generally the complacent who are least willing to take the risk of building a new labor party.

PART FIVE

CHAPTER THIRTEEN

THE MAIN DRIFT

DURING NOVEMBER, 1946, the mass public was polled for its opinion on whether "all corporations should or should not be required to put a union representative on their board of directors?" For most people the question contained a completely new idea, which makes it all the more startling that 42 per cent said they were in favor of including a union man.

The idea is no mere fancy of some poll-taker in search of his monthly quota of questions. It is in line with the very best liberal rhetoric, slightly extended; it is not outside the possibility of the co-operative relations earnestly desired by many labor leaders.

Co-operative relations between business and labor are rooted in the desire for peace and stability on the part of businessmen, labor leaders, and political officials. Such desires, with their monopolistic consequences, were back of the citywide labor-business cartel. Now, on a much larger scale, with consequences that go beyond pure and simple monopoly, a tacit sort of plan to stabilize the political economy of the U.S. is back of many current demands of the spokesmen of the three powerful bureaucracies in the U.S. political economy.

This conspiracy does not include the extremists in any of the camps. It is primarily a plan among the liberal spokesmen, although it is no doubt aided and abetted by the sophisticated conservatives.

Stabilization requires further bureaucratization of business enterprise and labor union. Given present industrial arrangements, it also involves amalgamating the union bureaucracy with the corporation's. This may occur either in the technical *place of work,* in the *economic enterprises* making up a given industry, or among the industries forming the *political economy* as a whole. So far there are American instances only of the first two kinds, except for one brief experiment with the third.

Peaceful Shops and Stable Enterprises

Business-labor co-operation within the place of work means the partial integration of company and union bureaucracies. By seeking to collaborate in making and administering company rules, the union is a megaphone for the voice of the worker, just as the company hierarchy is a loudspeaker for the voice of management. If the union is efficient, the worker's gripes will receive attention from the shop steward and, if necessary, go on up the union and company hierarchies to the president of the union and his lawyers and the president of the company and his lawyers. This is the power aspect of the arrangement and its mechanics from the worker's point of view.

But for something gained, something must be given. The integration of union with plant means that the union takes over much of the company's personnel work, becoming the disciplining agent of the rank and file within the rules set up by the joint committee.

The union bureaucracy stands between the company bureaucracy and the rank and file of the workers, operating as a shock absorber for both. The more responsible the union is, the more this is so. Responsibility is held for the contract signed with the company; to uphold this contract the union must often exert pressure upon the workers. Discipline must be brought to bear if unauthorized leaders call unauthorized strikes. The rank-and-file leaders of the union, the shop stewards, operating as whips within the plant, become rank-and-file bureaucrats of the labor leadership. As foremen are responsible to the company hierarchy, so shop stewards are primarily answerable to the labor union hierarchy, rather than to the rank and file who elect them.

On December 11, 1945, the Automobile Workers released a proposed agreement with the Ford Motor Company whereby the company and the union agreed that ". . . any employer or employees found guilty of instigating, fomenting, or giving leadership to an unauthorized stoppage of work shall be subject to discharge." In such cases the union would act as judge and prosecutor. Workers who follow unregulated militants, acting without due authority, are subject to penalties. To have no strikes is the responsibility of both company and union. They are disciplining agents for each other, and both discipline the malcontented elements among the unionized employees.

In November, 1946, a local of the United Steelworkers, another member of the new industrial aristocracy of unionism, signed a contract containing a "mutual responsibility clause" by which "the local union, any of its members, or the company" might be financially liable for the reasonable costs of "strikes, work stoppages, or lockouts of any nature or condition" that might occur. The international cannot be held responsible, nor can the local if it or a majority of its members do not participate in the strike. Presumably this means that the individual adherent to unauthorized strikes is to be individually punished.

"Such an agreement, even so watered down," says a national businessman's organ, is "typical of what management wants in new labor agreements." The union's motive for accepting such terms was a desire to continue "union security provisions." This was acceptable to the company officials who reasoned that such provisions "would be necessary if the union should be called upon to enforce its responsibility to management by disciplining contract-breakers." In addition, the union was willing to go along because an AFL union "was maintaining friendly relations with management and obviously was awaiting an opportunity to edge out the CIO and take over the whole jurisdiction." Since the great organizing drives of the Thirties, employers have gotten into the habit of distinguishing between "good responsible unions" and "bad irresponsible unions." The competition between AFL and CIO thus furthers responsible co-operation.

These examples of the bureaucratic integration of labor unions with business enterprises involve large industrial unions which deal with big corporations. The integration is often more far-reaching where a big union deals with an industry composed of many scattered small-scale business enterprises. In such cases, the union is the most stable element in the entire industry and takes the primary role as stabilizing agent. Here the co-operation assumes a more obvious relevance for the economics of the industry as a whole.

An agreement signed by the International Ladies Garment Workers Union in 1941 provided for "obligatory standards of efficiency in plant management and empowered the union to hale before the impartial chairman any manufacturer who failed to live up to these standards." "The businessmen of the industry," writes the official historian of the union, "retain the rights of management": the union "accepts the premises of free enterprise," but "imposes upon the management the obligation of efficiency." Because "there can be no security in an insecure industry," the union took upon itself the job of rationalizing the industry as a whole and insisting upon "efficient management and merchandising by the employer." In the entire industry, this union is the richest and largest single organization in "a jumble of jobbers, manufacturers, sub-manufacturers, contractors, and sub-contractors." It can afford, therefore, to take a statesman-like view. Each one of the contractors and jobbers and sub-manufacturers continues to get his profits under the planning and rationalization imposed by the union. It is not surprising that employers come to the "management engineering" department established by this union to ask and receive aid on time and motion studies, plant layouts, and other information designed to increase production.

Golden and Ruttenberg, men with experience in CIO steel, discuss labor-management co-operation in a manner reminiscent of any of several spokesmen for the garment industry talking of an "efficient" labor-business cartel. "Union-management co-operation tends to make management more efficient and unions more cost-conscious, thereby improving the competitive position of a business enterprise, and increasing the earnings of both workers and owners," write these steel unionists; and they quote with approval the happy managers of unionized plants and Ordway Tead's classic statement of worker reasons for business-labor co-operation: "There is a real sense in which the affiliated workers of an industry have more at stake in helping an industry than the salaried managers or the scattering of absentee stockholders."

The union most obviously acts in the economic interests of the worker in bargaining for increased wages, directly and indirectly. The union is a jobber of labor power, selling it as dearly as the market will bear. And the market increasingly narrows down to a dozen or so bargaining tables. Now, co-operation implies a definite and mutual objective between the co-operators. But the company wants its labor power to be as cheap as possible, whereas the union, in so far as it operates as a union is supposed to operate, wants wages as high as possible. If one enterprise gives higher wages than other competing enterprises, to maintain its level of profit it will have to charge higher prices, thus endangering its competitive relations with the other enterprises.

There is a solution: wages may be set for an entire industry, so that no one business enterprise will have cheaper labor costs than any other. Here on the industry level, true co-operation rather than compromise is possible: all the corporations forming the industry, along with the industrywide union, can pass on to the consumers (in the end, mainly the workers in other industries) the higher costs involved, and thus maintain high profits and high wages. Within the industry there is no real conflict between business and labor.

In their search for security and in the realization of their basic economic character and strategy, labor unions further the tendency to rationalize the job sphere by setting up job hierarchies and rules of conduct within the establishment. They further the rationalization of the social organization of work, and they extend the standardization and monopoly aspects of the economy. They would, as we have said, rationalize production without socializing it.

There are, of course, counter-tendencies. While one set of unions utilizes all technological developments, making semi-skilled and unskilled workers more important than skilled workingmen, other unions, such as the Musicians, look to the security of present members and fight for craft-like formations within the great industry.

Older craft unionists fought hard for job control through the closed shop to aid organization. Now the closed shop makes for peace and stability; it therefore fascinates many businessmen as well as many labor leaders. The electrical contractors, for example, fear legislation which would abolish the closed shop in their industry. The union, policing its contracts by this means, stabilizes its tenure; "cutthroat competition leading to chaos" might result from open shop conditions. Often businessmen see the closed shop as an asset in those areas of free private enterprise where there is free competition.

The big industrial monopolists show a similar concern to the degree that they understand the extent to which the new aristocracy of labor would go with its attempts to establish a form of profit sharing. In 1938, while business was still bad, the U.S. Steel Corporation suggested to Philip Murray that the Steel Workers Organizing Committee accept a wage cut. The union leader refused, but went on to demonstrate the possibilities of a more modern kind of union-management co-operation: "They advised against price cuts and put pressure on Washington in June, 1938, to delay a monopoly investigation of the steel industry, the TNEC hearings on steel, at a time when increased competition might have caused price and wage cuts. Pointing to the 'terror-stricken condition of the steel industry brought about by a system of cutthroat competition,' the chairman of the SWOC said in October, 1938: 'If the steel corporations cannot put their house in order, it is the avowed purpose of the organized steel workers in this nation to promote a constructive legislative program that will adequately protect the interests of the industry and its workers.'" That cutthroat competition had reduced the steel industry to terror was news to economists who had for decades been using the steel industry as the classic example of rigid monopoly pricing. It is clear that the labor leaders had lined up with the vested interests of the industry against the general business community, not to mention the public. "What would Judge Gary have said," Dwight Macdonald has asked, "if he had been told that fifteen years after his death, not only would his steel corporation be unionized, but that this union would come out as the protecting champion of the great monopoly price structure he had devoted his life to creating?"

Demands for stability in the plant and enterprises of an industry point to a third level of business-labor co-operation: the political economy as a whole. The more the implications of the concrete demands for peace and security are thought through, the more they point toward nationwide co-operation, under state control. Business-labor cartels can exist in a scattering of industries without governmental sanction, but as unions and trade associations grow bigger and make more co-operative deals, the state steps in and regulates the total structure of business-labor co-operation. Over the last two decades, the liberal state in America has felt the drive to stability and has been greatly moved by it.

The Liberal State

One of the trends characterizing U.S. society and accelerated by the New Deal is the increasing integration of real and, more particularly, potential democratic forces into the apparatus of the political state. This is part of the steady long-term shift in the locus of power from representative bodies, such as Congress, to administrative agencies, such as labor boards.

Often in this situation, politics becomes a battle between various pressure organizations represented by lawyers and technicians, not understood or participated in by the masses of people. As they bargain for economic power and maneuver for better positions, the leaders of these organizations must discipline their members. Their attempt to "bore from within" the state apparatus is accompanied by the desire to maintain their organizations intact, even to the point of ritualistically losing sight of their ends in their frenzy to maintain their means. The associations, including labor unions, lose their independence of action; thus they ensnare one another.

The New Deal was an attempt to subsidize the defaults of the capitalist system. Part of this attempt consisted in the effort to rationalize business and labor as systems of power in order to permit a continued flow of profits, investments, and employment.

Under the NIRA,* the businessmen of each industry were allowed to agree among themselves, and with the employees, on the terms of business. They could set prices of products and wages of workers. Such a scheme differed from the old business-labor cartel idea in its nationwide scope and in that the Federal government was policing "fairness," relaxing the anti-trust laws accordingly.

Most of what was written on labor in the Thirties says a great deal about section 7-A and the less well-known section 7-B of the NIRA. It is true that these sections gave the unions an official go-ahead to organize labor and to represent it in the code making. But to study only this aspect of the NIRA is to be guilty of a superficial, pro-labor bias in the interpretation of the meaning of the act. This act must be seen in terms of its meaning for business-labor co-operation on the level of industrial solidarity and within the political economy as a whole. What it amounted to was an attempt to governmentalize business-labor cartels, nationwide, industry by industry.

In its objective function, it was similar to the Italian idea of the corporate state: to unify the employer and the employee class within each industrial combine. It tried to give sovereignty to the monopoly unions and sovereignty to the trade associations, each in its proper sphere, and co-sovereignty to the trade associations and labor associations in their common spheres of action.

* National Industrial Recovery Act of 1933; in May, 1935, the Supreme Court declared the NIRA unconstitutional.

NIRA failed, first because not even the amount of political power delegated by Congress to Roosevelt was sufficient to enforce the co-operation; and at that time the unions were neither big enough nor wise enough in the ways of security-seeking to uphold the arrangement voluntarily. Secondly, the practical conservatives were strongly against NIRA; the small businessmen feared they would be squeezed out by the agreements between the monopolies of labor and of capital. They were of too much political importance to Roosevelt, a sophisticated conservative, to be ignored. Finally, by the time NIRA was invalidated, the economy was somewhat improved, so that those who had been frightened relaxed, feeling they might get out of trouble in some other, more old-fashioned way.

To be successful in industrywide bargaining, a union must be monopolistic. In its negotiating and policing work, it cannot allow one of its sectors, or some other union, to set a different pay scale and conditions for a specific local area. Nor can the corporative system be allowed to give its employees freedom to choose their unions. There must be a monopolistic union co-operating with a monopolistic trade association.

The Wagner Act * embodied in law a principle that is repugnant to the idea of monopolistic unions: the right of employees to choose their union representatives by majority vote, and the right to review or change that decision. The Wagner Act compelled all industries to observe the principle of choice, first legislated in the Railway Labor Act of 1926.† But the Wagner Act came into being under the spell, as it were, of the corporate state idea behind the NIRA and the experience of the boards operating under the NIRA. In the sequence of political fact, the Wagner Act was adopted to replace NIRA when it ended.

Unequal bargaining power between employee and employer, it was believed, leads to depressions "by preventing the stabiliza-

* The National Labor Relations Act of July, 1935. It was upheld by the Supreme Court in 1938.

† Its electoral machinery and other features were somewhat revised in 1934 and 1936.

tion of competitive wage rates and working conditions." The Wagner Act claimed to equalize this power. We want to make sure, its makers said, that (1) workers have the right to organize and to bargain collectively; (2) employers have no right to interfere with the formation of unions or to hamper their organizing; (3) the appropriate bargaining unit is decided for the workers' organization; (4) an election is held, if necessary, by which a majority of the workers in a unit may choose their union representatives; and (5) the union they choose is certified as the "exclusive bargaining agent" for that unit.

Elections under NLRB auspices determined which union was to be given the monopoly and excluded minority unions. The Wagner Act changed the basis of the monopoly by making it possible for the employees, by a shift in majority opinion, to destroy or to change the monopoly agent. It institutionalized the basis of monopoly for the union and, within the liberal state framework, guaranteed its democratization.

The power of the union is thus in part dependent upon the continuation of the governmental framework and in part upon the majority will of the employees. Union power is no longer directly dependent upon the strength it has accumulated and put into a direct arrangement with the employer. Every labor leader knew that the Taft-Hartley amendment of the law, enacted in the summer of 1947, might do much to break the power of the unions, particularly the power of those union leaders who had been leaning more on the national administration and its policies than on the massed force of the unionized workers.

One next step in this sequence of law is clear. The industrywide monopolies may be forced to shed their somewhat private character. They may become objects of regulation by government bodies who will outlaw strikes and compel arbitration of various kinds. They will next become, in practical effect if not formal law, organs of the state which protects their power, even as they have been during the late war. We cannot yet tell how fast the administration of the Taft-Hartley law will move in this direction. But the dialectic of business and labor and government has reached a stage where the state, in the interests of domestic stability and international security, increasingly appropriates the aims of the employer and expropriates or abolishes the functions of the unions.

This is the threat of increased labor-business co-operation within the system of private enterprise. This is the blind alley into which the liberal is led by the rhetoric of co-operation. This is the trap set by the sophisticated conservative as he speaks of the virtues of the great co-operation.

Where Does Labor Stand?

The labor leader is walking backwards into the future envisioned by the sophisticated conservatives. By his long-term pursuit of the short end, he is helping move the society of the United States into a corporate form of garrison state. The steps he has taken and where he now stands may be summarized as follows:

I. An enlarged scale of production leads to the corporate form of business enterprise; labor unions arise as a counter-force to this corporate form. The unions are economic attempts to equalize the bargaining power of the workers and the corporations. They give power to the worker for use against the power of property, although this fact does not appear in their operating ideology. Nevertheless, they would turn labor from a commodity into a job empire with some of the rights which property bestows upon the owners of the material facilities of production.

The liberal center's theory of labor, based as it is upon the historical experiences and practices of the unions, is anchored in this phase of union history. The fight of the practical conservatives against the unions is directed against their economic function paramount in this phase. The typical businessman in this public wants to break the power of the practical business unions. But other reactions in other forms also begin.

II. To counter enlarging unions, the business community forms trade associations. As histories of their activities make plain, their central aim is the destruction of labor unions or, at least, the neutralization of their practical power. The associations attempt to do this directly by co-ordinating the anti-labor activities of the employers, and indirectly, as managers of the political business of the corporations, by translating business's economic power into political power.

The very existence of the trade associations puts the labor-business fight into the political arena. They force labor into government up to its neck. During the World War I period and afterwards, they tried directly to break the unions; but since the late Thirties and especially after World War II, they have tried to control the unions through the government. Such political power and pressure as labor did exert upon the New Deal government was seldom effective against the trade associations.

The unions, to match industrywide trade associations, seek industrywide power; a strike seeks to set wage rates and conditions of labor in an entire industry rather than in a plant or a local area. The small businessmen are particularly hurt by industrywide agreements; their smaller plants do not have the efficiency to meet standards of labor costs generally modeled upon the economics of the larger dominant firms.

The piling up of business power in corporate monopolies co-ordinated by trade associations is paralleled by a concentration of union power. At the point of attempted negotiation, the "power centers," the big unions and the big corporations, dicker for smaller firms or smaller unions, resetting the pattern of labor-management relations.

Decisions within each power hierarchy become centralized, being made by top officers of big corporations and unions, not by shop stewards and plant foremen; the decisions become complicated and inflexible, for the men around the bargaining tables are unfree in that each talks for multiple interests and, given the great power each is handling, everything he says has larger political (class) overtones.

Along with corporations and trade associations, the unions increase the tendency toward monopoly and industrywide standardizations. Arrangements become more embracing and more rigid, while the possibility of crisis becomes more perilous. In their search for security and in their struggle against a government increasingly dominated by trade associations, the leaders of the unions find themselves more deeply involved with the national state.

III. Increasingly, this state becomes the regulator of the national labor force, a task previously performed by individual employers and their unions, with only the courts intervening. As the fight takes on crucial national significance, the state is the only group which can take over.

Not only are employer functions backed up or even taken over by the government, but the fight itself is governmentalized. Matters that were primarily economic now become political. Contrary to the liberal theory of the state, the government is not a neutral umpire using its impartial wisdom to effect a fair balance; it is increasingly a political instrument of employers, or at least a new amalgamation of business and governmental power. Confronted with state encroachment upon labor-business relations, the economic power of the unions declines. Every economic tactic is as dependent for its success upon the political authorities as it is upon the economic strength to withdraw the worker from the process of production.

The state takes over plants or mines when they are in trouble with the unions; it becomes the top personnel authority for the businesses involved; and the business managers down the line continue to operate the firm and the stockholders continue to receive the profits.

Under such conditions, for whatever express intent, strikes become more political than ever. Free collective bargaining becomes less a contest between the economic power of business and labor and more a contest between political pressures and influences. Using their economic power, unions become merely troublesome, unless they are backed up by political power.

✦

IV. In this political process, the labor leader faces a difficult problem. The state and the economy interpenetrate; during slump, war, and boom, the tie-ins tend to become ever closer. Yet labor unions as organizations and as memberships are oriented only in the economic sphere. They have no political program. Short-run decisions and pressures and struggles do not give any long-run answer to major political questions.

This is not merely an inadequacy of the labor leaders as a power elite; their organizations are primarily economic. In the cohesion of a union, for instance, it is the practical economic factor that is uppermost. It is the man who delivers higher wages who is most likely to succeed. If a labor leader begins to work for a political act not immediately and obviously involving an economic gain for his membership, immediately he will be accused of working for personal glory and selfish power. If he takes a longer-run political chance, he may get into short-term economic trouble with his members, who, at the present time, are often politically passive and politically and economically illiterate, not yet realizing clearly that they are living not in an economy separate from a political order but in a political economy.

In so far as the union is responsible, the reason for this apathy and lack of understanding began with the organizing slogans by which members were cajoled to join: they talked only about bread and butter. And there is no workers' education program adequate to remedy the bad beginnings.

Labor leaders, therefore, seem poor bets as far as political action is concerned. Many neither want nor are really able to participate in a political movement, for their character and the tradition of the organizations they lead have selected and formed them as different sorts of men: many are indeed the last representatives of the economic man.

V. Labor leaders as a whole are acting in the latter phases of the main political and economic development as if they were still in the earlier phases. They lag greatly, and this causes leak and friction. Yet in their drive for stability, using the old strategies and equipment, they tend, along with the coinciding forces of government and business, to modify the larger system in which they operate.

In order to secure the unions and to stabilize their business-like gains, the labor leaders allow their unions to evolve into institutions which integrate the industrial worker into a political economy that is changing from laissez-faire to monopoly and to a state capitalism with many corporate features. The labor leaders become part of a machinery which keeps them as leaders but makes them the go-betweens of the rank and file of workers and the class of owners and managers.

In our time, when capitalism is deeply troubled and labor unions emerge as strong stabilizing influences, the labor leaders drift toward some sort of over-all bargain with industrywide trade associations whose agents infiltrate governing agencies. They become keepers of stability and, under threat, move to join forces with established monopoly industry, to fight together against unorganized sections of the economy—small farmers, white-collar employees, consumers, little business. They would stabilize what they have.

The slogans of the liberal center justify these groupings as business-labor co-operation and view the state as a benevolent umpire and a great agent of compromise. But within a monopoly economy, the economics of co-operation and the politics of compromise lead to a strange coincidence of forces; this is a dangerous game.

The strategy of the labor leader in his present situation is to narrow the struggle by working for its institutionalization. Yet his fearful search for safety in legal and institutional guarantee means that he must act as discipliner of the labor force, the basis of any power he may have. He begins with the sanctity of union contracts and he moves toward control of labor-management relations by a government over which he has little real power.

Two habits of labor leader policy facilitate this trend. The first, which began on a large scale under Roosevelt and was strengthened by the wartime setup, is looking to the government or to particular politicians rather than to the workers. The second is thinking of his movement essentially as a minority affair, which must balance its power against others, rather than as a potential majority movement with which to reorganize modern society.

Given the state of power within the government and within and between the dominant political parties, governmentalization of the economy means subsidizing the free enterprise system at home and abroad.

The practical conservative's drive to break the unions ("all of them are crooked") rather than to shackle and use them ("let us make the unions responsible") upsets the coincidence of forces back of the main drift. Yet this drive makes for confusion and national inconvenience, which "the public" demands be remedied. In turn, the public's demand that something be done is the most ostensible and important prod to the state to move further along in the main drift. The state as presently constituted, and acting in a political milieu containing only the two major parties, can go only in that direction. The coming slump, intensifying the demands from all sides that something be done, will facilitate the whole process.

In the meantime, because of the present organization of political parties, this dialectic goes on behind men's backs, and particularly behind the backs of the labor leaders. Within the present party system, labor organizations and union members do not have the power of decision: they are not even able to confront the live alternatives. Day after day they hear the clamor of the public that something must be done; but they don't know what to do, and they are afraid.

CHAPTER FOURTEEN

ALTERNATIVES

THE MAIN drift goes on behind men's backs, but what do the men who lead see before them, and what are their plans? Not all leaders are confronted at all times with real alternatives, and only leaders of great stature ever see beyond the details of immediate and compelling decisions; ordinarily they do not gain the vision required to grasp their situation, the various ways out of it, and the possible consequences of each alternative.

Men in power are like men playing poker: no one of them knows just what he will do until the one next to him has done what the one next to *him* has forced upon him. That is a more realistic image than that of isolated thinkers confronted with clear choices of sharp alternatives. Yet ideas are relevant in this poker game of power.

The American labor leader does not usually initiate political programs and strategies. Generally he follows the ideology of traditional business unionism, which developed when organized labor was a minority stratum in the skilled labor market, and of liberal state unionism, which grew from traditional business unionism in contact with mass industry and from the welfare state notions of the New Deal.

Today neither liberalism nor business strategy avail against the main drift. If rigorously pursued, either idea may be economically troublesome to the executives of American society, but politically, both are merely aspects of the main drift. In the meantime, for new ideas which might open up a way out, the labor leader seems dependent upon the political intellectuals, whose ideas sometimes engage the attention and support of various political publics.

The question, "What is to be done?" may be answered by proposals of next steps, by statements of programs, or by exhortations of general principles.

Most members of the mass public, like many labor leaders, live below the high level of alertness that characterizes politically minded groups. Following scattered political expedients, they are usually creatures of the next step and take to general principles more readily than to programs. Many of the independent left have lost their will for next steps; entertaining only general principles, they sometimes mistake isolated next steps for morally motivated programs. Liberals and practical conservatives, between whom the main political struggle now goes on, are equally expert in the next step and the hortatory principle; neither of them has any program.

Programs state next steps leading to a principled image. Thus to have a program means to trace the consequences of any proposed next step upon the image of the world projected in principle. Only two political publics now seem to have programs; they represent the extreme political positions, the sophisticated right and the far left.

The program of the sophisticated conservatives is not usually stated in terms of its long-term consequences; nevertheless, it may be inferred from their proposals of next steps and their general principles. Always tainted with liberal rhetoric, its assertions are addressed to a mixed political public composed of the practical right, the liberal center, and the educated members of the mass public.

The program of the far left does not often clothe itself in liberal rhetoric in an attempt to win over or use the liberal center. In fact, by the public relations-minded standards of sophisticated conservatives, it is naïvely outspoken and stupidly rational. Yet when put together with the ideas of those independent leftists who are still thinking politically, it is radical in the literal sense. It attempts to get to the root of what is happening and what might be done about it.

The Program of the Right

Unlike their "practical" colleagues, the sophisticated conservatives see the world, rather than some sector of it, as an object of profit. They have planned a series of next steps which amount to a New Deal on a world scale operated by big businessmen. In so far as the New Deal was a program—or in so far as its expediencies may now be looked at together—it tried to make good the defaults of the capitalist system in America. Sophisticated conservatives objected only when, in so doing, the New Deal lifted national consumer power or helped small men whom New Deal theorists claimed to be also part of the capitalist system. To operate this system on a world scale it is necessary to think politically on a world scale.

Many sophisticated conservatives would make loans, which they say are huge, to foreign countries for political as well as economic purposes. They would "grant" money to countries like England, and "loan" money to countries like the Latin Americas; in their effort to stop the leftward drift of the world, whomever they could not control they would team up with. The amount of public money used, write *Fortune* editorialists, would depend on the willingness of U.S. private capital "to seize boldly upon the greatest chance, the greatest 'venture' it has ever faced." This money would be spent "in return for a franchise to live and do business in peace at a profit." That is a straightforward political statement of who would get what.

But where would the money come from? At first it would come "out of the hides of American wage earners, businessmen, and entrepreneurs"—out of taxes. And where would it go? "Nine-tenths of the money loaned would be spent in the U.S. for U.S. goods . . . it has no place else to go." It is as simple as that: we see here the New Deal type of mechanism for saving capitalism operating all over the world. Rather than merely pumping up the wage worker at home so he can buy, the plan is to pump up the world so that U.S. business can control all investments.

According to *Business Week,* Washington and Moscow are maneuvering into position for the eventual showdown. The export boom, as of the summer of 1947, "won't last many months unless the U.S. gives the world a new financial shot in the arm." Russia counts on "a slump in this country due to failure of the capitalist countries to restore trade. The real threat of war lies in the failure to restore this trade." The U.S. "is shaping a new eight-billion-dollar program. . . . Its purpose is to avert a threatened economic collapse in Europe and a violent cut in U.S. exports." The former would mean "political results that Washington would hardly welcome"; and as for the latter: "the U.S. could hardly escape the crash if we try to pull out just now." These are not isolated items; they represent the continuous reasoning of the sophisticated conservative in the middle of the Forties.

"We are asking the U.S. businessman," writes *Fortune,* "to think of Wendell Willkie's 'One World' not in fancy geopolitical terms, but merely in market terms." In describing the glories of capitalist expansion in terms of what father and son did, they ask: "Is this expansion from local ironmonger to 'national distribution' ordained to stop there? The task of expanding trade in stove pipe from a national to an international range is a tricky and often exasperating business, but there is money in it." This is the image of the profitable world of U.S. power, with Britain waning and Russia waxing strong.

Along with the U.S. public's money would go "the friendly collaboration of technical staffs." These latter would "help in the most efficient spending of the sums loaned." For to make foreign markets profitable for American businessmen, even if through subsidy by the taxpayer, "is something much nobler than sitting back and yammering at the State Department about 'policy,' as if we of the business community were not part of that and could not develop a policy *in our own terms.*"

The late war has brought about a world situation in which it is not necessary for a capitalist power such as the United States to resolve its internal contradictions in the classic manner of exporting at the point of a gun. War production and postwar boom should not obscure the ten-year slump that preceded. Everyone knew that the productive facilities could then have done what they did so easily during the war; everyone knew that for a time the governmental subsidy, which in economic fact the war was, would activate the system. Now it seems clear that, sooner or later, there will be another slump. Only if the world economy can be reconditioned can U.S. capitalism use it in order to allay her own internal cycle.

The dilemma of the U.S. abroad is clear: in order to set up and maintain an anti-Russian bloc, she must subsidize her late enemies, Japan and Germany, as well as her ally in arms and only competitor in the world market, Great Britain. But these countries cannot experience an expanded economy either, unless they share in the world market to some extent. Particularly is this true of Britain, which is using some of the three billion U.S. loan to compete with U.S. industry. Everybody wants to export, nobody can afford to import. "Britain has announced that it must sell 75 per cent more goods than prewar to balance its trade books. France's Monet Plan calls for an 87 per cent increase in export volume. . . . And so it goes . . . to maintain full employment," says *Business Week* in January, 1948, "it has been carefully estimated that our [U.S.] total export volume must be about three times that of the years just before World War II. Our exports of machinery and vehicles must be about five times greater."

This foreign program is now the spinal nerve of the sophisticated conservative's plan: its principle is a world profitable for U.S. business; its next steps are the massive politically guided loans, paid for by the U.S. people. We live and will continue to live in the shadow of World War III, which, according to the sophisticated conservative, is to be organized "conjunctively between business and government." There must be a "concert of policy between business and government."

The present boom is an economic echo of war; the government that originated this boom is, in fact, an active agent in its continuance. It has given heavy credits and loans to foreign countries, thus enabling them to place orders for capital goods with U.S. industry. It is spending large sums on military items and in subsidies of other sorts. The staggering after-tax profits made by corporations during and after the war have piled up, and there is a heavy cash reserve available on suitable terms for industrial purposes. The war dammed up a demand by stopping the production of durable consumer goods; it made the demand effective, for a time, by creating full employment and maintaining prices at relatively low levels for four or five years. The farmers, who of all sizable classes in the population benefited most economically from the war, have a continued chance for prosperity because of governmental price minimums and because a starving world hungers for the farm produce of the U.S. But each of these things may pass. Boom and war go together; unless there is a quick buildup for another war, it looks like slump.

All this is taken into account by the sophisticated conservatives. They say: if our program is not carried out, there will be serious military and political consequences on a world scale, as well as domestic economic consequences for which we cannot take responsibility. There will be a horrible slump in the U.S., and she will lie prostrate before Russia, who will thus win the world by default in the struggle of The Last World War. We cannot do business with Russia. "It is to businessmen that we must look, for they now have an almost everlasting power of choice."

In the history of capitalism, the sophisticated conservatives are doing an old job, with vigor and skill, under new conditions. Politically they would build up to a war with Russia, and economically they would figure out a way of getting rid of "excess production" until war production again brings profit to U.S. businessmen at home and abroad. It is a consistent view, and its image of our future is plain.

Foreign programs have their domestic reasons: it is their domestic troubles that interest the sophisticated conservatives in coming to the fore as policy makers for the right. Up to the Thirties, capitalist progress favored the ideology of the practical conservative. The business community of the United States has not been economically fascinated by foreign adventure. Even in its best years of foreign trade, less than 10 per cent of U.S. production has been exported. In the general framework of the political economy, not much has depended upon either the politics or the economics of imperialism. But the slump of the Thirties scared the right, and during this period its more far-sighted members began to understand how to avoid a recurrence. In its magnitude, the slump of 1929-39 was qualitatively different from earlier slumps. The United States entered the second World War without having solved the conditions of that slump. Her productive apparatus had not been fully employed for 10 years, and 10,000,000 workers were out of work. During the war, the United States enormously increased this productive apparatus. As Fritz Sternberg has shown, the U.S., in the middle Forties, can produce some 50 per cent more industrially and some 33 per cent more agriculturally than before the war.

Now there is no war. U.S. business must find a market for this potential flood of goods.

Only one major capitalist country came out of the last slump before the war: Nazi Germany demonstrated that unemployment in capitalist society can be solved by a war economy during peacetime. There are other ways besides a war economy of trying to prime the pump, but either they are not politically or technically possible on a large-enough scale or they weaken the class position of the conservatives and strengthen that of the workers and middle-class employees.

The liberal state might meet the problem by deficit spending on public works or by subsidizing consumption directly and indirectly, income being redistributed from higher to lower classes. The first method would require WPA's, new roads, family allowances, etc. The second might be accomplished by reducing the prices of consumers' goods while holding wages constant, or holding prices constant and allowing wages to rise, or by taxation graded sharply according to income levels, shifting income in some political way from real profits to real wages in order to increase effective demand.

In so far as they can avoid it, conservatives, both practical and sophisticated, will not seriously consider such techniques. To the contrary, the present anti-labor offensive is part of a pro-slump policy. In so far as labor is weakened, politically and economically, labor's share of the income is decreased, which means that the very purchasing power needed to stave off slump is being drained. Consumption would have to be raised 40 or 50 per cent above 1939, and there would have to be profit ceilings and price and investment controls, to prevent a slump by such internal means.

Reasonable people, who believe such added consumer powers will be politically given in order to prime the economic pump, overlook the political framework required for such economic mechanisms. Within liberal society, the system of economic balances has a power aspect; in a very real sense it is a precarious balance of class forces rather than a natural harmony of producers and consumers.

So long as national income is increasing and the system is expanding, the peaceful collaboration of labor unions and trade associations might work *economically;* but in slump, when there is no expansion, the collaboration will not work *politically.* Employers, if not also union leaders, will come to understand that they are not fighting over mere dollars and cents; they are fighting over power.

In such a balance of classes, the government, pulled and pushed by trade associations and, for a while, by labor unions, can be greatly weakened. Out of such perilous balance, there would come from the politically unaware public an urgent demand that somebody do something. In Italy, Germany, Austria, and Spain somebody did something.

The conservative way to economic balance, without disturbing the income and power relations between the classes, is deficit spending in foreign rather than in domestic fields, coupled with building a war economy in time of peace. Even the greatest conceivable expansion of foreign markets in the world today would not alone begin to neutralize the economic factors that are making for slump. The two go together in the American constellation of monopoly power. They form the program of the sophisticated conservative.

"It is not impossible," *Business Week* explained in 1946, "to envisage the day when a spokesman for military needs sits in on every major business decision." Above all a "business recession would quickly send industrial research departments scurrying for federal contracts." Since the war's end, "mobilization factors" assume more and more importance in business policy. Continual "contract development work," on cost-plus-fee basis, rather than a mobilization program when the war is upon us, is the order of the day. Disputes between business and military contracting officials over the terms are minor quarrels.

During the late war, vital decisions, including those of the wartime shape of the U.S. political economy, were often shared by the elites of military violence, monopoly capitalism, and political state. Big business took over many strategic positions of the wartime political economy. Mr. Forrestal, then the Secretary of the Navy, proposed that an administrative elite be developed more or less in the image of the military profession. Its members would be given "sabbatical leaves" in order to participate in "business activities." Informally, something like that is already operating: right after the war many generals went into, or back into, big business. Today, in peacetime, the Department of Commerce is calling many key businessmen important in the late war administration back to their posts.

Two of the most powerful officialdoms of American society, the big businessmen and the officer corps, thus come together within the framework of the democratic state. Those who monopolize the means of production and those who monopolize the means of violence have many interests in common, and any unity on their part obviously threatens democratic control of the political order.

The classic liberal theory of social development—from the unfree military state to the free industrial society—must now be telescoped into a model of a social structure at once military and industrial. What Herbert Spencer took to be a sequence of stages may turn out to be a dialectic, the synthesis of which is now in view.

That the United States has not had a military caste of much consequence means now that it is easy for members of non-military elites to be incorporated into the high ranks of the military. Direct commissions can easily be arranged for business elites, as they were for the railroad colonels of the late war. From the big business side of the alliance, C. E. Wilson, addressing the Army Ordinance Association, has asserted "that we should henceforth mount our national policy upon the solid fact of an industrial capacity for war, and a research capacity for war that is also 'in being' . . . anything less is foolhardy." In the early Thirties, the Nazi theoretician, Ewald Banse also proposed "preparedness science" as "the focus of all scientific work." "It might even be wise," Mr. Wilson publicly continues, to "give reserve commissions to outstanding industrialists to insure their interest and build a closer bond between them and these services." From the union of the military, the scientific, and the monopoly business elite, "a combined chief of staff" for America's free private enterprise is to be drawn.

Mr. Wilson and Mr. Forrestal are logical and realistic spokesmen for their respective interests; they voice the economic and military requirements of the main drift. Each proposal supplements the other; together they present an image of a militarized capitalism in the defense of which they would conscript America.

Their plans solve the two main problems, mass unemployment and world war. Mass unemployment is done away with only by war, and war—as President Roosevelt once remarked—will never be done away with until full employment is attained. According to Mr. Wilson, however, war is "inevitable in our human affairs . . . a basic element in evolutionary peace."

Changes in a social structure as well articulated as this often proceed by bargains between the leaders of various organizations. They may each enter the bargains for different reasons and they may come out of them doing things they never expected. It is not at all impossible that American society may be conscripted for monopoly business on the model of an army garrison under the perilous image of peace by mutual fright.

If the sophisticated conservatives have their way, the next New Deal will be a war economy rather than a welfare economy, although the conservative's liberal rhetoric might put the first in the guise of the second. In the last transition from peace to war, WPA was replaced by WPB.

The establishment of a permanent war economy is a long-time trend. Its pace and tactics will vary according to the phase of the slump-war-boom cycle dominant at any given time. In the phase of inflated boom with great fear of slump, the practical rightists have the initiative, but in the longer historical perspective, they are merely advance shock troops of the big right. Carrying out the old-fashioned policies of the practical conservatives will lead straight into slump. Then the sophisticated conservatives will take over policy-making for the business class as a whole.

The practical conservatives fight the unions; taking a short-run economic view, they try to smash them. In doing so, they further deprive the economy of the purchasing power needed to avoid slump. When the slump comes, the sophisticated conservatives, whose view will be dominant, may continue the labor-smashing policies of the practical right or, if they need the labor leader and his organization as a disciplinary force and can count on co-operation, they may try to capture the labor leader in order to monopolize all chances of independent organization among the rank and file.

The labor leader has to fight the practical conservative who would destroy his job and his union, but in the end, he will have to come to some kind of terms with the program of the sophisticated conservative. In fighting the Utopian capitalist of the practical right, however, the labor leader often assumes the liberal tactics and rhetoric of big business co-operation; he asks for the program of the sophisticated conservative; he asks for a place in the new society which the sophisticated conservative envisions, and which the main drift is bringing. He is not only caught between two evils, but in fighting the one, he is exposing himself to the other. Economic disaster hangs over his head, and in struggling against the political forces leading to it, the labor leader takes a political road and uses a liberal ideology which would bind him to the political economy of the sophisticated conservative.

It is a question of timing and of phases. The program of the practical right means slump. The program of the sophisticated right means war to avoid slump or to recover from it. This cycle of utopian and military policies for capitalism, with its oscillations of slump and war, will end in a corporate state presiding over an industrial society in a war condition, with or without labor leaders. When the military state is joined with private monopoly power, a permanent war economy is required to maintain the productive apparatus in a condition of profitable utilization and society in a state of acquiescent dread.

The Program of the Left

Confronted with the main drift and the program of the right, the American left is now powerless, distracted, and confused. Over most of the world the left has been beaten; and in the last 40 years, when it has won, its victory has often passed into its Thermidor. Men have not won freedom or security, but have remained in the rack of capitalist society or have been quickly geared into an equally alien apparatus of state control.

The program of the right can be presented as an implementation of what is now happening in and to the world, but no left program can honestly be asserted in such a compelling way. What is happening is destructive of the values which the left would implant into modern society: nowhere are leftward forces linked with endeavors that are moving effectively against the main drift. Instead there are scattered tendencies and defenses, and ideas and plans carried by equally scattered intellectuals. The left is neither anchored in the sequence of events nor linked securely with large forces of rebellion. It is socially meager and economically unused. Any statement of its goals and strategy is likely to appear abstract and anti-climactic after an analysis of the linkage of the right's program with the main drift.

The ideas available on the left today are less a program than a collective dream. We choose this word "dream" carefully, for given their powerless condition and lack of movement, what is said by left intellectuals inevitably seems dream-like in quality. We shall not attempt to analyze the historical experience of European socialist parties in their relations with labor unions, nor account for the absence of a socialist movement in the United States. We do not write as party historians nor certainly as party tacticians, for there is no party which we would seriously address. We shall attempt to do only one thing: to make the collective dream of the left manifest. In doing so we shall not try to remove the naïveté of formulation that is now so often part of the low state of American socialist theory.

The social imaginations of left intellectuals in America were greatly stimulated and expanded during the slump of the last decade. During the war, as seems to be the case in modern wars, much ground was lost, and many who were once radical have now given up. Yet the war and its results destroyed many liberal myths and revealed many conservative intentions and consequences.

On the ideological side, the left would replace the myths and compromises of liberalism by concrete analyses and plans. The present impasse of the left prompts its adherents to take new bearings, and drawing upon the last century of left tradition and ideas, to build a plan of attack, a strategical program, and an image of the future. Any survey of left tradition reveals that its aim, stated briefly, has been to democratize the structure of modern society. The left is easily derailed; it forms and re-forms its camps wherever men would exercise their democratic will. When classic socialism was compromised by social democracy, by petty trade unionism and political mugwumping, twentieth-century syndicalism and guild socialism arose as an attempt to restore the more direct democratic impulses of classic left tradition; and today, when the Communists have become the foreign agents of a bureaucratic tyranny, the left struggles to free itself from their influence and to reform as an independent force.

Classic socialism shares its master purpose with classic democracy. The difference between Thomas Jefferson and Karl Marx is a half century of technological change, during which industry replaced agriculture, the large-scale factory replaced the individual workshop, the dependent wage and salary worker replaced the independent proprietor. Left movements have been a series of desperate attempts to uphold the simple values of classic democracy under conditions of giant technology, monopoly capitalism, and the behemoth state—in short, under the conditions of modern life.

In contrast with the left's dream, the formal democracy of twentieth-century America is confined to a narrow political area; the rest of man's life, particularly his work, is left out. Industry, the leftist believes, is now the domain of autocratic decisions which affect people more decisively than anything Congress, hedged in by administrative agencies, might do. Within its enlarged administrative structure, even political democracy is becoming less and less direct; the distant control over the representative makes him unreal to the people, and a creature of forces at the hub. Formal democracy, the leftist continues, does not allow men the opportunity to rule themselves nor offer them the chance to learn self-control in the process of administration.

The left would establish a society in which everyone vitally affected by a social decision, regardless of its sphere, would have a voice in that decision and a hand in its administration. To so democratize modern society, to rebuild it upon the principles of immediate freedom and security, requires that the main drift be stopped, that society be rid of its increasingly managed movement through slump and war.

Power won by election, revolution, or deals at the top will not be enough to accomplish this. In the day-by-day process of accumulating strength as well as in times of social upset, the power of democratic initiation must be allowed and fostered in the rank and file. The leftist believes that a movement must be built powerful enough to put into practice the policies required to stop the main drift and, at the same time, implant into the very mechanisms of society the democratic impulses which it instills and releases in its members. During their struggle, the people involved would become humanly and politically alert.

These are immense goals, but nothing less is possible to the democratic left. What these goals mean to the leftist can be made clear by considering how he strives to move toward them and what instruments he feels are available and required.

As the right focuses its program upon the business leader and makes its demands of the business community, so the left focuses upon the labor leader and makes its demands of the laboring community. Business leaders and labor leaders are the two handles which right and left would grasp; they represent the larger groups which these politically alert publics would set in further motion. The program of the left, however, so far as the labor unions are concerned, attempts to seize upon the root of the matter: man in the process of his work.

I. The unions, in the left's view, should seek to establish a workers' control over the social process of work. This means that in every workshop or its equivalent the unionized workers would continually strive to encroach upon the functions now performed by owners of industry and their appointed managers. The only limits to this encroachment are set by the union's power. Within the union, the organized unit of work is taken as the basis of organization, and the rest of the union built up from there. The workshop, as G. D. H. Cole has said, contains "the most important outposts, though by no means the most important citadels, of capitalism." It is there "that the workers can most easily concentrate their power and take over positive functions." Within the company, the plant is to be taken over by the union to the fullest extent of its power. Ideally, if all management personnel did not show up for work, the plant could be effectively operated by the workers and their unions.

The trade union thus becomes the immediate political community of the worker. Within it, issues that directly affect his daily life are posed for argument and decision. The union contract is seen as a changing constitution of an industrial government, the union as a self-governing agency of the social process of production. No intelligent leftist thinks hours and wages are unimportant, but just as important and often more so are the detailed conditions of work, especially authority in the shop. The union becomes the means of a social revolution in the working life of the worker; it transforms his daily working existence.

This is the beginning point, for the work men do is the central fact of the waking hours of their lives. The questions that touch them concern the organization of their work. If the conditions of labor are oppressive and unfree, if the laborer at work is disciplined by men over whom he has no control, if he is paced by technical and human machinery he does not understand, then, according to the left, his whole life is oppressive. He can be made free only by a democratic organization of the productive process within each plant, shop, office, and place of work in an industry. The questions at issue are precisely those that have been within the prerogatives of management.

To enlarge the democratic power of the worker in the shop, the unions would have to strive to take from the employer the right to appoint supervisors and foremen; the unionized workers would elect their immediate authorities, thus making "the discipline of the shop a matter, no longer of imposition from without, but of self-regulation by the group as a whole." Those who are doing the work would choose their leaders for the work. The union would strive to substitute its democratic organization for the organization of the company by seeking genuinely collective contracts in which the workers' own collective regulations for hiring and firing are substituted for the companies'.

It is not enough, according to the leftist, that the worker be represented on governing bodies by labor union officials. To have a real and felt control over the sphere of his own work, the worker himself must have a more direct chance to have his say. The representative of labor within the plant would function only part-time, retaining his job in the plant.

The unions would proceed toward the establishment of a

democracy inside the workshop in accordance with the principle of independence of labor action. This means independence from the employer and from the state, both of which encroach upon shop organization. The unions would not accept, much less seek, "joint control" or membership in labor-management production committees; they would seek to transfer power over the workshop from the employer's agents into their own hands. A shop stewards' committee elected by the workers would strive to be recognized by the employers, but the employer would have no representative sitting on it. Contracts would at all times be of as short duration as possible, and moreover, they would terminate at the same time those of other unions terminate.

Independence of labor action means continual workers' control at the point of production, which means that the union would attempt to replace management function by workers' control at every point where its power permits. The union would proceed as if it were going to become the organizer of work within this society and the basis for a social reorganization for a future democratic society.

In order to proceed with such a program the unions as they now exist would have to be drastically modified at two points: they would have to greatly expand the basis of their membership, and they would have to be solidly united:

The unions must organize the unorganized, ceasing to be aristocracies of labor, however large, and becoming coextensive with people who work for wages or salary. They must become representative of all the lower strata, not only in order to have the power needed, but because under present conditions, and more so in slump, such an enlargement of members will energize their policies.

The unions would thus become organizations in which the solidarity of all labor becomes real; the unions would unite. They would change from "a congeries of mutually suspicious and often conflicting units into a rationally organized body, following in the main the industrial form of organization, and binding together the whole of the trade unionist workers into a single effectively directed force, really capable of united action on matters of common concern."

To encroach upon management's power over the social organization of work, to expand union membership to be coextensive with all wage and salaried work, to unite in order to be able to exert their accumulation of power most effectively—these require that labor unionists pay attention not only to the shop but to the economics of the industry, as well as to the political spheres of the whole society.

Technical and economic planning is not a politically neutral technique. In fact, no plan capable of solving the slump-war-boom cycle and maintaining full production and employment would be accepted by the conservative members of the main drift or by their liberal allies. Any such plan would inevitably threaten and destroy existing property relations. Therefore every such plan would be advanced by labor and the left along with an exposé of the concrete political and economic reasons for the resistance to it. Instead of trying to educate the Secretary of Commerce or the corporate officialdom, the left would try to educate the people involved. To do otherwise would be to treat political issues as if they were technical problems and to assume, in accordance with the liberal rhetoric, that the economic system of monopoly capitalism is harmonious and rational. To do that would demoralize the workers who believed in the plan. It is acting in an irrational class society as if it were a rational co-operative one.

Neither slump nor war will be avoided within the present American system. To solve these twin issues in a leftist way, the living standard of the U.S. people would have to be raised enormously. It will not be so raised within the present framework. The American right in the modern capitalist state would "solve" the problems of slump by war, or by a permanent war economy. Neither slump nor war, the leftist believes, will be avoided if American society is not economically transformed.

✦

II. The left's economic program for the unions involves a continuous bookkeeping for given industries and for the economy as a whole. A running balance sheet of human needs and economic production, and a public statement of the relations of prices, wages, and profits for each major industry and for the total economy would be kept. Whenever the output appeared to be dropping below what is required for continued full production and employment and the highest possible level of consumption, the union would take up the issue in its negotiations with the industries involved and the union movement with the headquarters of rightist power.

Plans for increasing or maintaining production would immediately be made, in close consultation with the production workers involved. This planning is seen as part of the control from below that is the keystone of the democratic aim of the unions. On the left, plans would be so worked out and so discussed that "each man . . . in control of any particular stage of the process must be aware of the relation of his role in production to that of every other man. That," as Rea Stone puts it, "is the essence of planning."

When their plans are rejected, the unions would follow up with the demand that the industry involved be "nationalized" and that the workers be allowed to run it according to the plans they have set forth. This demand, according to the left, should be put forth positively: if "they" can't do it, we can. Since the rise of the Soviet state, leftist thinkers have become clearer about the meaning of their demand to de-privatize industry, although many aspects of the matter require further clarification. It is not a fetish with them; no leftist believes that such a move would solve all the problems with which he is confronted. But as one concrete link in their program, it is decisive for all leftists.

In left circles today, the slogan of nationalization means nothing unless it is accompanied by concrete plans for socialization involving workers' control. In industrially backward countries, such as India, nationalization may be advanced by struggling capitalists in order to accelerate the countries' progress to modern capitalism. In advanced countries with centuries of capitalism behind them, such as England, nationalization may be resorted to in order to shift the losses and risks of profitless industries off the shoulders of capitalists and onto those of taxpayers. Nationalization and socialization are thus by no means identical.

In the left dream, socialization is a central end; nationalization is seen as an often dangerous means to that end. To nationalize the means of production and distribution without socializing the concrete organization of work, and therewith man himself, is only too likely to result in the incorporation of union bureaucracy with state bureaucracy, both being burdens on the alienated worker and barriers to his daily freedom at work. The left would socialize the means of production in order to further the humanization of man himself. It is in the workshop, more than in the electoral district, that the new man of a free society must be developed. That is why the leftist believes that workers' control, more of it or less of it, should be the first and the continual demand in every union negotiation and strategy.

In addition to socializing the work process, the object of nationalizing industry, in the words of G. D. H. Cole, "is to make the conduct of industry subject to considerations of public policy and to co-ordinate all the industries concerned in accordance with a general plan directed by the working class movement." The public policy most relevant is how to avoid slump without resort to war economy. Short of nationalization, and during the transition, the key demand of the left and of its unions is drastic redistribution of real income, to be accomplished by a sharply graduated income tax, a lifting of indirect consumers' taxation, greatly advanced wages, and greatly reduced price levels.

In the highly developed U.S. production plant there is no necessary disharmony between public control of economic decisions and workers' control within the shop. The modern political imagination has not even begun to be exerted on the potential forms of democracy at this point; according to the left, decentralized shop control and centralized economic planning are entirely compatible. Men in their roles as consumers are distinct from men in their roles as producers, in the first case obviously having more to do with the external relations than the internal conduct of an industry.

Such an economic program for the unions is merely one or two steps from the demands now being raised by the vanguard unions. Labor has moved, as Nat Weinberg, Research Director of the UAW, has recently said, from a bargaining situation based on "the momentary power relationship, as between a local, generally a small employer and a local, frequently a craft union," to a situation in which it has a passive interest in the figures on industrial activity, but without hope of changing the general economic environment which conditions union effectiveness. Recently a third stage has begun: "Some unions, at least, now look upon statistics as social tools . . . as instruments for the measurement of the social performance of our economic machine." Mr. Weinberg reminds us that "the first major collective bargaining campaign was fought out over the wage-price-profit relationship" only in 1945.

Before the rise of the CIO, the small-scale unions, "functioning in the peripheral areas of the economy," made it "futile for labor to think in terms of an over-all economic program. . . . Leaders of the craft unions could function effectively at the expense of the vastly larger group of unorganized wage and salary workers." But already leftist leaders see that 14,000,000 organized people "can make progress only with and not at the expense of the community." Now the organized workers are definitely in the mass-production industries "where the crucial decisions are made which determine the material fortunes of all the American people, and labor is face to face with the decisive power in the economy and conscious of a new responsibility for the welfare of the community as a whole."

III. Just as the shop program is the foundation for the economic program, so the economic program is the base for the political program which the left would have the unions take up. But workshop and economic programs will be bitterly fought on the political front; without a political program, and the accumulation of political power, labor's shop and economic plans do not have a chance.

Labor's political program must rest upon labor's economic strength; but that strength, no matter how hard won, will be shattered if it is not used politically. Yet political triumphs, no matter how great, may mean little or nothing within the present system if they are accompanied by economic failure. Action in each must open possibilities in the other, although in the general view of the left, behind the man in the political organization stands the man in the union, and behind the man in the union stands the man in the shop. Indeed, if those in shop and economy are to do the work assigned them by the program of the left in the transformation of modern society, they need a political wing as independent in its activity and as vigorous in its sphere as the unions are in theirs.

The reason for an economic underpinning for any political action on the part of the left goes beyond the formal fact that political power rests upon economic power. A socialist political program could not be successfully carried through in this society unless training were provided in the more direct democracy of daily life, in the shop and in the unions. Those who are serious about democracy must begin by giving the impulses of man a chance to realize themselves creatively in work. That is the basis for a politics of democratic socialism. Yet there is no need for leftists to limit their struggle to the shop and the economy.

Today, knit together as they are by trade associations, the corporations steadily translate economic strength into effective and unified political power. The power of the federal state has increased enormously. The state is now so big in the economy, and the power of business is so great in the state, that unions can no longer seriously expect even their traditional short-run economic gains without considering the conditions under which their demands are politically realizable. If the democratic power of numbers is to be used against the concentrated power of money, it must in some way create its own political force. It is the aim of labor's political organizations steadily to translate the economic strength of organized labor into effective and unified political power.

This translation, the left believes, can be neither effective nor unified if it is doled out in little supports of various segments of the two major parties. The left would create an independent labor party to undertake political and economic moves which in daily practice reveal the sovereignty residing in the people. Unlike the sophisticated conservative, who can use the existing political apparatus to implement the main drift, the unions must create their own instruments of political struggle. The leftist would urge the labor leader to engage with him in the creation and use of political and economic action against the main drift. Independent labor action in the economic sphere means independence from labor-management co-operation; in the political sphere, it means independence from liberal governmental attempts to mediate and shackle union action, and from entanglements with either of the major parties.

To have peace and not war, the drift toward a war economy, as facilitated by the moves and demands of the sophisticated conservatives, must be stopped; to have peace without slump, the tactics and policies of the practical right must be countered and overcome. The political and the economic power of both must be broken. The power of these agents of the main drift is both economically and politically anchored; both unions and an independent labor party are needed to struggle effectively.

The left would have labor's political party protect, facilitate, and co-ordinate the struggle for economic and shop democracy, push for a political interlude between wars, in which the distribution of domestic power would have primacy over foreign affairs, prepare the people for a fruitful role in the next slump, establish an intellectual forum and build a public, in order that an orderly and continuous re-evaluation of ideas and plans might take place.

Labor's party would defend politically the effort to create new democratic areas in the spheres of work and economy, and the effort to organize and to use more broadly the solidarity of labor action. It would serve as a means of keeping the unions independent of employers' organizations and the apparatus of the state. It would try to initiate, enlarge, and focus human autonomy beyond the sphere of production and beyond the labor unions. It would foster all the direct action it could among consumers, co-ordinating this work, industry by industry, with demands and plans for rational and full production set forth by the workers involved in production. The party would facilitate and prompt union action. It would be an agent in turning a collection of unions into a labor movement.

The American left focuses its political attention and energies more on domestic politics than on foreign affairs. It now believes that America is the center of initiative for world power and that the present powers in America cannot and will not do anything along lines that might avoid war.

Western Europe is incapable of political initiative; what happens in Europe, clutched in the squeeze play, is more a result of what Russia and the United States do than what any power on the peninsula of Europe tries to do. Unlike Russia, the United States emerged from the late war with productive facilities intact and with a greatly increased potential. Men who would act for economic and political freedom have more of a chance—no matter how small, difficult, and perilous—in the United States, a parliamentary democracy, than in Soviet Russia, a totalitarian state. Power harnessed to this idea, when gained in America, will count for more because of the industrial weight of this country in foreign affairs.

It is in the United States that the political interlude between wars will be crucial. To create new political and human chances for European and for world culture, the left would create new political choices within the political economy of the United States. That, it believes, is the realistic beginning for the formation of a third camp in a world polarizing for war. The left would exert all its efforts to enlarge this political interlude; if there is no such interlude, the left knows that there is little chance of realizing any part of its program.

In order to convince the people in the political interlude, the left knows that the unions must do more than increase their power. They must organize power democratically. Just as on the economic front in the unions, so on the political front in the political party, the left would examine every means used in its struggle for power to see if that means develops democratic initiative.

Those who desire decisive changes in the existing system must stress the transformation of the people from a passive public to an executive organ. Existing organizations as they now stand cannot be depended upon to carry the people through the slump, nor can any projected organization, unless the principle of its foundation and operation is democratic in the simplest and most uncomplicated sense.

In the party, man as consumer would be especially important; in this area direct democratic action is possible and effective. Instead of relying upon voluntary price cuts by businessmen, or automatic market reductions, or governmental control, the leftist would have consumers establish direct price-control committees in union, neighborhood, and city. Together they would refuse to pay higher prices and higher rents. This involves the creation and defense of a wide network of consumer co-operatives, linking dirt farmers and labor unionists, and enlarging the areas of self-government in the economic area. Only by such means, the leftist believes, will people come to realize clearly the basic relations of the economic system in which they live.

The emphasis of the left upon rank-and-file awareness and active control, in union, party, and co-op, seems to other political publics a naïve belief in democracy, or even in man. But for the left, it is only what democracy means, when taken seriously and practically. In view of the coming slump, this is now more important to the leftist than ever. If he would make that slump politically fruitful, there must be developed, before and during it, people who have the initiative and self-reliance not to "take things lying down." As slump sets in, labor would grow as a movement rather than decline as a wage-bargaining institution. The labor party would be active in this transformation, serving as a link between labor and the unorganized, and between labor and certain sectors of the middle class; it would guide the labor leader in his approach to these elements, relating the labor-left program to the welfare and values of middle class and unemployed, in order to win them over during the slump.

In every area where people are politically organized, the left makes up its mind about which parties it would co-operate with and which it would reject, according to which attract the people most militant and vigorous in their demands, whose leaders or members are most imaginative about democratic tactics that will strengthen the will of the rank and file, and which allow more chance for an effective voice in group policy from the activated rank and file.

It is clear that if the unions are to enlarge their sphere of operations, they must enlarge the sphere of their perception and knowledge. Today vision involves an organization capable of seeing what is happening with a hundred eyes, figuring out what might be done about it with a hundred minds, and stating all the probable consequences of each possible move in order that they may be assessed. That is not the job of isolated thinkers but of a team of men who can devote their combined talents to the task.

The labor party would have to attract and develop teams of such men. Now they are scattered and their efforts are not co-ordinated. To function at their best and to accomplish something, they would have to be brought together into a forum for debate and mutual correction, and they must have a critical public which, regardless of size, is indispensable for any careful political thinker.

Modern techniques of social observation and analysis have not yet begun to be developed for political use. It is the left's desire to capture the political intellect in order to gain a continual re-evaluation of its going program and in order to make public a continuous "bookkeeping" of the U.S. political economy.

To those who object that the program the left advances can only attract another little group that cannot win, the left intellectuals reply: You may be right; no one knows; we do not believe it. Even if it were so, we would still be for the attempt. We are among those who have decided to throw in with "the little groups that cannot win." In fact, the big groups never win; every group loses its insurgency; maybe that is all that is meant by winning. It is a question of where one decides to keep placing one's weight.

CHAPTER FIFTEEN

THE POWER AND THE INTELLECT

FOR INSURGENT leaders, the terrible quality of politics lies in the fact that they cannot usually choose allies; they must often choose a path first and hope to create allies afterwards. If the labor leader goes against the main drift, he will be fighting hard against powerful social actors rather than allying himself with them. For a while he will be strategic in the creation and maintenance of a new power bloc. Rather than make deals on the top with powerful interests, he will have to accumulate power from the bottom. Thus the leader and the rank and file must keep in step; but now, if he would fight the main drift, the labor leader must take the first steps. He must modify the character and enlarge the scope of the labor union in America. He must widen the base of his own power by creating allies for the fight.

The as yet unorganized wage workers and certain elements of the middle class would have to become part of labor's bloc. Among the wage workers, the labor leader would accumulate power; in order to permit and facilitate the utilization of power, he would win allies among the middle classes. If the power is to be used for democratic ends, every step of the strategy must counter the main drift; to do that, the labor leader would have to utilize intellect, and foster a contact between it and power within a coalition set sternly against the main drift.

The U.S. Workers

The political and social potential of the U.S. workers, and the conditions under which they might take the historical initiative, are not known. Yet several things are clear: whether they fight the main drift with any effectiveness depends upon the extent and the character of their organization, the level and direction of their political alertness, and the way in which they are able to react to the next slump.

Union organization has come in waves, proceeding historically from the top strata down. The aristocracy of industrial workers has recently been added to the aristocracy of skilled workers. There are still skilled and semi-skilled workers not in unions, but almost none of the unskilled underdogs are in the unions. Just as the addition of an industrial aristocracy to the union world has made a difference in the shape of the unions during the last decade, so would the addition of the underdogs in the next decade, if they were appropriately organized.

The underdogs—those who get the least of what there is to get —are not the lowest stratum within U.S. society; they are largely outside of it. Those who are underprivileged economically are also underprivileged socially and psychologically. They have developed habits of submission; they do not now possess the means to see and hear what is going on, much less to have opinions about events beyond the narrow range of their daily routines. They lack the information that is required to understand a world where the determining causes in their lives lie beyond their direct vision.

The underdogs lack the hardy self-confidence and capacity for indignation common to middle-class people. Their indignation is short-lived and often concerned with moral trivia. They have not been defeated; they have never tried. Defeat presupposes the impulse to dare, of which underdogs know little. They do not participate in many of those areas of middle-class existence which form the main stream of American culture.

The underdogs are not much interested in national or local elections, nor do they vote as regularly as do the middle and upper classes. In 1944, only 53 per cent of the lower fourth voted, as compared with 84 per cent of the upper fourth. They do not know who are their representatives in Congress or much about such governmental affairs as the establishment of price ceilings. They are ignorant and often too timid to judge the weighty questions which poll-takers and politicians offer them. Their withdrawal and isolation is literally of such an extent that they do not know what they might wish for. To endure this life requires a low level of aspiration which softens the will and creates apathy.

The condition of the underdog is an important aspect of class relations in America today. The liberal sees it as a problem of "adjustment and participation." Those set against the main drift see it differently: the withdrawn should be remade inside a new kind of union community; then they will be ready to participate. A type of man must be built into a human being outside the present system of society so that he may be able to shake it to its foundations.

Under appropriate conditions, the underdogs are likely to become solid union members; from among them rank-and-file militants can be recruited. The huge and sudden success of many CIO drives of the Thirties owes much to the fact that in the steel towns and coal villages, as well as in Akron and Flint, the unions dipped into the lower ranks of the semi-skilled and the unskilled workers. That was the first time they were organized on such a scale in the history of U.S. unionism. For many of these people the union came as a civilizing force, although a limited one. If the less skilled were in the unions in large numbers, the unions might have a chance to form an adequate culture apart from the culture that prevails, and thus break at least the cultural ties to the main drift.

For the union to become an instrument of social transformation, the people of the union must think of it as their creature; they must want to know all about it and want to run it in as much detail as possible. Those unions whose members approach this are usually born of a direct struggle, such as the sit-down strikes a decade ago; the industries in which they organize have tough union policies: everything has been gained bitterly over long periods of time. Moreover, many of the members have been underdogs for whom the union has served as a vehicle of socialization. The auto worker who is an ex-miner, or the son of a miner, for example, has experienced a great release as he goes from a closed community into a great industrial area. His frustrations and rejections have been channeled into the union; inside its generous industrial framework he has found acceptance. Above all, unions that approximate such communities have in them leaders who are political and genuinely democratic in outlook and method.

Only a small percentage of the underdogs are now in the unions, and the unions are by no means handling them in a long-run, intelligent manner. A mass of such people might experience the union and its world as their own social world, as their link with the larger society. The way in which they are organized, the very slogans and tactics used, are crucial not only to the meaning the union will assume for them, but also to the role that unions of socially organized underdogs will play in American life.

To organize these people in unions that would become their major communities would be to build inside this society something of a new society. It would create an arena in which politics would become so much a part of the life of the worker, so connected with his daily work and his social routine, that political alertness would be part of his human alertness as a social being.

We speak here of ideal conditions in order to speak of how they may be approximated. It is not so much indirectly through the labor party as it is directly through the union as a community that the political consciousness of the U.S. worker can be aroused. Or better, it is by a close interlocking of the two.

The political apathy of the American worker is an apathy about engaging in electoral politics when there are no issues which he feels deeply or understands fully. He votes neither for Tweedledee nor Tweedledum. Yet on more stirring occasions, the U.S. worker may "vote with his feet." The American worker has a high potential militancy when he is pushed, and if he knows what the issue is. Such a man, identified with unions as communities and given a chance to build them, will not respond apathetically when outside political forces attempt to molest what is his.

It makes little sense for leaders to complain that workers are politically acquiescent and at the same time to support either of the two major political parties. Such support only takes away their chance to organize politically and to alert men to politics as live issues. The activities of these parties alienate people from politics in its deeper meanings and demoralize those on the edge of political consciousness. Every time the labor leader supports a candidate of either party, he injures his chance to lift the level of political attention and intelligence of the workers.

Political acquiescence and lack of organization and leadership are mutually involved. Political apathy is not a function only of leadership; certain conditions in the life of the worker, and in the history of the United States, lie back of it.

Many of the major historical and psychological factors which formerly made for acquiescence among American working people are now defunct. If the frontier was a "safety-valve," it is no more. If immigrant peoples came in on the bottom of the society to do its dirty work and to lift all social strata, they will not come again. No longer will the mixed streams of migrants fragmentalize the working population into nativity, culture, religious, and language groups. No longer will such a lower class compare life in the U.S.A. with peasant levels in pre-industrial homelands.

Advertising slogans that attempt to build loyalties to business firms and the business system already seem banal; they will sound completely hollow when the next slump hits. The expanding market, with its promises of better jobs and chances to be your own little business boss, now contracts; better jobs and little businesses that pay off are not forthcoming to everyone who works hard for them. The rise in the volume of the educated may continue, but education will *mean* less and less as jobs required to realize on it decline in number. The chance to climb from wage-worker to white-collar jobs, which gives the economically spurious but socially real feeling of ascent and individual progress, even now shows signs of decreasing, or at any rate, of giving less income. The personalization of success has been possible, but how long will the personalization of failure into individual guilt continue?

The long trends making for acquiescence and continued loyalty to a failing system now flatten out and begin to decline. The recent historical experience of the working people in America has shaken loose many of the ideas which have lagged behind the changed structure of events. Within one generation the people of this country have been subjected to two world wars and one great slump.

The slump of the Thirties was qualitatively unique in the history of American capitalism; nothing like it had ever happened to Americans. If everyone who was working in 1929 had continued to work until 1939, each one could have taken a vacation for one year and two months and the loss in national income would have been no greater than it actually was. In terms of the total of all the goods and services available to the people, the free private enterprise system was set back 33 years; the average citizen had about as much available to him in 1932 as he had in 1899.

Yet the slump of the Thirties did not break down the historic mentality of acquiescence. Coming as it did after a long boom, it did not seriously jar the mentality of workers nourished by boom conditions and expectations of more boom to come. Reactions to the last slump were economically anchored in the great upward curve of 1865 to 1929, which, although interrupted from time to time, was experienced as a steady social advance. The old ideas built into the worker mentality over the long years persisted; the slump of the Thirties did not eradicate the optimistic mood. However severe, it could still be seen as a bottom of a cycle that would regain its peak. But only a war economy pulled the system out of the last slump.

The American people did not decide to enter or not to enter war in 1941. On the contrary, as a writer for *Fortune* has said, they "were eased into war by a process of discrete gradualism and manufactured inevitability." Mr. Stimson himself has written:

"The question was how we should maneuver them [the Japanese] into firing the first shot without allowing too much danger to ourselves. It was a difficult proposition." Furthermore, entry and participation in the war and its aftermath have not meant mass sacrifice and destruction for Americans, but on the contrary, a "steady crescendo of boom." Along with this, the war was sold not in context with ideology and much less with truth; it was sold by advertising men the way they sell outdoor moccasins and automobiles.

Wartime unity held labor unions in its shackles, not because of any positive factors, but because of the outside fascist threat, and the gains in power and prestige enjoyed by the pro-Roosevelt leaders of labor during the war. Yet even so there was widespread insurgency among the rank and file against top labor officials. For instance, during the wartime coal strike, there was great worker sympathy for the miners; if he had wanted to, John L. Lewis undoubtedly could have made that sympathy active by appealing to the rank and file of other unions. In the 1942 convention of the UAW, the rank-and-file leaders of 1,000,000 men loudly rejected many a policy of the top men; some 40 per cent voted against the no-strike pledge of their top leaders; yet they had no policy of their own to substitute, and no leaders then arose to show them one. The 1946 strike at General Motors was virtually called by the workers.

"Slowness of inception of U.S. labor action," a *Fortune* writer asserts, "is no guarantee that, once started, it will not speedily reach extremes." It is well to remember what happened in the Thirties: in two years, 4,000,000 workers not only organized and engaged in strikes, but many of them sat down in factories in order to back up their demands. Even during the war, wildcat strikes were significantly earnest. Such strikes, no matter how quickly and effectively suppressed, are prime indices to militancy, for they are against both employers and union chiefs, and often against the government as well. The relative quiet of labor, during periods of quiet, should be kept in mind, but so should the sit-down men who "stood ready to resist to the death any violence used to evict them."

Even though the slump of the Thirties did not completely shake loose the illusion that things always automatically return to normal, still it was a dress rehearsal on a considerable scale. The coming slump may well be a big show. Its historical timing and magnitude may well implant the insurgent impulse in the American workers. It will come after a period of war-born boom. After the show of productivity the workers have witnessed, it is unlikely that they will accept the fact of poverty again. The war and its aftermath of prosperity have demonstrated that there are ways out of unemployment and poverty. It is also clear that, in the lifetime of a man, two major wars have occurred, and that neither has availed anything, except to pull the most effectively industrialized country in the world out of a slump.

Slumps and wars have come fast and close together. The people will tend to see the new slump as a continuation of the old one; they will also see a continuation in the buildup to another war. Perhaps they will connect slump and war to each other, and connect both with the kind of society they are trying to live in. It is the job of left union, left party, left intellectual to spell out these connections. Expectations will be high and distrust of do-nothing authorities will be higher; it remains to turn expectations into demands; people may demand a way out short of war.

This next time, as never before in the history of U.S. labor, a sizable number of workers will enter the slump organized in some sort of unions. A massive leftward tide in U.S. labor is not impossible. In large part, whether it follows through or is sidetracked is up to the labor leaders.

Mere deprivation, for a while, will not start a movement, for simple deprivation may lead to apathy. With deprivation must come the rejection of the symbols and myths that justify the authorities and the acceptance of counter-symbols that will focus the deprivation politically, inculcate the truth about common interests and common struggles, and offer some hope of winning a better tomorrow. For this there must be the intellect as well as the power. The American labor unions and a new American left can release political energies, develop real hopefulness, open matters up for counter-symbols only if they are prepared to act boldly and win over the less bold by their success.

The Middle Classes

The labor leaders and the U.S. workers are not alone if they choose to fight. They have potential allies of pivotal importance. All those who suffer the results of irresponsible social decisions and who hold a disproportionately small share of the values available to man in modern society are potential members of the left. The U.S. public is by no means a compact reactionary mass. If labor and the left are not to lose the fight against the main drift by default and out of timidity, they will have to choose with whom they will stand up and against whom they will stand.

The labor leader is often timid of public reaction should he act vigorously. He can overcome this fear by considering the composition of the "public" which reacts to the uneasy balance of class forces by clamoring that something be done. The labor leader's fear of the "public" is due to his lack of analysis of it and his failure to judge aggressively the organizability and political potential of each of its main elements. It is a fear that reflects the former position of labor unions as a minority acting in a continually hostile environment. That fear cannot be overcome by compromising gestures nor by capitulation, but by viewing some sections of the public as potential supporters and some as enemies. The first should be organized. The second should be fought.

The American people have undergone a decisive occupational change in the last two generations. Today, only about 20 per cent of the population can in any way be called free enterprisers; some 25 per cent are new middle class and 55 per cent are wage workers of factory and farm:

	1870		1940	
Free enterprisers		33.4%		20.0%
Farmers	24.2		10.4	
Businessmen	8.3		8.4	
Free professionals	0.9		1.2	
New middle class		5.8%		25.0%
Office workers	0.7		9.9	
Salespeople	2.6		6.3	
Salaried professional and technical	1.7		6.2	
Managerial	0.8		2.6	
Wage workers		60.8%		55.0%
Urban skilled	10.1		11.9	
Urban semi-skilled and unskilled	21.4		35.6	
Rural workers	29.3		7.5	
Total		100.0%		100.0%

Seen from the standpoint of the labor unions, and of a labor party, the main facts are that wage workers as a whole have not increased, as nineteenth-century socialist theoreticians believed, but that a new middle class of salaried workers has. These white-collar people are potential union members. Even now, some 15 per cent are in unions (43 per cent of the wage workers are unionized). The farmers, although their numbers decline, are still crucial politically, and the smaller businessmen, who seem to maintain a rather even statistical keel despite a great turnover of individuals, are more crucial politically than their numerical strength indicates.

In 120 years, the farm stratum has been cut from 72 to 18 per cent of the working population. This rural stratum is by no means homogeneously composed of family-owned and family-operated farms. In fact, farm technology has been whittling down the numbers of precisely that kind of farmer. If the polarization of the old rural middle class continues as it has over the last 70 years, it will destroy the middle-class character of farming and split the stratum into subsistence farmers and wage workers on the one hand, and commercial farmers and farm corporations on the other. This trend had been slow because the techniques required were not applied on a scale comparable to that in industry. Now the concentration tendencies in agriculture begin to accelerate. Between 1910 and 1935, the proportion of farms between 20 and 499 acres dropped from 70 per cent to 58 per cent, whereas those over 500 acres rose from 29 to 40 per cent. Between 1935 and 1945, the number of farms dropped 13 per cent, whereas the average size of the farms in acreage rose 26 per cent. Many marginal producers are eliminated as farm land becomes more concentrated, farmers fewer and richer.

From the upper side, farming is becoming a big business, tying in with canners and packers and distributors. The big farmer is an enemy of labor; labor cannot win him any more than it can win big business. It should not toady to big farmers, it should fight them and their projected farm system, not directly, but by forming co-operative arrangements between the small farmers and the wage workers.

Consumer co-ops as part of the institution of the union, or closely joined with it, can provide a direct linkage with small farmers, who could thus be given a larger share of the consumer's dollars. At the same time, if such union co-ops were going concerns on a large scale, food prices could be lowered. Economic links of that sort, binding union and small farmer, would underlie the common political activity against big farmers and big business, including monopolies of seed, equipment, and transport.

When the slump comes again, the small farmer will be among its first victims. The difference between administered prices of big industry and market prices for farm produce shook the rural people to their very foundations last time. To prop them up again, governmental bottoms would have to be more ample than is in the small farmer's political power.

✦

To the lower class, the small business people are often the most apparent representatives of the "higherups"; but upper-class people make a firm distinction between small and large businessmen. Small businessmen are often "upper" in terms of income, but in terms of occupational origin and job history, intermarriage and education they are closely connected with the wage and salaried workers. The upper class judge more on status and background; the lower more on income and the appearances of it.

Small businessmen frequently are used as a front by larger business concerns. They are out in front in the common denominator of voluntary organizational life, the chambers of commerce and the "Service Clubs." The labor leader who talks fearfully of the "public" often has small businessmen in mind. He knows that smaller businessmen often act as the grass roots of larger business. To capture them for labor means to fight the roots which big business has put down in the small business community. As things now stand, small business serves as one of the main pressures exerted on the state, for the backbone of the typical political constituency is very often a column of small businessmen whose influence on organized wage and salaried workers is very great.

It would be foolish for the labor leader to attempt to win over the small business strata, and the practical right which is based upon them, by compromise and appeasement. Often there is no coincidence of interest between labor and these small-fry exploiters. Such elements are firmly entrenched in the cities and towns, and today they are an even more spiteful enemy of democracy than big business.

Yet their power over a city can be broken; that has been shown and is being shown in those few localities where labor has moved into the city hall. When that happens, the crucial middle groups who hang in the balance and whose interests are one with the workers', but who are psychologically hard to win, will come over.

Labor's approach to the smaller middle-class elements should neither exclude them nor toady to them. Both strategic genuflection and ideological capitulation are fatal. They can be won over only if labor is strong and shows its strength in vigorous, adequate action, publicly attached to issues of wider community importance. Pronouncement of and struggle for simple questions of wages and hours for organized labor alone will rightly be interpreted as special pressure for a special interest. That is what alienates and often incurs the enmity of many unorganized middle-class elements.

In the coming slump, which in all likelihood will be the political interlude for U.S. society, any narrowing of the trade unionists' aims and methods will make that much easier the mobilization by fascist demagogues of the unemployed and the middle class, especially its disgruntled lower-middle-class elements. If such mobilization appeared more or less successful, there is no reason to suppose that the sophisticated conservative would not financially back the demagogues.

There is now ample historical evidence that "in full political crisis, the middle class first turns to the working class," as a *Fortune* writer has asserted, "and makes an about-turn to the fascist right only when persuaded that the working class cannot or will not carry through a social revolution."

The alliance between labor and the middle classes involves an active search for real and practical points of coincidence between them. But when there is no real point of coincidence, then no attempt to toady should be made. Labor must be wise in the perils of expedient involvement, carefully analyzing the results of any compromises it would make.

Economically and psychologically, the urban middle class of small businessmen and white-collar employees is the least homogeneous and the most "in-between" stratum in the U.S. population today. The middle class as a whole has undergone great shifts since the rise of organized labor:

	1870		1940	
Free enterprisers		85.2%		44.5%
Farmers	61.7		23.0	
Businessmen	21.2		18.9	
Free professionals	2.3		2.6	
New middle class		14.8%		55.5%
Clerical	1.8		22.0	
Salespeople	6.5		14.1	
Salaried professional and technical	4.4		13.7	
Managerial	2.1		5.7	
Total		100.0%		100.0%

The meaning of the figures for labor's strategy is clear: white-collar workers should now be a central target of union organizing drives, for both economic and political reasons.

The big political point that emerges from any study of white-collar people is that only when labor has rather obviously won out in a city, if then, will the white-collar worker join a union. If the leaders of labor are included in compromised committees in the chamber of commerce, then such white-collar groups as may exist in a city will certainly be easy prey for business-oriented leaders. Lenin's remark that the political consciousness of a stratum cannot be aroused within the sphere of relations between workers and employers may be only a half truth for factory workers, but it seems doubly true for white-collar employees. Their occupational ideology is politically passive; they are not now engaged in any economic struggle except in a scattered way. In the various middle-sized cities they form the rear guard of either business or labor, but in either case they are rear guard.

Economically the white-collar employees belong with wage workers, but they have to be appealed to on a wider issue than simply that of wages and hours. They should particularly be appealed to on price issues. When prices outrun consumers' income, people either have to get more pay or be priced out of the market. In both cases, the unorganized white-collar workers fall behind. In the middle Forties, labor has missed an enormous chance to unionize white-collar people by the most militant possible appeal on the price issue.

Theories of the rise of the white-collar people to power are often inferred from the facts of their numerical growth and their indispensability in the bureaucratic and distributive operations of mass society. Only if one assumes a pure and automatic democracy of numbers does mere growth mean increased power. And only if one assumes a magic leap from occupational function to political power does technical indispensability mean power.

The numbers must be organized, the indispensability made politically relevant. Now the white-collar workers have neither political awareness nor rudimentary organization. It is the task of labor to build unions for them and to do so in a way that makes the road to increased security and freedom clear.

The allies of the main drift are able to exploit heavily the unfinished task of the unions: their failure to organize widely. To win allies among the middle class, labor must organize more deeply and widely among the wage workers, and among the white-collar and farm employees. Unionization and political alliances go together; each facilitates the other; together they make up labor's approach to problems of "public reaction."

A labor party would co-ordinate and time these drives and alliances. No one union or set of unions can take on that task. In the slump, various organizations of neighborhoods and unemployed groups will rise. The labor party would firm them up, give them continuity, and offer them orientation. It would accumulate and focus the economic power of the unions in a political manner, and foster links beween their powers and those of the allies of labor among the middle class.

The sophisticated conservatives' program, cloaked in liberal rhetoric and abetted by the clamor of the practical conservatives, may swing the middle class of farmers and small business and white-collar people into line through fear and organized insecurity. The program of the left, if realized in time, can stop the main drift only if it succeeds in counter-organization among these middle-class elements.

The Labor Intellectuals

The labor intellectual has been the political gadfly of the labor leader. In and around the labor movements of all countries, whenever he has had the chance and often when he has not, the intellectual has taken upon himself the task of raising the level of political awareness. That he has succeeded only in rare instances and for short periods of time is revealing of labor leaders, of labor intellectuals, and of the character of the unions and their memberships.

Labor leaders in America have shied at the word "intellectual" ever since Samuel Gompers broke with his own socialist past and began the business-like trek from ideas to pure and simple unionism. They will continue along the main drift unless they seize upon the kind of experience that is available to the intellectual craftsman and join it to their own power and experience.

Just as many labor leaders have made their adaptations, so have many intellectuals. In terms of career, many opportunities have opened up between the two wars and especially during the late war. The two greatest blinders of the intellectual who today might fight against the main drift are new and fascinating career chances, which often involve opportunities to practice his skill rather freely, and the ideology of liberalism, which tends to expropriate his chance to think straight. The two go together, for the liberal ideology, as now used by intellectuals, acts as a device whereby he can take advantage of the new career chances but retain the illusion that his soul remains his own. As the labor leader moves from ideas to politics, so the intellectual moves from ideas to career.

There are many types of men included in the term "intellectual." Even the four types of labor intellectuals we shall discuss briefly differ widely in the kinds of skill they possess and in their relations to the policy makers of the unions. But each is pro-labor and each tries to influence the making of policy and the shaping of strategy. Each has somewhat different aims so far as his relations with labor unions are concerned; in trying to achieve these aims, he uses different means and in the process becomes a different type of operator.

1. The labor leaders have been using professionally trained intellectuals as staff assistants for some time. They have had to: big business and big government have employed such personnel, and the unions have had to follow in order to do battle the way battle is now done.

These professionals face labor's problems with the labor leaders on a day-to-day basis, but because of their education, they might be expected to have a more far-sighted, or at least a different, view of things. They are on the leader's staff, but they do not share his power; they can only borrow it when he wishes to make the loan.

No power usually means no status; lack of status, as well as of power, is usually aggravated by the fact that some labor intellectuals serve the unions only part-time. In many unions the prestige generally accorded the well-educated is denied the research director or editor of a union paper. Given this situation, we might expect certain tensions to develop between leaders and staff.

As a research man or an educational director, an economist or a lawyer, the staff intellectual is concerned with problems which the labor leader faces and hands to him for solution. But in his weekly relations with the leader, the staff intellectual tries to influence the leader by attempting to see problems in advance and to set them up in one way rather than another. To influence policy, he has to be expert in spotting the problems which will most interest the leader but which go a little beyond the range of the leader's own perception. He is often a man quite skilled in intellectual workmanship, and yet any power to influence affairs that he may possess depends more upon the leader's attitude toward him than upon his intellectual ability.

This personal dependency on the leader means that the staff intellectual is usually in an insecure position, as is revealed by the caution with which such men proceed when policy-relevant issues arise. In so far as he does not go beyond the leader's range of interests and values, the staff intellectual acts as a technician implementing a set policy rather than as a direct influencer of policy.

Within each union bloc, the intellectuals think as the leaders of their respective union blocs think. This is certainly true of AFL intellectuals, especially editors of publications. But the CIO research and education directors are more independent, and—since they are retained at the pleasure of the CIO elected leaders—they may be influencing the CIO policy makers to a greater extent than do the staff thinkers of the AFL.*

II. The intellectual as an official, an active member, or a promoter of a radical party has been in and around the unions since they began in this country. Labor leaders are fully aware of this kind of intellectual and of his activities. Indeed, so deep is the impression he has made that many labor leaders tend to think that all "intellectuals" are this type.

In working within the unions, the radical party intellectual follows the "line" of his party. Often he turns to the factory workers and the immediate leaders of their unions; he works to influence and sometimes to gain formal power within the unions by organizing "party cells" within various locals and plants and cities. He operates as a publicist and politician in the unions, even as does the labor leader himself.

The party intellectual goes into unions on a level with the sergeants and lieutenants of the labor movement, the shop stewards and committeemen. He strives to strengthen the power of these rank-and-file leaders within the unions and within the laboring community—against the top officials of the union if need be. He knows that labor leaders at the top come and go. He supports those who come to the front in times of change and who

* *See* Notes and Sources, p. 311.

can capture the imagination of the rank and file during periods of tension. By selective support, he tries to move labor from pure and simple unionism to recognition of the role that larger and more political action can play in winning even pure and simple demands.

III. Many intellectuals are not tied to any organization; it would seem that they could become masters of their own mentality. But the price such intellectuals pay for this chance, when they take it, is lack of direct power.

Not many labor leaders know intellectuals as free-lance researchers. Such types have not been available very long; in so far as their skills have been used by power groups, they have largely been used in the service of big business.

The free-lance research intellectual is "free-lance" only so far as labor unions, government agencies, business firms, and political parties are concerned. He is not usually a regular employee of either of these three, although he may drift in and out of all of them in a consultative capacity. He is often a college professor, but he may also be a journalist or, even more likely, a research technician for one of the mass media or for their adjuncts, or a lawyer. By definition, however, he has no constant foothold in the institutions of labor or in institutions which continuously deal with the unions.

Research men are highly skilled in the techniques that American social scientists have developed in the last decade. Moreover, those among them who are pro-labor may be not only technicians but idea-men whose research imaginations are enlivened by the problems of labor. Such intellectuals now have no influence on the policy makers in labor unions. Many of them want to work in the service of labor, but somehow they never do.

The free-lance is not only powerless; he is often naïve about the kind of power needed to influence a labor leader. Neither knowledge nor experience necessarily lead to policy-making power in a trade union, and certainly power is not often influenced by admonitions, particularly if they are well-founded in the leader's own shortcomings.

The small party and the union staff intellectuals are usually much wiser about the facts of power than the free-lance intellectuals. The party intellectual usually knows that the only way he can influence the union official is to organize a power base of party members in specific locals or plants. The staff intellectual may wait cautiously for years before he attempts to influence policy without paying the price the radical party man, or the labor leader himself, is willing to pay. But the free-lancer often seems to think he can influence by the sheer magic and wisdom of his talk.

IV. The effective intellectual member of the team of power and ideas will have to combine features of the party intellectual, the staff thinker, and the free-lance research man. In his actual working operations, he must unite these three roles into a triple-threat ability; and he must become an all-around fixer. He must be able to organize a new local in a fresh and open city. He must, in brief, master every skill that is needed to be a labor leader. He must be what we may call a union-made intellectual.

One of the major clues to the political history of U.S. unions has been the absence of union-made intellectuals: men who combine solid trade union experience, preferably of militant character, with the degree of self-awareness and wider consciousness associated with the best sense of the term intellectual. There are such men in a few of the newer unions, and we can base our description on them.

They became involved with the unions during the Valley Forge days of the organizing campaign. Then and later they struggled for an education in the big sense of the word: self-awareness and political consciousness. Minor parties facilitated this education, and many self-made intellectuals served a stretch in the Communist Party; they abandoned it in the Thirties because of its restraining character, or if later, because the union-made intellectual was generally skeptical about the war.

Unlike many non-union intellectuals of more academic or journalistic types, the union-made intellectuals compete with each other in terms of the activity to which their ideas lead. They are not intellectuals for the sake of being intellectuals or because they have nothing else to do. They are union thinkers, with a big job on their hands.

Such men are in themselves a link between ideas and action; this affects the healthily extrovert shape of their mentality. With them the gap between ideas and action is not so broad as to frustrate and turn their minds inward; they compete by having their ideas acted out, for better or for worse; they are not just waiting and talking.

The role of such union-made intellectuals within a union and between the union and other elements of the U.S. population would be difficult to overestimate. They serve as a bridge between pure and simple unionists and the professional intellectual members of the staff. They also serve as a strong link, a set of opinion leaders, between the political world of left-wing ideas and democratic ferment, and the economic world of the unionists and the companies. Within the union they act as leaven, lifting it beyond mere pork-chop contentment. As members of the anti-Stalinist left-wing intelligentsia, they serve as a link between the union world and the middle-class leftward intelligentsia and free-lance technicians, who would go all out for unions if unions gave them the chance.

Non-union intellectuals will cluster around a union if the union has such union-made intellectuals at the top and down its hierarchy. Such men could form a center of identification for all intellectual elements in America who feel homeless and without power. They offer avenues of intellectual activity. In this sense the union-made intellectuals are a vanguard; they can turn the unions into vanguard organizations.

One basic test of a union's democratic vigor is whether or not it generates a broad stratum of union-made intellectuals, and whether or not such home-grown radicals can find or create channels upward to the top and downward and out to the shop stewards and the rank and file. In the end, such men are the only guarantee of the union of power and ideas.

The Leaders of American Labor

Some labor leaders have both the vision and the will to meet the situation they are in; they are themselves so close to the radical intellectual that they will welcome his co-operation. Other labor leaders lack vision but have will: they feel that something ought to be done, but they do not know what. Their hearts are in the right place, they may even feel a little guilty about the role they play in the practicalities of union and public life. Among these, the intellectual will find men who might welcome him if he does not frighten them. And there are those labor leaders who have the vision but who do not have the will. They are the most guilt-ridden in the union world. Often they are men who were once socialist, but who made the great compromise, deserting large ideas for little power. Finally, there are labor leaders without the will and without the vision.

Vision is relative to knowledge, will to character. But vision is also relative to the chances a position and career give you to see; and will is also dependent upon the exigencies of holding one's own in the organization one leads or the career one pursues. Many labor leaders have been so tied up in the immediate present, pressuring for their cut in the existing arrangements of power, money, and status, that they have not begun seriously to question the system itself nor the conditions under which even their liberal demands could be securely realized. Only a certain type of labor leader will coalesce with a certain type of intellectual and fight the main drift.

Generally, the lower in the union hierarchy the radical intellectual goes, the more likely he is to find colleagues among labor leaders. The higher he goes, the more apt he is to find leaders who are with the main drift. The man at the top may be a pure and simple unionist who doesn't stop to ask questions about "theoretical notions": he doesn't see the main drift. Or, if he does, he is more likely to see within it the opportunity to stabilize his own power and position. In either case, he does not want the co-operation of the labor intellectual. It is primarily among the ambitious secondary leaders and the alert rank and file that the labor intellectual can relate his skill to going operations.

Many labor leaders fail to understand the power of their own unions; they want time and security to consolidate their gains. But to organize 14,000,000 people in unions, and to hold them, is to mount a locomotive which one cannot slow down for every whistle stop. The labor leader can play the role of the brakeman only at the risk of losing his seat as engineer.

The situation of the unions is such that the labor leaders cannot narrow the fight now and shackle it in a successful drive for security; they must broaden it—by completing their organizing work and by politicizing the aims and the strategy of their movement. If there are to be any fights for labor in America a quarter of a century from now, labor leaders must complete, in the Forties and Fifties, the work they began in the Thirties.

Our study of the character of America's labor leadership—the positions they occupy, their career-lines, and the traditions and anxieties that impel them—does not lead us to expect that they will join issue against the main drift, unless as a group they undergo severe modification. But we must take an over-all look at American labor leaders with an eye to assessing their capacities to meet the issues which confront the unions. Just how fit is this leadership to cope with the situation at hand? The answer to that question must be given statistically: some leaders are and some leaders are not fit, and some are in between. Thus the question has to be put: How many are, how many are not, and how many may be?

In terms of our information on the labor leaders, we can set up these minimum criteria for the leader "adequate" to the situation: He must have a realistic image of business, which means that he will see the immense power and influence of business and its associations on national affairs, and that he will recognize the intent of business to break or shackle labor unions. Politically, he must see that the two dominant parties are blind traps, not fit instruments with which to cope with his political situation. He must be for a labor party, at least within the next ten years. He need not be a "third-party" member because in most states he cannot be at the present time.

The men who might be capable are not necessarily engaged in action today, but they hold views which suggest that under the threat of events they would be more likely to take the correct and adequate path, and less likely to drift into the trap. These are men who are more likely to take the next steps to leading against, rather than with, the main drift.

According to these standards, which are not very rigorous or trustworthy, 8 per cent of the CIO and 4 per cent of the AFL leaders qualify: they are dissatisfied with the major parties and they are for a new labor party; they know big business is powerful and they believe its intent is to break labor unions.

Immediately below this "elite," 9 per cent of the AFL and 19 per cent of the CIO leaders hold a militant view on at least three of the four points. If we relax our criteria and add these two groups together, 13 per cent of the AFL and 27 per cent of the CIO leaders stand at the top of our scale.

About 35 per cent of the AFL and 43 per cent of the CIO leaders occupy a fence-sitting position. They score militantly on only two of the four points at issue. Below them are 53 per cent of the AFL and 30 per cent of the CIO leadership who score either all negative, or positive on only one point.

These are the labor leaders lined up along the scale of possible opposition to the main drift. Whether this drift will win or whether it will be fought to the end depends to some considerable extent upon these men. If they do not change and do not act in some manner adequate to the situation, they will not measure up to their responsibilities to the rank and file nor will they be

Militancy score:	AFL	CIO
A	4%	8%
B	9	19
C	35	43
D	38	24
F	15	6
Total cases	205	157

able to carry out that extension of democracy which alone can preserve such elements of it as now prevail. But if they choose to make the struggle, they will not be alone.

The fight against the main drift will not take place unless the American workers are so hit by the coming slump that they will modify basically the outlook and alertness of our present labor leadership. Between the leaders and the led in the union world, more than in most others, there is a kind of step-by-step, long-term balance, the whole of which rests upon the state of the nation in its slump-war-boom cycle. The strength of the labor leader is with the rank and file; without it there would be no labor leader. But without leaders, the rank and file will not be strong at crucial times and places.

The union leader is an organization man. In the end, he will change as does the character of his organization. That works both ways: to the right and to the left. Regardless of autocracy in the unions, in the long run the members will either destroy the leader or they will get some leadership out of him. The fortune of the labor leader depends more directly than that of any other power elite upon the character and timing of the coming slump and upon how the workers will react to it. When appropriate conditions move the masses, action of a larger sort is entered into with enthusiasm. It is then that leadership is tested and those men who have been plied with the security of routine and soaked with the fear of action fall by the way.

If people show strength, they will find leaders. There are in the unions a handful of union-made men, now without much power, who see what is happening and who will be ready, when the time comes, to take the chance of leadership. There will be more such men. Even in our short political lifetime, we have witnessed an entirely new labor leader elite come to the fore. In another slump, it will happen again. The labor movement in America is still building. The AFL is only two generations old; the CIO, one-third of one generation.

✦

To have an American labor movement capable of carrying out the program of the left, making allies among the middle class, and moving upstream against the main drift, there must be a rank and file of vigorous workers, a brace of labor intellectuals, and a set of politically alert labor leaders. There must be the power and there must be the intellect. Yet neither the intellectuals nor the workers at large are in a position to take up an alliance and fight against the great trend. The unions are the organizational key to the matter; and neither intellectuals nor rank and file are now running labor unions in the United States.

This is where labor stands: there are labor leaders who are running labor unions, most of them along the main drift; there are left intellectuals who are not running labor unions, but who think they know how to run them against the main drift; and there are wage workers who are disgruntled and ready to do what must be done.

It is the task of the labor leaders to allow and to initiate a union of the power and the intellect. They are the only ones who can do it; that is why they are now the strategic elite in American society. Never has so much depended upon men who are so ill-prepared and so little inclined to assume the responsibility.

NOTES AND SOURCES

I

I AM INDEBTED to many people for guidance and assistance, but five individuals have been crucial in the making of this book:

J. B. S. Hardman of the Inter-Union Institute, which provided approximately one-third of the funds for the poll materials incorporated, has guided my thinking about unions over the last two years. He will not be in agreement with many of the conclusions, but without his aid I should not have reached them.

Helen Schneider, formerly of the Bureau of Applied Social Research, with whom I have been for two years happily associated in several research endeavors, prepared an analysis of the poll materials incorporated in the book. Her memorandum was especially valuable in the critique it provided of the meaning of the questions asked the labor leaders.

Hazel Gaudet Erskine, formerly with the Bureau of Applied Social Research and the Columbia Broadcasting System, designed a set of preliminary tables, checked my sample, and is responsible for much of the statistical work behind Chapter Three. In addition, I have had the benefit of her detailed criticism of the second draft of the manuscript.

Maud Zimmerman, now of Sarah Lawrence College, pre-tested several drafts of the questionnaire and performed the laborious task of administering the mailing and reception of the three waves of interviews.

Ruth Harper Mills was in charge of the preparation of the manuscript; her general editorial work and advice have been indispensable; without her six months of work, the book would have been delayed at least another year. In addition, she has relieved me of other research burdens in order to permit my working on this manuscript.

II

Beatrice Kevitt thoroughly edited the next-to-the-last manuscript, greatly improving its readability. I wish to thank her for generously giving of her time and skill.

In its various phases, the manuscript has been read and criticized by many friends and colleagues, among them: Louis Clair of *Modern Review*, Hans Gerth of the University of Wisconsin, Richard Hofstadter of Columbia University, Leo Lowenthal of the Institute of Social Research, Robert S. Lynd of Columbia University, Dwight MacDonald of *Politics* magazine, Robert K. Merton of Columbia University, William Miller of New York City, Irving Sanes of New York City, Clarence Senior of the Bureau of Applied Social Research, Columbia University, Adolph Sturmthal of Bard College, Harvey Swados of Nyack, New York, and Nat Weinberg of the United Automobile Workers.

Their advice has greatly facilitated my work and clarified its results at many points. I wish to thank them, and to say that they are in no way responsible for such deficiencies or errors as remain.

III

The following men in the labor unions have generously given me their aid in connection with two polls of labor leaders. None of them are in any way responsible for the questions which I have asked or for the analysis presented. Boris Shiskin, economist, AFL; I. M. Orburn, Secretary-Treasurer, Union Label Trades Department, AFL; James B. Carey, Secretary-Treasurer, CIO; Kermit Eby, Assistant Director, Department of Research and Education, CIO; J. G. Luhrsen, Executive Secretary, Railway Labor Executive Association; Glenn R. Atkinson, Railroad Labor Organizations, formerly with OPA; Marion Hedges, Research Director, Brotherhood of Railway Trainmen; Phil E. Ziegler, Grand Secretary-Treasurer, Brotherhood of Railway Clerks, AFL.

IV

This book is the third report of a research project on the characteristics of American labor leaders which I have had under way since 1941. Report No. 1, with which I was assisted by Mildred Atkinson of the University of Maryland, was published in the *Public Opinion Quarterly* (Summer, 1945). That first report was the pilot study of the present work, and some of the figures and formulations in the present book are taken from it. Report No. 2, a preliminary statement of the poll materials incorporated in this book, is printed in *The House of Labor,* edited by J. B. S. Hardman (New York: Rensis Press, 1948).

V

I know of only two previous statistical studies of trade union leaders. Both of them use the data contained in *American Labor Who's Who* (New York, 1925): P. A. Sorokin, "Leaders of Labor and Radical Movements in the United States and Foreign Countries," *American Journal of Sociology* (November, 1927), pp. 382-411; Louis Stanley, "A Cross-Section of American Labor Leadership," Appendix III, pp. 412-20, of *American Labor Dynamics,* edited by J. B. S. Hardman (New York, 1928). The latter study by Stanley provides tabular information on officials of the AFL and of independent unions which I have used to establish trends in various connections. These distributions include 788 persons directly connected with labor unions, 682 of them with the AFL. Unfortunately, we are not told their positions in the unions, but they are separated from the non-union people listed in *American Labor Who's Who,* many of whom are journalists, political party figures, and executives of various labor serving associations. Information on "The 1924 Leaders," contained in the present book, has been computed from Stanley's tables on leaders directly connected with unions.

In addition, there is one study of local labor leaders in two Connecticut towns which provides census-type data on 44 leaders: Samuel Koenig, "Social Backgrounds and Attitudes of Labor Leaders, with Special Reference to New Haven and New Britain, Connecticut," *Sociology and Social Research* (January-February, 1941), pp. 264-65.

* * * * *

Introduction: What Are Labor Leaders Like?

On the distinction between unions as armies and as town meetings, *see* A. J. Muste, "Factional Fights in Trade Unions," pp. 332-48 in *American Labor Dynamics*, edited by J. B. S. Hardman (New York: Harcourt, Brace, 1928). On the labor union as an enterprise, *see*, under different terminology, Selig Perlman, *A Theory of the Labor Movement* (New York: Scribner's, 1928). On the powers of property, *see* Franz Neumann, *European Trade Unionism and Politics* (New York: League for Industrial Democracy Pamphlet, June, 1936).

Chapter One: The Political Publics

A first draft of parts of this chapter was printed in the May-June, 1947, issue of *Labor and Nation:* C. Wright Mills, "Five Publics the Polls Don't Catch." The estimate of Communist Party turnover is from Arthur M. Schlesinger, Jr., *Life*, July 29, 1946. The reference to "troublemakers" in the steel unions is to an item in C. S. Golden and H. J. Ruttenberg, *The Dynamics of Industrial Democracy* (New York: Harper's, 1942).

Chapter Two: The Mass Public's View

The facts concerning radio's handling of labor news are drawn from Lila W. Sussman's article, "Labor in the Radio News, an Analysis of Content," *Journalism Quarterly*, Vol. XXII (September, 1945). I am indebted to Susan Cane for her spot examination of labor in the daily press.

Some of the figures for the table on "In and Out of the Unions" are taken from Mills and Thelma Ehrlich, "The People in the Unions," *Labor and Nation* (January-February, 1947). They were tabulated from a poll performed by the National Opinion Research Center, then at the University of Denver, which we borrowed. NORC is not responsible for any errors in the results we present, or for our interpretative analysis. We wish to thank Clyde Hart, director of NORC, for his generosity in allowing us to analyze and present these materials. Other figures are from M. J. Ulmer, "The Post War Business Population," *Survey of Current Business* (January, 1947); the *Statistical Abstract of 1946* (Adult population in 1945, p. 14; Employed labor force over 20 years of age, p. 175); and the *Sixteenth Census of the United States: the Labor Force*, pp. 98 and 100. As to the proportion of leaders and active members among the "Union-involved," *see* John Huber, "This is Labor," *Labor and Nation* (August, 1943), p. 26. For comments on the apathy of trade union members in British unions, *see* "Inside the Unions," *Planning* No. 249 (May 10, 1946), a broadsheet issued by Political and Economic Planning.

The mass public's opinions of labor unions and leaders are all taken from the file of such opinions maintained by the Labor Research Division of the Bureau of Applied Social Research, Columbia University. This includes all relevant materials from all the major polling organizations, notably Roper, Gallup, and NORC. Two previous analyses of this data, by Mills and Hazel Gaudet Erskine, have been drawn upon in the preparation of this text; both appeared in *Labor and Nation:* "Labor's General Score with the Public" (November-December, 1946); and "Anti-Labor Legislation" (March-April, 1947). Daniel L. Camp prepared some special tabulations of materials on file with the American Institute of Public Opinion Research from which I have drawn.

A great many questions asked the mass public by the polling organizations have been biased against labor unions. Recently some 155 questions asked about labor by the major polling organizations between 1940 and 1945 were examined in fine detail by an expert on polling, A. Kornhauser ("Are Public Opinion Polls Fair to Organized Labor," *Public Opinion Quarterly* [Winter, 1947]. *See* criticism of this analysis in *POQ* [Summer, 1947]). Of the 155 questions examined, 3 per cent were biased pro-labor, 42 per cent were neutral, and 55 per cent were biased anti-labor. Moreover, the questions which have been asked tend to be focused on union faults, on features of the union world that one would expect to be publicly condemned, or upon restrictions on the unions that have been proposed: some 81 questions fall into that category. Only 8 questions, on the other hand, are focused upon the more positive features of unions; the remaining 66 are neutral or doubtful in their focus. Certain polling organizations are more guilty of anti-labor bias than others: approximately three-fourths of Dr. George Gallup's questions during this period are "in the negative direction." The polls "Taken as a whole," this study concludes, "are clearly not fair to organized labor." Yet recognizing this bias, we can, if we exercise great care, use the results of the polls in our attempt to gauge the public's attitude toward the labor unions.

The question, "Are you in favor of unions?" was asked in August, 1936, June, 1937, October, 1938, May, August, and December, 1939, May, 1940, May and November, 1941, May, 1942, and May, 1943.

Any "popularity contest" of labor leaders runs into the fact of mass ignorance. If, for instance, people are asked to pick from a list of labor leaders those whom they most approve and those whom they most disapprove, they must of necessity choose both their favorites and their least liked from among leaders with whose names they are acquainted. To counteract this factor of familiarity as much as possible, we have in the text scored the results of this popularity contest by computing the ratio of approval to disapproval.

Chapter Three: The Houses of Labor

I have taken factual material for use in my statement of organization from several standard labor economics texts, notably, Carrol R. Daugherty, *Labor Problems in American Industry* (Boston: Houghton Mifflin, 1941), and Richard Lester, *Economics of Labor* (New York: Macmillan, 1947). A good general statement is to be found in the Winter, 1946, issue of the *Harvard Business Review*, "Understanding Union Administration," by Philip Taft, and another in F. Peterson, *American Labor Unions* (New York: Harper's, 1945). I have also interviewed on this problem staff members and other representatives of various internationals.

My figures on the internationals and the history of their memberships are from an unpublished manuscript "The White-Collar Unions," and from a set of tables run from Hollerith cards on which I have punched the information contained about each of the 182 internationals in F. Peterson's *Handbook of Trade Unions,* as well as other, scattered sources. I wish to thank Mr. Roslow for assisting me in the coding of these materials.

To speak only about the average size of unions may obscure significant variations. The leader of the International Association of Sideographers, which contains 48 members, carries a different administrative burden than the chief of the Automobile, Aircraft and Agricultural Implement Workers, which numbers upward of 1,000,000 members. It is well to remember that even at the late wartime peak, only 30 internationals (or 17 per cent) contained over 100,000 members, and 79 (or 46 per cent) of the internationals contained less than 25,000 members. The number of locals in an international is a further clue to the administrative scope of the top leaders. An international may contain anywhere from a few to over 5,000 locals, but the average (median) number of locals for all internationals is around 166.

The membership figures for the AFL, CIO, and independent unions of the first quarter, 1947, are from *The Directory of Labor Unions in the U. S.* (Bureau of Labor Statistics, Bulletin No. 901, Washington, D. C., May, 1947).

Both the AFL and the CIO contain local unions that are directly affiliated with them without an intermediary national or international organization. In 1940, for example, directly affiliated locals in the AFL numbered 1,450, containing a total of 250,000 workers, and in the CIO, there were around 300 directly affiliated locals, with 210,000 workers. Most of those in the AFL are in small communities where there are not enough employees in each craft for separate locals. It is the operating policy of each of the blocs to assign them as soon as it is expedient to appropriate internationals.

The AFL is further complicated by 4 Departments and 720 Department Councils, which consist of sub-groupings of unions in related trades or crafts. This arrangement, however, is merely an administrative convenience for the internationals involved; they attempt to minimize and to adjust jurisdictional issues among the locals of the various internationals. Some of the departments—ones for coal and metal miners, for instance—were abolished after the unions involved had resolved their jurisdictional squabbles.

The tabulations of all unions into craft, amalgamated craft, and industrial types was made from a roster drawn up by Carrol Daugherty, *op. cit.,* pp. 531-38. In 1915, Glocker ("Amalgamation of Related Trades in American Unions," *American Economic Review,* Vol. V, p. 554) revealed that of 133 internationals, only 28 were organized strictly according to craft. *See* also Solomon Blum, "Jurisdictional Disputes Resulting from Structural Differences in American Trade Unions," *University of California Publications in Economics,* Vol. III, No. 3X (Berkeley, 1913). A study by D. J. Saposs and Sol Davidson ("Structure of AFL Unions," National Labor Relations Board, Research Memorandum No. 8, Washington, D. C., May 15, 1939, Mimeographed) indicated that of 81 AFL unions, only 12 were *strictly* craft in organizational form. The classifications used were quite rigorous and complicated.

As of August, 1940, here are the percentages of the three types of unions organized during three historical periods, computed from Daugherty:

Period of origin:	CRAFT	AMALG.	INDUS.
Before 1914	77%	60%	47%
1914-1934	16	20	25
1935-1939	7	20	28
Total	43	91	36

Average size of membership for the three types of unions organized in these periods is as follows:

	Average Size of Reported Membership		
Period of origin:	CRAFT	AMALG.	INDUS.
Before 1914	20,100	57,300	119,000
1914-1934	5,570	18,500	77,300
1935-1939	2,630	24,300	81,950
All unions in 1940	16,200	43,000	98,500

Data on fees and dues are available in Philip Taft, "Dues and Fees in Labor Unions," *Quarterly Journal of Economics* (February, 1946). *See* also *New York Times,* February 10, 1946, for detailed statements of dues for all CIO internationals; and also "How Much to be a Union Man?" *Business Week,* August 17, 1940. The study of tenure of office from 1910 to 1941 was made by Philip Taft, "Opposition to Union Officers in Elections," *Quarterly Journal of Economics* (February, 1944). The data on specific unopposed elections in unions are also from Taft, "Understanding Union Administration," *Harvard Business Review* (Winter, 1946).

Chapter Four: The Split Runs Deep

The ages of the labor leaders and their educational levels are taken from an original poll. This study includes: the leaders of the national AFL and CIO unions—the presidents and the secretary-treasurers; the presidents and secretaries of the AFL and CIO state organizations; the leaders of the city centrals (AFL) and the city industrial councils (CIO). Among these men are found practically all the big names of labor as well as hundreds who are not nationally known. There is no doubt that the power of decision in the world of the unions resides with these leaders, and especially with the heads of the national unions.

The sample for our study was based on lists provided by the AFL and CIO of their leaders on the national, state, and city levels. The dates of the lists for the various categories varied somewhat, but in general our reference date is the late spring and early summer of 1946. In the following table we have, as it were, mapped out the population from which the sample was drawn:

	AFL	CIO	TOTAL
National			
Presidents	99	38	137
Secretaries	85	38	123
State			
Presidents	50	36	86
Secretaries	48	32	80
City heads	756	222	978
Total	1,038	366	1,404

Three waves of questionnaires were sent out. A questionnaire went to each of the CIO leaders represented in the accompanying table. Questionnaires were sent to every national and state officer of the AFL. Since there were so many AFL city heads, we addressed a questionnaire to every other leader. We sent a total of 1,026 questionnaires. The first wave was put into the mails on May 8, 1946; the second, mailed on May 24, was sent to all those who had not responded to the first mailing; the third, mailed on July 3, was sent only to certain categories of personnel. In accompanying letters, anonymity was guaranteed the individuals who responded. In the end we obtained a sample of 410 usable returns from these categories, or 40 per cent of the number we had attempted to poll. (The independent unions were also polled, but our sample was too small for exact study. We also have fragmentary materials on 82 editors and research and educational directors—*see* Notes to Chapter Fifteen.)

The response was larger among the CIO leaders than among those of the AFL. Because of this, it is technically difficult to throw together the returns from these two union blocs. We could, of course, do so by weighting our sample, but we do not think that is wise. It is more convenient, and just as interesting for our purposes, to treat our data as two samples—one of the AFL and one of the CIO. We have compared the samples and the populations in the AFL and the CIO by the various positions involved. This comparison shows rather clearly that the sample obtained does not differ significantly from the population as a whole in any single category of personnel. Here is the population and the sample of labor leaders by positions:

	AFL		CIO	
	Population	Sample	Population	Sample
National				
Presidents	15%	13%	10%	12%
Secretaries	13	14	10	9
State				
Presidents	8	6	10	15
Secretaries	7	12	9	10
City heads	57	55	61	54
Total number	660	232	366	178

If we knew even a few facts about the labor leader population as a whole, we could then compare our sample with these facts about the population. But all we know, apart from position, is the region of the country in which the leaders reside. In the table below, we compare our sample with the population of leaders in terms of the four major regions of the country. It will be seen that the two distributions do not differ in any significant way.

	AFL		CIO	
	Population	Sample	Population	Sample
Northeast	23%	25%	37%	31%
North Central	40	41	36	38
South	24	20	16	17
West	13	14	11	14
Total number	660	230 *	366	177 *

* Two of the AFL men and one CIO man are from outside the U.S. proper—Canada and Alaska.

Even when we break down the geographical distribution into finer units, we find that the sample is a very close regional approximation to the population that it represents.

We might be afraid that our sample is biased in that the labor leaders who refused to respond to our questionnaire are in some significant way different from those who did answer. How can we find out if this is so when we know nothing about the universe we are interested in?

This technique is frequently used in mail surveys: One can assume that the investigator was satisfied with the replies he received as a result of his first attempt. In that case, all who had not answered in the first wave would be non-responders. We have information about some of these non-responders, however, for some of them answered waves two and three. We may compare those who replied to wave one with those who replied to waves two and three (in our hypothetical reasoning the latter represent the non-responders to wave one). If they are different, we have reason to believe that our sample is not a representative one—that our sample does not reflect the universe.

Mail polls often tend to be biased by education: the more educated people respond more frequently than those who are less educated. We cannot check the educational composition of all labor leaders with that of those in our sample, for nobody knows the educational composition of all labor leaders. Yet the range of education within our sample is quite wide, and there are very great educational differences between the AFL and CIO leaders. Should any educational bias exist, it would, of course, affect the absolute educational levels of our leaders. But the relative standing between the AFL and the CIO with respect to education might still be valid. Finally, we do have the check provided by the data obtained in the different waves. We can compare the educational level of those who responded to our first mailing with the educational level of those who responded to the later waves.

	AFL		CIO	
	Wave 1	Waves 2 and 3	Wave 1	Waves 2 and 3
Some high school or less	56%	62%	43%	42%
High school graduate or more	41	35	54	54
No answer	3	3	3	4
Total number	127	105	130	48

Very little difference is found between the two waves: in the AFL, a slightly higher proportion of the less-educated responded in the second wave (62 per cent as against 56 per cent), but this difference is not statistically significant. In the CIO, there is also no significant difference. We have followed this same procedure of comparing the answers to the first wave with those in the later waves in connection with all of the opinion questions which we asked the labor leaders. In no case do the answers differ significantly between the first and the later waves.

It is known that mail polls tend to be biased in terms of the amount of interest in the subject and knowledge of the topic which you are polling. (*See* E. A. Suchman and B. McCandless, "Who Answers Questionnaires?" *Journal of Applied Psychology* [December, 1940], p. 753 *ff. See* also references cited in H. A. Edgerton, S. H. Britt, and R. D. Norman, "Objective Differences Among Various Types of Respondents to a Mailed Questionnaire," *American Sociological Review* [August, 1947]). In the present case the questions concern the labor leader's career and personal opinions; it is, therefore, a sample of interested people. Speculatively, we do not know why some of them should be any more interested in such a topic than others.

Still, it may be claimed that those who didn't answer might in some significant way be different from those who did—that they might be more or less co-operative, or more suspicious of pollers. We have no definitive answer to this. The only way to find out would be to know what our non-responders are like—by personal interview, if necessary. Our budget made this procedure impossible. Such evidence as is available, and especially the fact that there are no significant differences between those who answered the initial request and those who answered only after additional prodding, gives us confidence in this sample of labor leaders.

The ages of corporation officials are from *Fortune* (February, 1940), p. 51, and from TNEC Monograph No. 11, by M. E. Dimock and H. K. Hyde, Table X, p. 46. *See* also Taussig and Joslyn, *American Business Leaders* (New York: Macmillan, 1932). The ages of governmental officials were computed from information in A. W. Macmahon and J. D. Millett, *Federal Administrators* (New York: Columbia University Press, 1939).

For a long time the AFL leaders have tended to be less well educated than non-AFL leaders. A study in 1924 (Stanley in *American Labor Dynamics*) showed that 47 per cent of the independent union leaders and 66 per cent of the AFL leaders were of the grammar school level. But the AFL leaders, like the rest of the U.S. population, have been slowly getting better educated. Over these two decades, there has been some lift in the educational level within the AFL, although available figures do not permit us to say just how much it has been.

Data on the education of business executives are found in Taussig and Joslyn, *op. cit.;* I have taken the education of corporation executives as of 1940 from unpublished tabulations made by Virginia B. Miller; the corporations are those listed by Berle and Means as the 200 largest plus all those not so listed but studied by the TNEC (Monograph 29, pp. 346-47). The data on government officials is from Macmahon and Millett, *op. cit.*

Chapter Five: The Self-Made Men

The data on the Middle Western city are from a study organized by the Bureau of Applied Social Research. Complete results will be published by Harper's under the title, *Influence: A Study of Stratification and Opinion Leaders.* The city was selected as typical of its size group and region on the basis of 37 statistical indicators run on all cities of its size group in the Middle West.

The proportion of the population that is foreign-born depends, of course, upon how many people immigrate into the country. Mass immigration into the U.S. was stopped by law about 25 years ago. That means that the proportion of the foreign-born has steadily declined. In 1910, for the urban white population, the figure was 24.2 per cent; but by 1940, the proportion was 13.4 per cent.

As with the general population, so with the labor leaders: over the last twenty years the trend has been toward more native-born leaders. In one 1924 sample (*American Labor Dynamics*), 29 per cent of the AFL leaders were foreign-born; today the AFL figure is 10 per cent. The only possible historical comparison with the CIO today is with the independent unions in 1924. At that time, 50 per cent of the leaders of independent unions were foreign-born whereas today in the CIO, 11 per cent, and in the independent unions, 14 per cent are foreign-born.

The older a person is, the more likely he is to be foreign-born. This is true for the labor leader as well as for the U.S. population. Here are the proportions of foreign-born in the various age groups for the 1940 white male population and for the labor leaders.

Age:	WHITE * MALES	AFL	CIO
Under 35	2%	..	3%
35-44	14%	5%	7%
45-54	23%	10%	17%
55 and over	25%	19%	29%

* Computed from *The Sixteenth Census of the U.S. 1940,* Population—Nativity and Parentage of the White Population, Table 5, p. 35.

It is of interest to notice that more of the labor leaders of foreign origin than the native-born have fathers in the small business strata. Thus in the AFL, 17 per cent of the leaders who were born in the U.S. of U.S.-born fathers, as compared with 26 per cent of the leaders who are foreign-born of foreign fathers, have fathers in the small business class. In the CIO, the figures are 12 and 33 per cent respectively.

The figures on U.S. males, occupational distribution, are taken from my forthcoming book, *The New Middle Class: A Study of White-Collar People,* and are a special "recodification" of census data. Thanks are due to Oxford University Press for permission to present these figures before their publication in that volume. The figures on the occupations of the fathers of business executives as of 1928 are from Taussig and Joslyn, *American Business Leaders,* recomputed from Table 20, page 88.

Answers to the question, "What was your main occupation before you became a trade union official?" may be biased: most unions require that an individual have an employment record in the trade, industry, or occupation being organized before he can be elected to a union position. It may therefore be that the labor jobs claimed as the main occupation of the labor leaders are reflections to some unknown extent of this administrative fact. However, in view of the occupations of the fathers reported, I do not feel that this is a very serious bias in the figures presented.

I am indebted to a conversation with Earl Brown of *Life* magazine for several points made in connection with types of organizers. The distribution of income among the national and local officers, shown below, is computed from Philip Taft's essay, "Understanding Union Administration," *Harvard Business Review* (Winter, 1946), pp. 253-57. I have compared some of these figures with those from the AFL given in the *Postal Record* (December, 1943), pp. 440-41, and found the two commensurate.

Sixty-two international presidents, 1944:

SALARY	AFL	CIO	IND.	TOTAL
$14,500-30,000	15%	6%	40%	14%
9,500-14,499	22	18	..	20
4,500-9,499	48	53	60	50
2,000-4,499	15	23	..	16
Total cases	40	17	5	62

Top national officers, other than presidents, of sixty-two internationals:

SALARY	AFL	CIO	IND.	TOTAL
$12,500 and over	10%	..	8%	7%
9,500-12,499	10	6%	15	9
7,500-9,499	21	16	..	17
4,500-7,499	38	19	54	34
2,500-4,499	21	59	23	33
Total cases	71	37	13	121

Full-time paid local officers:

WEEKLY SALARIES	LOCAL UNIONS
$90-125	18%
66-85	21
45-65	26
Highest regular rate in trade—foreman's rate	35
Total cases	84

The salaries of business executives are from R. A. Gordon, *Business Leadership in the Large Corporation* (Brookings Institution, 1945), especially pp. 275, 280, 281, 299. These 264 executives were heads of companies in public utilities, industrials, and railroads. Forty-four per cent of the industrial executives received more than $87,500 and around 19 per cent took more than $112,500. Another study (John C. Baker, *Executive Salaries and Bonus Plans* [New York: McGraw-Hill, 1938], p. 181) in 1936 indicates the spread of executive compensation in 44 large industrial corporations: the top men got on the average $93,000; the bottom men averaged around $24,000; and the total average (median) for the whole group was $35,000. *See* also TNEC Monograph No. 11 by Dimock and Hyde. We do not, incidently, in this comparison have systematic data on expense accounts of business and labor leaders.

The quote from Mother Jones is taken from Harold Seidman, *The Labor Czars* (New York: Liveright, 1938), pp. 257-58, as are several other points about the style of life of labor leaders. The quotes from Dubinsky and about Dubinsky and Hillman are from Benjamin Stolberg, *Tailors' Progress* (New York: Doubleday, 1944), *see* pp. 88, 186, 224, etc. I have also consulted with benefit on such points R. R. Brooks, *When Labor Organizes* (New Haven: Yale University Press, 1937), especially pp. 260-62.

Chapter Six: The Liberal Rhetoric

The quote on employers "stupefied by class dogma" is from Murray and Cooke, *Organized Labor and Production* (New York: Harper's, 1940).

Chapter Seven: The Racketeer Business

In this chapter I have used Harold Seidman, *The Labor Czars* (New York: Liveright, 1938) both for facts and for the general tieup of business unionism and business-labor racketeering; also Walter Chambers, *Labor Unions and the Public* (New York: Coward-McCann, 1936); Lester, *op. cit.;* Stolberg, *op. cit.;* Dean Sullivan, *This Labor Union Racket* (New York: Hillman-Curl, 1936); Joel Seidman, *Union Rights and Union Duties* (New York: Harcourt, Brace, 1943); G. L. Hostetter and T. Q. Beesley, *It's a Racket* (Chicago: Les Quin Books, 1929); Edward Levinson, "Business Prefers Racketeers," *The New Republic* (November 27, 1935); and M. I. Gurfein, "Racketeering," *Encyclopaedia of the Social Sciences,* Vol. XIII (New York: Macmillan, 1934), pp. 45-49.

Chapter Eight: Labor's Image of Business

In the answers to the question of who has more influence in national affairs—business or labor—the figures on the proportion thinking business has more power are minimum. Some who answered "labor" qualified "if labor could deliver the vote, etc." They talked in terms of potential power.

The question on the intention of business was worded: "Do you believe that, on the whole, the larger businesses in the United States: (a) Accept the principle of collective bargaining and deal with the unions in good faith . . . (b) They tolerate unions and deal with them as far as they have to but no further . . . (c) They are trying to 'break' the unions." The three alternatives form a rough scale of trust in business intention from a labor union standpoint. As mentioned in the text of this chapter, however, the element of time needs to be present to make the (c) and (b) alternatives exclusive. That this is a deficiency in the wording of the question is shown by the fact that some 20 per cent of the total group of respondents checked both (b) and (c). The idea of these respondents, as indicated by their comments, is clear: Business really wants to break the unions and intends to *whenever the opportunity arises or the time comes.* But we did not ask about the *conditions* of business putting into effect its intention; we asked about business's intention as the respondent saw it. Therefore, the 20 per cent who checked both (b) and (c) have in our text tables been tabulated in the (c) group.

Yet that does not entirely solve the trouble, for we know from the comments that at least some of the respondents, who checked (b) only, really believed that business was trying its best to break the unions but couldn't do so because of existing laws. These few cases, as is standard in such check questions, were coded according to their comments as well as the check mark. There were still, however, respondents who checked only the (b) statement and made no comment. It is entirely possible that at least some of these really should be in the (c) group, but they have of course been tabulated as (b). That is why the percentages reported as believing that business is out to break the unions are absolute minimums; they are probably 5 or 6 per cent greater, but there is no way to improve the accuracy of that particular count. However, an indirect check indicates that perhaps the error is very slight indeed. It would in most likelihood be the less-educated respondents who, checking (b), would nevertheless believe the (c) statement but not take the trouble to make a remark. Perhaps the better-educated CIO leaders were less docile about checking the question and not making a comment than the less-educated AFL leaders. But this is not the case: the CIO leaders were no more likely to double-check the alternatives or to make qualifying comments than were the less-educated AFL leaders.

Chapter Nine: Programs and Expediences

In general, 95 per cent of the AFL leaders who believe that business is out to break the unions also believe that the unions should have a long-range program, whereas 87 per cent of those who are more trustful of business intent believe that the unions should look to the future with the aid of a program.

Henry David's article, "One Hundred Years of Political Action by Labor," is an excellent brief account, especially of AFL policy and practice (*Labor and Nation* [November-December, 1946]). *See* also a previous statement by him in *Labor Problems in America,* edited by E. Stein and J. Davis (New York: Farrar, Rinehart, 1940). I have also consulted Robert Hunter, *Labor in Politics* (Chicago, 1915). On labor's political strategy of collective bargaining applied to politics, *see* Selig Perlman's lectures to the ILGWU, published by the union in 1945: "Labor in the New Deal Decade." I have found W. E. Walling's *American Labor and American Democracy* (New York: Harper's, 1926) a good statement of labor's traditional political role and attitude toward government. It is pro-AFL in viewpoint. *See* also for the AFL's role and outlook *Labor and Politics* by Mollie Roy Carroll (New York: Houghton Mifflin, 1923), especially Chapter VIII.

The quote on "social politics" is from Dubinsky, found in Stolberg, *op. cit.,* p. 198. On political pluralism, *cf.* Francis W. Coker, *Recent Political Thought*

(London, Appleton-Century, 1934), especially pp. 503 *ff*. The quotation on the ILGWU is from Stolberg, *op. cit.*, p. 345. The quotation on the steelworkers and the leaders, "Witherspoon and Barton," is from Golden and Ruttenberg, *The Dynamics of Industrial Democracy*, pp. 57-58.

Chapter Ten: Party Ties

On the general topic, *see* "Labor's Role in the Election," Joseph Rosenfarb, *Public Opinion Quarterly* (Winter, 1944), pp. 376 *ff*., from whom I have quoted. On the 1940 Lewis episode, *see* Irving Bernstein, "John L. Lewis and the Voting Behavior of the CIO," *Public Opinion Quarterly* (June, 1941). The labor vote, 1936-44 is from *The Gallup Political Almanac* (Princeton: 1946), pp. 205-206. On the ILGWU and Dubinsky quotes, *see* Stolberg, *op. cit.* The quotation from A. A. Berle, Jr., is from the magazine *'47* (November, 1947).

Chapter Eleven: Communists and Labor Leaders

Our primary sources on Communism and the labor movement are: spot interviews over the last several years with labor leaders both in and out of Communist factions; several journalistic histories of labor during the Thirties, containing documented items about Communist activities, especially Herbert Harris's *Labor's Civil War* (New York: Knopf, 1940), and Edward Levinson's *Labor on the March* (New York: Harper's, 1938); the files of the *Daily Worker* and *New Masses,* and those of labor and other non-Communist papers. The magazine, *Business Week*, on this as on so many other items of labor union news, is very carefully documented and factual. The files of the *New Leader* provide a shrill liberal anti-CP line and news. *Labor Action*, the weekly organ of the Worker's Party, contains far-left views and news.

The lineup of the CIO unions according to Communist factions or control has been developed from and checked against all relevant sources. *See* particularly Andrew Avery in the *Chicago Journal of Commerce,* between June 24 and July 11, 1946, and between January 13 and January 31, 1947. These are written from the standpoint of a sophisticated conservative and are quite factual. *See* also: Research Institute of America's pamphlet, "The Communist in Labor Relations Today" (March, 1946), and U.S. Chamber of Commerce's pamphlet prepared by E. Schmidt, "Communists Within the Labor Movement."

The quotations from Harold J. Laski are taken from *The Secret Battalion* (The Labour Publications Department, Transport House, Smith Square, London, S.W. 1), pp. 12 and 14.

Chapter Twelve: Old Parties, New Parties

See notes for Chapter Ten. A good brief discussion of the mass public's view of "third parties" is found in NORC's bulletin, *Opinion News* (September 15, 1947). On views of the major parties and a new party, *see* G. H. Smith and R. P. Davis, "Do the Voters Want the Parties Changed?" *Public Opinion Quarterly* (Summer, 1947).

The figures on minority party vote were computed from the *Statistical*

Abstract of the U.S. Census, 1946, p. 299. On the Socialist Labor and Socialist Parties, *see* E. M. Sait, *American Parties and Elections* (New York: Appleton-Century, 1939), p. 187 *f.* For figures on Socialist Party membership and votes, *see American Labor Year Book* (New York: Rand School, 1925), p. 141. On the 1912 election, *see* H. F. Pringle, *Theodore Roosevelt* (New York: Harcourt, Brace, 1931); for 1924, *see* K. C. MacKay's doctoral thesis, *The Progressive Movement of 1924* (New York: Columbia University Press, 1947), from which I have taken facts and quotations. Also *cf.* Matthew Josephson, *The President Makers* (New York: Harcourt, Brace, 1940). On the common denominators of Progressive movements, *see* B. P. Dewitt, *The Progressive Movement* (New York: Macmillan, 1915). On the AFL policy of 1910, *see Convention Proceedings* (1910), pp. 16 and 103, and *Forty Years of Action* (1920), both cited by W. E. Walling, *American Labor and American Democracy* (New York: Harper's, 1926).

The quote from Hillquit is from MacKay, *op. cit.*, who quotes it from Lewis Gannett, "A Party Struggles to Be Born," *Nation* (March 4, 1924), p. 240. For notes on PAC, *see* Joseph Rosenfarb, "Labor's Role in the Election," *Public Opinion Quarterly* (1944) p. 376 *ff.* For an excellent analysis of Wallace's political history and behavior, *see* Dwight MacDonald, *Henry Wallace* (New York: Vanguard, 1948).

After our sample of labor leaders had answered the question on a national party, we followed up with: "How about in local (state and city) politics?" Contrary to our expectations, very few labor leaders are for a new party on one level (e.g., local) and against it on the other (e.g., national). The patterns of response on the national and the local are not statistically different. When cross-tabulated, the following table results:

For a new party:

NATIONALLY	LOCALLY	AFL	CIO
Yes	Yes	11%	18%
No	No	83	74
Yes	No	2	5
No	Yes	4	3
Total cases		227	176

It should be mentioned that a close examination of the comments made to the new party questions *now* and *eventually* indicates that it *is* the timing and not the different wording of the questions that accounts for the differences in the answers. The respondents interpreted "gains for labor will best be made by" in the same way as "I would prefer to work for labor's viewpoint by . . ."

The difference in the timing of the new labor party can be made the basis for an over-all classification of labor leader reaction to the idea. By combining their answers we obtain the following picture:

For a new labor party:

NOW	EVENTUALLY	AFL	CIO
No	Yes	11%	26%
No	No	76	51
Yes	Yes	11	22
Total cases		229	177

Chapter Thirteen: The Main Drift

The quotations from the Automobile Workers' proposals were printed in the *New York Times*, December 11, 1945; the facts on the Steel Workers' local agreement in *Business Week* (June 7, 1947); those on the ILGWU type of agreement are from Stolberg, *op. cit.* The quotes on business-management co-operation and Ordway Tead's statement, cited by Golden and Ruttenberg, are from their book, *The Dynamics of Industrial Democracy.*

I am indebted to an unpublished manuscript by Dwight MacDonald for the point about the Steel Workers Organizing Committee. The quotation on the TNEC hearing is from R. A. Lester, *Economics of Labor* (New York: Macmillan, 1947), p. 852. In the discussion of governmental actions, I have learned much from Bernard H. Fitzpatrick's *Understanding Labor* (New York: McGraw-Hill, 1945), a conservative but penetrating book. I am not able to go along with his conclusions, but his analytic perception of what is involved has in several places been fitted into the pattern of my argument. In my formulation of the main drift, I have found Franz Neuman's work on the German labor movement (*see Behemoth* [New York: Oxford University Press, 1942], and the LID pamphlet cited above) valuable, as well as the idea of "power centers," advanced by Fred Harbison and Robert Dubin in their excellent book, *Patterns of Union Management Relations* (Chicago, 1947), *see* pp. 182 *ff.;* and an unpublished manifesto by Louis Clair and Lilian Symes, "Where We Stand." *See* also Adolf Sturmthal, *The Tragedy of European Labor* (New York: Columbia University Press, 1943).

Chapter Fourteen: Alternatives

Quotations represented here as from sophisticated conservatives have been taken mainly from *Business Week* and *Fortune;* for example, *Business Week* (September 14, 1946; June 7, 1947; November 1, 1947), and *Fortune* (June, 1947). The figures from Fritz Sternberg are from his excellent book, *The Coming Crisis* (New York: John Day, 1947). In connection with the program of the left, I have reread with benefit G. D. H. Cole, *Guild Socialism: A Plan for Economic Democracy* (New York: Stokes, 1920), and G. D. H. Cole and W. M. Mellor, "Workers Control and Self Government in Industry," *Bulletin of New Fabian Research Bureau, No. 9* (1933), as well as various syndicalist literature. The quotation from Rea Stone is from her article, "The American Worker" (Internal Bulletin of the Johnson-Forest Minority, Issue No. 8, September 4, 1947, Mimeographed), and that from Monatte, "Trends in French Unionism," *Modern Review* (August, 1947). The quotations from Nat Weinberg are taken from his speech before the American Statistical Association, New York, December, 1947.

Chapter Fifteen: The Power and the Intellect

A number of key facts on the habits and characteristics of the underdogs have been brought together by G. Knupfer in her doctoral thesis, *Indices of Socio-Economic Status* (New York: Columbia University Press, 1946). The occupational tables presented in this chapter are taken from my forthcoming book, *The New Middle Class: A Study of White-Collar People.* The quotation by the *Fortune* writer on the middle classes during political crisis is from Sherry Mangan in "The State of the Nation: Minority Report," *Fortune* (October, 1943). The Stimson quote on how war came is from the *New York Times,* 22 March 1946, p. 15, col. 4.

We have at hand systematic information on 82 of the better-known and more influential of labor's staff intellectuals: 37 are editors of AFL and CIO papers, and 46 are directors of research and education within the unions. Although this small group cannot be taken as representative of labor's staff intellectuals as a whole, it does include most of the key people in this bracket.

The editors of the labor papers are quite different from the directors of research and education. This is particularly true of AFL editors, who are not nearly as well educated as staff men of the CIO. Their union careers are also very different. The AFL editors entered the labor world long before the other intellectuals, and for the most part, they rose in a way similar to that followed by the elected leaders: most of them led their local units before taking their present posts. All the other types are more likely to have entered their present union posts without having held previous jobs in a trade union. On the whole, the AFL editors think like the elected AFL leaders. Like them, they feel labor should try to gain its ends by working within existing parties, that the AFL and CIO should get together and achieve unity. They are split pretty evenly in their opinions as to whether or not labor has long-range objectives and as to whether or not there is any serious threat of fascism in this country. Only a few of them are fearful of business's intentions with respect to labor unions. At the opposite pole of the staff world of the unions are the research directors of the CIO. They differ from the AFL leaders as do the elected CIO leaders; but among the CIO staff intellectuals, these differences are magnified and accentuated. Whereas the AFL editors seem to reflect and generally to go along with AFL opinion-leadership, the CIO research and education specialists seem to be more "extreme"; they not only go in the general direction of the CIO leadership but seem, in fact, to go beyond it.

CIO leaders are much more likely than AFL leaders, for example, to be fearful of business's strength and suspicious of its motives. CIO research directors are even more fearful. The general CIO leadership is more "alert" to the menace of fascism than other labor leaders. Almost unanimously, CIO research and education experts feel there is great danger of fascism in this country. On the question of eventually setting up a third party, a fifth of the AFL leaders favor such action; among the CIO leaders, support for a third party comes from twice that number. But among CIO research and education directors, three-fourths are in favor of eventually setting up a third party to gain labor's objectives.

I have taken some points on the union-made intellectual from my essay "Grass Roots Union with Ideas," *Commentary* (March, 1948).

INDEX

Addes, George, 195
AFL, *see* American Federation of Labor
amalgamated craft unions, 55, 59-60
American Federation of Labor, 49, 54-58, 60-61, 66, 68
  age of leaders in, 69-71
  business, estimate of power of, 133-39
  business policy in labor relations, estimates of, 140-45
  and CIO, differences between, 68, 73-74, 82-83
    on Communist issue, 186
    in estimates of power of business, 134-36
    in experiences with Communists, 198
    between leaders of, 98
  and Communist Party, 195-96, 197
  education of leaders in, 71-73
  "fascist" threat, view of, 146-47
  as federation of political machines, 5
  estimate of power of, 137
  labor party, view of, 211-13
  labor programs, view of, 155-58
  and labor unity, 74-83
  occupational background of leaders in, 92-94
  party affiliations in, 172-76, 183-84
  and party politics, 162-63
  racketeering, role in, 129-32
  and third party movements, 204-8
Anarchist Party, 182
anti-Communist attitude of labor leaders, reasons for, 190-92
anti-Communist drive of CIO, 191, 199
anti-Communist liberals, 22, 23
anti-labor attitude, of news media, 32-34
  of popular culture media, 34
anti-unionism, anti-Semitism and Jim Crowism, comparison with, 77
  as represented by practical right, 24-25
aristocracy, of craft labor, 117-18
  of industrial labor, 118-20
autocracy in union government, 116
Automobile Workers, United, 6, 100, 193-95, 198, 224, 259, 272

Banse, Ewald, 248
Berle, A. A., Jr., 184
Berry, G. L., 64
Bevin, Ernest, 169
big businessmen and officer corps, 247
bi-partisan politics, 160-63, 171-85, 201
  and labor leaders' view of labor party, 213-14
boom (*see also* slump-war-boom cycle), politically alert publics during, 29
Brandeis, Louis, 19
Bridges, Harry, 44, 85
Brindell, Robert, 130-31
British trade unions, 38
Broach, H. H., 128
Brophy, John, 65
building trades, jurisdictional allocations in, 5
Building Trades Council, San Francisco, 125

Bull Moose Party, 203
bureaucracy in the labor union world, 98
bureaucratization of business enterprise and labor union, 223-24
business, intent in labor relations of, 140-45
and labor racketeering, 125-26
labor's image of, 133-49
business agent of union, 5, 50-51
as labor racketeer, 123-25
as springboard to union career, 97-98
business executive, income compared with labor leader's, 100-2
business-involved people in United States, 35
business intent in labor relations, difference in views of national, state, and city labor leaders on, 141-43 [237
business-labor cooperation, 112-21,
in craft unions, 117-18
government role in, 229-33
in industrial unions, 118-20
integration of union and corporation: in enterprise, 224-27
in plant, 224
in political economy, 227-29
labor racketeering as, 122-26
business-labor relations in U.S. political economy, 233-38
business-like approach to union career, 95-96
businessmen, labor leaders' views of, 147-49
business unionism, 117-18
and communism, 191
and labor racketeering, 122-25, 131-32
political strategy of, 163
Business Week, 25, 241, 243, 246
Byrnes, James, 208-9

Call, 20
capitalism, adventure, 131
capitalism (Cont.)
industrial, 131
and sophisticated conservatives, 244
and unionism, 7
Capone, Al, 127-28
Carey, James, 194
Carpenters Union, 5, 60, 64, 118, 206
Chicago Federation of Labor, 205
"Christian Socialism," 96
CIO, *see* Congress of Industrial Organizations
city body of international union, 57-58, 97-98
views of leaders, on intent of business, 141-43
on labor party, 212
class bias against unions, 42-43
Cloakmakers, Joint Board of, in ILGWU, 197
Clothing Workers, Amalgamated, 55, 64
Coefield, John, 171
Cole, G. D. H., quoted, 258
Commerce, Chamber of, 133, 168
Committee of Forty-Eight, 206
Communist Party, 22-23, 66, 182
and AFL, 195-96, 197
charges of liberal and left-wing opponents, 199-200
and CIO, 194-99
far left, similarity to, 22
and labor leaders, 187-200
labor unity, fear of, 198
liberal center, appeal to, 192
Nazi-Communist pact, effects of, 199
political characterization of, 22
political status of, 27-30
social composition of, 23
unions, view of, 23
U.S.-Soviet wartime co-operation, effects of, 196-199
as viewed, by far left, 189, 192
by independent left, 182, 192
by liberal center, 187-89
by mass public, 186-87

Communist Party (Cont.)
as viewed (Cont.)
by practical right, 187
by sophisticated conservatives, 187-88, 192
Wallace candidacy, support of, 209-10
Communist relationships of labor leaders, 192-99
Conference for Progressive Political Action, 205-6
Congress of Industrial Organizations, 49, 53, 54, 56-58, 60-61
and AFL, differences between, 68, 73-74, 82-83
on Communist issue, 186
in estimates of business power, 134-36
in experiences with Communists, 198
in leaders, 98
age of leaders in, 69-71
anti-Communist drive of, 191
business, estimate of power of, 133-39
business policy in labor relations, estimates of, 140-45
and Communist control, 195-99
education of leaders in, 71-73
"fascist" threat, view of, 146-47
labor party, view of, 211-13
labor programs, view of, 155-58
as federation of political machines, 5
formation of, 56
labor, estimate of power of, 137
and labor unity, 74-83
occupational background of leaders in, 92-94
party affiliations in, 172-76, 183-84
political strength of, 179-80
slump, impetus of, 68
conservatives, *see* practical right: sophisticated conservatives
conservative way to economic balance, 246
consumer co-ops, 276
Coolidge, Calvin, 24, 206-8
corporate state, 121
corporation executive, as opportunist, 154
and union leader, relative power of, 134
CP, *see* Communist Party
craft labor, aristocracy of, 117-18
craft unions, 55, 59-61
Croly, Herbert, 19
Curran, Joseph, 45, 107

Davis, John W., 206-8
Debs, Eugene, 204
delegate bodies of union, 51
democracy, and socialism, 251-52
in unions, 66-67, 106, 116
in United States, weaknesses of, 252
Democratic Party, 172-78, 183-84
democratic power of worker in shop, 254
depression, *see* slump
Dubinsky, David, 45, 85, 96, 132
on labor in politics, 163, 182

Electrical, Radio, and Machine Workers of America, United, 194
electrical work, capital-labor cartel in, 128
elites, military, capitalistic, political, relations of, 247-50
employers, domination of labor market by, 7-8
Emspak, Julius, 194
estimates of chances as factor in labor leaders' view of labor party, 214-15
expediences among labor's leadership, 153-70

far left, 15-16
business-labor relations, view of, 117
Communists, similarity to, 22
view of, 189, 192

far left (Cont.)
economic program for unions, 257-59
foreign program of, 262
labor disunity, view of, 74
labor leaders, view of, 16
labor party, value of, 262-65
view of, 202
political characterization of, 15
political program of, 259-65
political status of, 27-30
powerless condition of, 250-51
program of, 240, 250-65
social composition of, 16
sophisticated conservatives, similarity to, 27
unions, view of, 16
Wallace candidacy, view of, 210
workshop, program for, 253-56
Farmer-Labor Party, 205-6
Minnesota, 181-82
farmers, 275-77
Farmers Union, 20
"fascist" threat, labor leaders' views on, 145-47
fear of failure as factor in labor leaders' view of labor party, 215-17
Fitzgerald, Albert, 194
Ford Motor Company, 6, 224
Forrestal, James, 247-48
Fortune, 25, 241, 242, 271-72
free enterprisers, 275, 279
Fur and Leather Workers, International Union of, 193
Furuseth, Andrew, 103

gangster, in labor racketeering, 126-28
garment trades, 8
Gary, Judge, 229
General Motors Corp., 100, 272
goals of labor, 158-60
Golden, Clinton, 167, 226
Gompers, Samuel, 54, 130-31, 205
on party politics, 171-73, 205, 206
Green, William, 44-45, 54, 78, 85, 96, 130
Green, William (Cont.)
on Communism, 198

Hardie, Keir, 96
Hillman, Sidney, 64, 199, 209
Hillquit, Morris, 207
Hochman, Julius, 96, 182
House Labor Committee, 26
Hutcheson, William, 5, 60, 64, 171

ideology, of labor leaders, lack of, 164-70
in union career, 95-96
ILGWU, *see* Ladies' Garment Workers Union, International
independent electoral party, and labor, 161
as sidetracked by New Deal, 181
independent left, 17-18, 240
business-labor relations, view of, 117
Communists, view of, 188, 192
labor party, view of, 202
political characterization of, 17-18
political status of, 27-30
powerless condition of, 250-51
program of, 250-65
social composition of, 17
unions, view of, 18
Wallace candidacy, view of, 210
Independent Party, 206
independent unions, 56, 60
age and experience of leaders in, 70-71
education of leaders in, 73
industrial labor, aristocracy of, 118-20
industrial unions, 55, 59-61
intellectuals, labor, *see* labor intellectuals
intellectuals, non-union, 286
international representatives of unions, 5, 50
international unions, 49-52
methods of formation of, 52
officers of, 49-50
heads, as locus of power within union world, 52

IWW (International Workers of the World), 17

Jones, Mother, quoted, 102-3

Kingdon, Frank, quoted, 210

labor, goals of, 158-60
  and labor racketeering, 125-26
  in party politics, 162-63
  power of, as viewed by labor leaders, 136-37
labor action, independence of, 255-56
labor disunity, 68-83
labor intellectuals, role of, 281
  types of: free-lance researcher, 284-85
    official, active member, or promoter of radical party, 283-84
    professionally trained, 282-83
    union-made, 285-86
labor leader (*see also* labor leaders; labor leaders' views)
  anti-Communist attitude, reasons for, 190-92
  and Communists, 187-200
  and conservatives' program, 249-50
  and corporation executive, relative power of, 134
  as disciplinarian, 8-9
  engineering type of, 131
  as general, 3-4
  ideology, lack of, 164-70
  income of, 100-2
  as labor contractor, 6-7
  and main drift, 266-74
  managerial type of, 131
  method of study of this book, 9-10
  nativity of, 84-88
    as factor in political affiliation, 175
  as opportunist, 153-54
  as parliamentary leader, 4-5

labor leader (Cont.)
  party affiliation of, 171-76, 183-84
  personal aspirations of, 149
  as political boss, 5, 106
  political meaning of personal advancement of, 105-6
  pre-union occupation of, 91-95
  probable role in new labor party as factor in his attitude, 217-18
  pro-Communist relationships of, 192-99
  as public figure, 13, 104
  as rebel, 7-8
  as self-made man, 84-108
  slump, political role in, 29-30
  and small businessmen, 277
  social and occupational origins of, 88-90
  as spokesman, 111-21
  style of life of, 103-5
  task of, 291
  union career of, 95-99, 106-8
  as viewed, by far left, 16
    by liberal center, 21-22
    by mass public, 31, 41, 43-46
    by sophisticated conservatives, 26-27
  vision and will of, 287-91
labor leaders (*see also* labor leader; labor leaders' views
  AFL and CIO, differences between, 68-74
  age of, 68-71
  associated conditions of timidity toward new labor party, 218-19
  education of, 68, 71-73, 91
  experience of, 70
  job areas of, 58-59
  labor unity, estimates of chances for, 79-80
    explanation of variances in opinions on, 80-83
    opinions on, 77-79
  main drift, capacity to fight against, 288-90

labor leaders (Cont.)
members, relationship with, 62-67
segregation from, 104-5
militancy score of, 289
political affiliations as compared with general public, 172
political ideas to practical politics, shift from, 165-70
programs of, 153-70
tenure in office of, 64
well known and little known, 44-45
labor leaders' views, on businessmen, 147-49
on business policy in labor relations, 140-45
on business power, 133-39
on "fascist" threat, 145-47
on labor, power of, 136-37
on labor in politics, 163-70
on labor party, 211-13
reasons for, 213-19
on labor programs, 155-60
on major political parties, 176-78
on public reaction, 274
labor movement abroad, 169
labor news, presentation by mass media of, 32-34
labor party, 201-19, 280
attempts to form: before World War I, 202-4
after World War I, 204-8
far left, desire for, 15
value to, 262-65
labor leaders' views on, 211-19
Labor Party, American, 182-83, 205
of Cook County, 205
of Illinois, 205
labor racketeering, 122-32
AFL, role in, 129-32
and business, relationship of, 125-26
as business-labor co-operation, 122-23, 125-26
and business unionism, 122-25, 131-32
labor racketeering (Cont.)
economic conditions inviting, 127-29
gangster in, 126-28
and labor, relationship of, 125-26
and politics, relationship of, 125-26
labor relations, intent of business in, 140-45
labor union, *see* union; unionism; union organizations
labor unity, AFL and CIO, variances in opinion on, 80-83
arguments pro and con, 75-77
union leaders' estimates of chances for, 79-80
union leaders' opinions on, 77-79
as viewed by political publics, 74-75
labor vote, 179-85
Ladies' Garment Workers Union, International, 103, 182-83, 226
LaFollette, Robert, 203-4
campaign of 1924, 165, 206-8
congressional hearings, 25
Laski, Harold, quoted, 199-200
left, *see* far left; independent left
left intellectuals, views on labor unity, 75-77
left-wing charges against Communists, 199-200
Lehman, Governor, 182
Leninist left, *see* far left
Levy, L., 182
Lewis, John L., 6, 44, 55-56, 64, 65, 78, 85, 132, 196, 272
Communists, relationship with, 193, 198-99
political strength of, 179
liberal center, 19-22, 237, 240
business-labor relations, view of, 113, 117
Communists, charges against, 199-200
view of, 187-89
labor, theory of, 233
labor disunity, view of, 74
labor leaders, view of, 21-22

liberal center (Cont.)
political characterization of, 19-20
political status of, 27-30
social composition of, 20
unions, view of, 21
Wallace campaign, view of, 210
Liberal Party, 183
liberal rhetoric, 111-21, 171, 181, 204
liberal state, 229-233
liberal way to economic balance, 245
lobbying and labor, 161-62
local business-labor political cartel as backbone of racketeering, 125-26
local unions, 49, 50-51, 57-58
salaries of officers, 101
Locomotive Firemen, Brotherhood of, 64

McCarthy, P. H., 125
Macdonald, Dwight, 229
Mahon, William, 64
main drift in American politico-economic development, 3, 25, 223-65, 266-67
allies of, 280
and labor leaders, 281, 287-91
means of averting, 281
Marshall Plan, 210
Martin, Homer, 198
mass public, 13-14, 23, 240
Communist Party, view of, 186-87
labor disunity, view of, 74
labor leader, view of, 31, 41, 43-46
labor leaders' nativity, view of, 84-85
news and popular culture media of, 32-35
politically alert public, relationship with, 31-32
political opinions, means of acquiring, 31-32
in slump, 28, 31
third party, view of, 201
mass public (Cont.)
unionism, bias in opinions concerning, 85
unions, view of, 31, 35, 39-46
class bias, 42-43
specific criticisms, 41-42
Matles, James, 194
media, mass, labor news in, 32-34
popular culture in, 34
as viewed by labor leaders, 138-39
membership of unions, 35-40, 53
vote of, 180-81
Merrill, Lewis, 191
middle class, new, 275, 279
middle classes, political role of, 274
social composition and psychology of, 278-81
Middle West, political factors in, 175
militant approach to union career, 95
Mine Workers, United, 44, 64, 103, 198, 206
Minnesota State Federation of Labor, 205
minority party vote from 1896 to 1944, 203
Mitchell, John, 66, 103
money, as root of business power, 137-38
Murray, Philip, 44-45, 56, 78, 100, 119, 132, 209, 228
Communists, relationship with, 194, 199
Musicians Union, 44, 100

NAM, *see* National Association of Manufacturers
Nation, The, 15, 19, 20
National Association of Manufacturers, 14, 133, 162, 188
National Labor Relations Act, 231
national unions (*see also* international unions), 49
New Deal, 160, 163, 165, 181-85, 208, 229, 241
New Leader, The, 15, 19, 20
New Republic, The, 15, 19, 20

newspapers, handling of labor news by, 33-34
NIRA (National Industrial Recovery Act), 230-31
NLRB (National Labor Relations Board), union elections, 38, 39-40, 232
Non-Partisan League, 182, 206
of Minnesota, 205
of North Dakota, 205
NRA (National Recovery Administration), 132

occupational changes of American people, 274-76
occupational origins of labor leaders, 88-91
as factor in political affiliation, 175
occupations of labor leaders before union affiliation, 91-95
Office and Professional Workers of America, United, 191
O'Neil, Charles, 6
opportunism in labor's program, 153-54
organizers, union, 98-100

PAC, *see* Political Action Committee of CIO
Partisan Review, 17
party affiliation of labor leaders, 171-73, 183-84
determining factors of, 173-76
party lines of Communist Party, 196-99
party politics and labor, 160-63
peace and war, 261
Perkins, George, 203
personalization of business-labor relations, 113-14
Petrillo, James, 44, 100
planning as politics, 256
Plumbers Union, 171
Plumb plan, 205
PM, 20
political action among workers, conditions of, 266-74
Political Action Committee of CIO, 180, 208-9
political apathy of worker, 269-71
political approach to union career, 95
political campaign of 1906, 162
political demands, of far left, 15
of independent left, 17-18
politically alert publics, *see* publics, politically alert
politically passive public, *see* mass public
political publics, *see* publics, politically alert
Politics, 17
politics in labor, *see* bi-partisan politics
politics, and labor racketeering, 125-26
"pork-choppers," 5
power, and intellect, 266-91
strategy of, 239
in union world, locus of, 63-65
practical right, 23-25, 240
anti-union activity of, 233
business-labor relations, view of, 113
Communists, view of, 187
labor disunity, view of, 75
political characterization of, 23
political status of, 27-30
slump, attitude toward, 245-46
social composition of, 23
and sophisticated conservatives, relations of, 249
third party, view of, 201
unions, views of, 24-25
pressure politics and labor, 161-63
Printing Pressmen's Union, 64, 206
programs of labor's leadership, 153-70
Progressive, Wisconsin, 20
progressive parties, history of, 203-8
Progressive Party, 183, 204-8
property and labor unions, 7-8
public, mass, *see* mass public
public experience with unions, 35-39

public opinion, importance to labor leader, 14
leaders of, 32
publics, politically alert, 13-30
labor disunity, view of, 74-75
labor leader, view of, 13-14
mass public, relationship with, 31-32
slump, changes under conditions of, 27-30

racketeering, labor, *see* labor racketeering
radio, handling of labor news on, 32-33
Railway Labor Act, 231
Randolph, A. Philip, 45
rank-and-file leaders of unions, 37-39
rank and file of labor, control by, 66-67
and labor racketeers, 125
and main drift, 266-74, 290-91
as viewed, by far left, 16
by independent left, 18
by sophisticated conservatives, 27
reformers, 153
regionalism as factor in political affiliation of labor leaders, 174-75
Republican Party, 172-78, 183
responsibility of labor and management, public's view of, 45-46
Reuther, Walter, 6, 44-45, 107-8, 132, 193, 195, 209
revolutionary party and labor, 161
right, *see* practical right; sophisticated conservatives
Robertson, D. B., 64
Roosevelt, Franklin D., 179, 181-83, 208
Roosevelt, Theodore, 203-4
Ruttenberg, Harold, 167, 226

satisfaction with present political parties as factor in labor leaders' view of labor party, 214
Schlesinger, Benjamin, 182
Seaman's Union, 103
Seidman, Harold, 126
shop steward of local, 51
as springboard to union career, 97-98
Sigman, Morris, 103, 182
slump, 185, 256, 261, 263-64, 276, 290-91
drift toward, 3, 24, 242-43
labor party, role of, 280
mass public during, 31
methods of avoiding, 244-46
political effects of last, 81
politics of, 27-30
as result of practical right's program, 249
of the Thirties, 271-73
union split in last, 68
slump-war-boom cycle, 9, 67, 121, 290
small businessmen, 275-78
and labor leaders, 277
Smith-Connally Act, 208
socialism and democracy, 251-52
Socialist Party, 182, 204, 206
socialists, revolutionary, 153
social phases of union career, 102-5
sophisticated conservatives, 25-27
business-labor relations, view of, 113
and capitalism, 244
Communists, view of, 187-88, 192
domestic program of, 244-50
far left, similarity to, 27
foreign program of, 240-44
labor disunity, view of, 75
labor leaders, view of, 26-27
political characterization of, 25
political status of, 27-30
and practical right, relations of, 249
program of, 240-50, 280-81
social composition of, 25-27
third party, view of, 201
unionism, view of, 25-26
Spencer, Herbert, 247
spokesmen, 111-21

stabilization, drive for, 223-24, 229
Stalinists, 210
state body of international union, 57-58, 97-98
  views of leaders, on intent of business, 141-43
    on labor party, 212
Steel Workers, United, 100, 194, 225
Steel Workers Organizing Committee, 228
Sternberg, Fritz, 245
Stone, Rea, quoted, 257
Stone Workers Union, 100
Street Railway Workers, Amalgamated, 64
strikes, public reaction to, 41-43
Socialist International, 22
Socialist Party, 20
success patterns inside union, 97-99, 106-8

Taft-Hartley Act, 24, 75, 209, 232
Tead, Ordway, 227
Teamsters Union, 64, 100
third parties, history of, 202-8
third party, 165, 172-76, 181, 183-84
  for labor issues, 201-19
Thomas, R. J., 193-94, 195
Tobin, Daniel, 64, 100, 125, 171
trade associations, 233-34
trade unions, *see* union; unionism; union organizations
Trade Union Unity League, 197
Trainmen, Brotherhood of Railroad, 207
Trotskiest left, *see* far left
Truman, Harry, 208-9

UAW, *see* Automobile Workers, United
underdogs in U.S. society, characteristics of, 267-69
union (*see also* unionism; union organizations)
  as army, 3-4
  as democratic society, 4-5
  functions of, 6-7
union (Cont.)
  as instrument of social transformation, 268-69
  members, active, 37
    inactive, 35-37
  as political community of worker, 253-54
  as political machine, 5
  rank-and-file leaders of, 37-38
  as regulator of labor market, 6-7
union careers, beginnings of, 95-96
  career lines in, 97-99, 106-8
  incomes in, 100-2
  social phases of, 102-5
union funds, centralization of, 63
union-involved people, percentage in United States, 35-36
unionism (*see also* union; union organizations)
  and capitalism, 7
  class bias against, 42-43
  disunity in, 68-83
  familiarity of public with, 35, 39
  and property ownership, 7-8
  specific public criticisms of, 41-42
  as viewed, by Communists, 23
    by far left, 16
    by independent left, 18
    by liberal center, 20-21
    by practical right, 24-25
    by sophisticated conservatives, 25-26
unionism, business, *see* business unionism
union leaders, *see* labor leader; labor leaders; labor leaders' views
union officer and corporation manager, relative power of, 134
union organizations, 49-67
  assessments and dues in, 62-63
  autocracy in, 116
  conventions of, 62-63
  craft and industrial, 55, 59-61
  democracy in, 66, 106, 116
    test of, 286-87
  elections in, 62, 63-64
  history of, 53
  industrial composition of, 60-1

union organizations (Cont.)
international, 49-52
leaders and members, relations between, 62, 66-67
local, 49
membership, figures of, 53
national, 49
occupational composition of, 61-62
organizational machine of, 62, 65-66
sizes of, 53
state and city, 57-58, 97-98
union organizers, 98-100
unions, *see* union; unionism; union organizations
union world, bureaucracy in, 98
locus of power in, 63-65
U.S. Steel Corporation, 228
UOPWA, *see* Office and Professional Workers of America, United, 191

votes, as root of labor power, 136-37

wage workers, 275
wage-worker component of union membership, 61
Wagner Act, 231-32
Wagner-Murray-Dingel Health bill, 160
Wallace, Henry, 20, 200, 202, 209, 211
war (*see also* slump-war-boom cycle), 185, 256, 261, 271-73
drift toward, 3
functions of labor leader in, 9
political publics during, 29
prevention of, 24
war economy, as goal of sophisticated conservatives, 248-49
drift toward, 261
Weinberg, Nat, quoted, 259
Wheeler, Burton K., 206
white-collar component of union membership, 61
white collar employees, politics of, 279-80
Whitney, A. F., 45
wildcat strikes, 9
Wilson, C. E., 248
Woll, Matthew, 130
workers, conditions of political action among, 266-74
political apathy of, 269-71

University of Illinois Press
1325 South Oak Street
Champaign, IL 61820-6903
www.press.uillinois.edu